GLOBAL FINANCIAL CRIME

ISTITUTO PER GLI STUDI DI POLITICA INTERNAZIONALE

In association with the Istituto di Studi di Politica Internazionale.

Global Finance Series

Edited by
John J. Kirton, University of Toronto, Canada, Michele Fratianni, Indiana
University, U.S.A. and Paolo Savona, LUISS Guido Carli University, Italy

The intensifying globalisation of the twenty-first century has brought a myriad of new
managerial and political challenges for governing international finance. The return of
synchronous global slowdown, mounting developed country debt, and new economy
volatility have overturned established economic certainties. Proliferating financial
crises, transnational terrorism, currency consolidation, and increasing demands that
international finance should better serve public goods such as social and
environmental security have all arisen to compound the problem.

The new public and private international institutions that are emerging to
govern global finance have only just begun to comprehend and respond to this new
world. Embracing international financial flows and foreign direct investment, in both
the private and public sector dimensions, this series focuses on the challenges and
opportunities faced by firms, national governments, and international institutions,
and their roles in creating a new system of global finance.

Also in the series

Sustaining Global Growth and Development
G7 and IMF Governance
Edited by Michele Fratianni, Paolo Savona and John J. Kirton
ISBN 0 7546 3529 5

Governing Global Finance
New Challenges, G7 and IMF Contributions
Edited by Michele Fratianni, Paolo Savona and John J. Kirton
ISBN 0 7546 0880 8

Global Financial Crime

Terrorism, Money Laundering and Offshore Centres

Edited by
DONATO MASCIANDARO

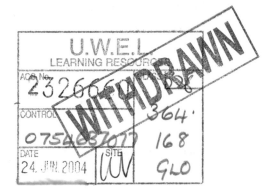

ASHGATE

Published by
Ashgate Publishing Limited
Gower House
Croft Road
Aldershot
Hants GU11 3HR
England

Ashgate Publishing Company
Suite 420
101 Cherry Street
Burlington, VT 05401-4405
USA

Ashgate website: http://www.ashgate.com

British Library Cataloguing in Publication Data
Global financial crime : terrorism, money laundering and offshore centres. -
   (Global finance series)
   1.Money laundering 2.International finance - Corrupt
   practices 3.Terrorism - Finance 4.Banks and banking,
   Foreign 5.Financial institutions - Law and legislation
   I.Alworth, Julian S. II.Masciandaro, Donato, 1961-
   364.1'68

Library of Congress Cataloging-in-Publication Data
Global financial crime : terrorism, money laundering and offshore centres / edited
by Donato Masciandaro.
      p. cm. -- (Global finance)
Includes bibliographical references and index.
   ISBN 0-7546-3707-7
   1. Money laundering. 2. Transnational crime. 3. Terrorism--Economic aspects. I.
Masciandaro, Donato, 1961- II. Series: Global finance series.

   HV6768.G56 2004
   364.16'8--dc22

                                                                        2003025531
ISBN 0 7546 3707 7

Printed by TJ International Ltd, Padstow, Cornwall

Contents

List of Contributors

Vito Tanzi Inter-American Development Bank and United Nations

George Peter Gilligan Department of Business Law and Taxation, Monash University, Melbourne

Barry A.K. Rider Director, Institute for Advanced Legal Studies, London

Friedrich Schneider Linz University

Donato Masciandaro Paolo Baffi Centre, Bocconi University, Lecce University and Institute for International Political Studies

Alessandro Portolano Bank of Italy, Rome

Julian Alworth Econpubblica, Bocconi University

Chizu Nakajima Director, Centre for Financial Regulation, Cass Business School, City University, London

Foreword

Vito Tanzi

Until the early 1990s few people had heard the term 'money laundering'. If they had, they probably associated it with the process of removing damaged or dirty bills from circulation to replace them with newly printed ones. If few had heard the term, even fewer would have known what it meant. Over the last decade, the term has gained much wider recognition among the general public. Many are now aware that it refers to a phenomenon related to activities that are not socially acceptable.

Over this period, there have been many newspaper articles about the leaders of countries such as the Philippines, Nigeria, Pakistan, as well as other individuals that allegedly stole large sums whilst in power and deposited these sums in places where the money was safe because banking secrecy or other rules made access to it difficult or impossible. These stories have helped to heighten interest in this phenomenon on the part of the public and have shown that the activities to which 'money laundering' refers are not trivial.

As was inevitable, the phenomenon has also attracted the attention of experts and academics. In recent years, many articles and books dealing with money laundering have been published and specialized journals dealing exclusively with this phenomenon are now available to those with a deep interest in it.

Money laundering makes one think immediately of a process by which something that is not clean becomes clean. It thus starts with the concept of dirty money. However, the money is obviously not dirty in some physical sense. Rather, its dirtiness refers to the way it was obtained. Behind the concept of dirty money there is the view that the money has been obtained in some illegitimate, illegal, or criminal way. Thus, at the origin of dirty money, there must be some dirty or antisocial activities – activities that have been prohibited by society.

In earlier years, money laundering was largely connected with the proceeds from traditional criminal activities as well with the avoidance of particular economic regulations, such as those that prohibited the exportation of capital. More recently, money laundering has been connected with more modern crimes. For example, the smuggling and the marketing of illegal drugs or weapons has at times generated huge earnings to those who engage in these activities.

In 1988, Forbes magazine placed Pablo Escobar, the notorious drug smuggler from Colombia among the richest people on earth. His fortune was estimated to amount to several billion dollars. This wealth needed to be invested in activities that would not attract the attention of the authorities of different countries. In other words, it had to be cleaned or laundered.

Since the tragic episode of September 11, 2001, a new activity has been connected with the phenomenon of money laundering, namely terrorism. The perpetrators of acts of terrorism need money to carry out their terrorist activities. This money must get to them in ways that do not attract attention. In this particular case it is not necessary that the origin of the money is criminal. In fact, this money could come from legitimate activities. Rather, it is its use that is criminal. In any case, there is a strong interest on the part of those who participate in acts of terrorism as well of those who send the money to hide its origin and its destination.

Although the amount of money connected with terrorist activities is not likely to be large and is certainly much lower than that associated with drug trafficking or with weapons smuggling, for obvious reasons the link between money and terrorism has given a strong stimulus to the general fight against money laundering. The American government has taken the lead in this fight and has given it an international character. Various international institutions have stepped in to assist in this fight.

This new book, *Global Financial Crime,* is a welcome addition to the growing literature on the subject. I am confident that it will be much appreciated by those interested in the subject and should also contribute in some way to the fight against black money and the activities connected with it. The book brings together contributors with skills from different disciplines and the accumulated knowledge of experts who can cast new light on the topic. The book not only surveys the existing literature and reports on many of the ongoing initiatives in the fight against money laundering but it also tries to break new ground and to bring new insight by using innovative tools and much originality in discussing and in explaining the phenomenon. The authors emphasize the role that incentives play in this phenomenon and the costs associated with fighting it. The book also discusses why the laundering of drug money may be different from the laundering of terrorist funds. This difference must be taken into account in the fight against black finance.

This book is particularly interesting in the discussion of the difficulties in defining various phenomena and in assessing the costs and the benefits of initiatives that aim at eliminating all forms of money laundering. Should the objective be to reduce to zero the possibility of engaging in money laundering? But even if this were possible, how costly would reaching this goal be? Are we sure that a world with total transparency in financial transactions and with strict rules that prohibit any informal financial transactions would necessarily be a better world?

In various parts of the book, the conflict between national sovereignty and the need for a global strategy is addressed. Nobody would like to have an independent international police force. At the same time a strategy fragmented among various national police forces and justice systems has obvious limitations.

I hope that this book will receive the attention that it deserves. I also hope that it will help in the important fight against a phenomenon that cannot be allowed to grow.

Introduction

Donato Masciandaro

New York, September 2001; Riyadh and Casablanca, May 2003. The first date is that of the horrific attack by international terrorism on the orderly development of civil society; the second recalls the tragic pursuit of terrorism's deadly strategy of intimidation.

The risk from terrorism has impacted heavily upon the evolution of the international financial markets and their regulation. Right from 12 September 2001, a crucial query began to circulate with insistence within the world economy, and not just there: what will change for the banks and stock markets of the world after the apocalypse of New York?

Naturally, the initial summations dwelled on the painful observation of the costly tribute paid in human lives and on the unknowns linked to the possible crumbling of trust in the normal course of economic and financial activities.

Meanwhile, however, the world immediately began to question, with a longer perspective, how this would affect a cornerstone of recent developments in the international financial markets: the 'neutrality' of the capital exchanged there.

There is no doubt, in fact, that the increasing fluidity of international financial interchange in recent decades has depended, all other things being equal, on the de facto 'neutrality' attributed to the capital handled in the markets, as far as its origin and final destination are concerned. Capital, in other words, has increasingly tended to have neither nationality, colour nor odour: it has been 'faceless' capital, moved exclusively by expectations of remuneration.

Nevertheless, in a context where the 'war against terrorism' has become a worldwide priority, assuming as an essential strategic objective the dismantling of the forms of financing to fundamentalist groups, it was inevitable that authorities and public opinion would become extremely sensitive regarding the exact origin and destination of such capital.

The end of capital neutrality implies that the principle of free circulation does *not* consider all financial flows: if a given amount of capital is of criminal origin, is earmarked to finance terrorist activity, or possesses both characteristics, it must be blocked and intercepted.

The war against capital laundering or, as it were, *black global finance*, intended as an effort against the financing of both terrorism and organised crime, thus occupies the centre of the agenda of national policymakers and international institutions. It is a fact that the first official act of the Bush Administration in the war on terrorism was precisely a declaration of 'financial war'.

At the level of economic analysis, the end of capital neutrality poses an interesting dilemma: what relationship exists between the quest for efficient allocation of resources – a cardinal principle of market economies – and safeguarding the integrity of financial flows themselves – also a fundamental principle for proper development of a market society – from the risks of contamination related to the activities and purposes of terrorist and criminal organisations?

The financial war on terrorism and organised crime is based on four basic postulates. The first Postulate is *Vulnerability to Terrorism Financing Risk*. The world network of the banking and financial industry, beyond the specific awareness of the majority of individual intermediaries and professionals who work in it, is the linchpin of the mechanisms that permit the financing of international terrorism.

The second Postulate is the *Equivalence between Terrorism Financing Risk and Criminal Capital Laundering Risk*. The mechanisms that facilitate the financing of terrorism are the same that permit the laundering of the illicit capital of transnational criminal organisations, a phenomenon long the subject of concerned attention on the part of authorities and regulators.

The third Postulate is *Offshore as a Catalyst of Terrorism Financing Risk*: the mechanisms of financing terrorism and laundering criminal capital can function in a world financial network because in that network there are 'weak' nodes or 'black holes' represented by offshore financial centres (OFCs).

The fourth Postulate is the *Equivalence of Offshore Centres as a Catalyst of Terrorism Financing Risk and Fiscal Damage Risk*: the weak nodes in the network are particularly dangerous because they not only facilitate the financing of terrorism and the laundering of criminal capital but also facilitate unfair tax competition among sovereign nations; this last problem is also increasingly a subject of concern to policymakers.

Our four postulates emerge from an examination of the documents of the international organisations dedicated to the war on terrorism financing. In May 2002, for example, the OECD Council at Ministerial Level affirmed that (page 1):

> The scope for financial crime has widened with the expansion and increased integration of financial markets. Money laundering, terrorism financing and tax crime have to the changed in both nature and dimension. Today the potential for financial abuse can threaten the strategic, political and economic interest of sovereign states. Widespread financial abuse undermines the integrity of the international financial system and raises new challenges for policymakers, financial supervisors and enforcement agencies. In certain jurisdictions such abuse may go so far as to undermine the democratic basis of government itself.

And again (page 2):

Poorly regulated financial markets not only open up new opportunities for financial crimes but also threaten the stability of the international financial system. As new technologies reduce the importance of physical proximity to major on-shore financial centres, so a new generation of Offshore Financial Centres (OFCs) has emerged. Remote jurisdictions bereft of natural resources and too isolated to benefit significantly from the global economy have established OFCs characterised by strict bank secrecy, criminal penalties for disclosure of client information and a policy or practice of non-cooperation with regulatory, supervisory and law enforcement agencies of other countries. This new generation of OFCs has succeeded in attracting brass plate banks, anonymous financial companies and asset protection trusts.

A global strategy to prevent and combat international terrorism has been defined in the international forums. This strategy identifies 'uncooperative' countries and territories and uses the threat of sanction. The fulcrum of the financial war consists of blacklisting recalcitrant parties.

Considerable work on the OFCs has been done by the Basle Committee, IOSCO, FAFT, UN, OECD, and the G-7 Finance Ministers. In 1999, the Financial Stability Forum established an ad hoc Working Group, that submitted a Report in March 2000.

The first official 'blacklists' included several countries all over the world. Looking just at the action by FATF (Financial Action Task Force), this OECD-connected organisation has now monitored up to 45 countries which represent 8 per cent of total GDP, 15 per cent of overall population, and 25 per cent of world foreign bank deposits. In June 2003, the FAFT revised its Forty Recommendations for combating money laundering and terrorist financing, calling for special attention to business relationships and transactions with persons, including companies and financial institutions, from countries that do not apply the FAFT Recommendations. And, as the OECD pointed out, other OFCs may exist or emerge.

The objective of this volume is to analyse the robustness of the four postulates that form the basis for the financial war on terrorism and organised crime, investigating possible origins and effects in order to gauge the effectiveness of the design of regulatory policy.

To do this, we must study the relationship existing between international movements of capital and the role of offshore centres, with respect to three different themes: the financing of terrorism, the laundering of illegal capital and tax competition.

Obviously, the complexity of the topic does not concern just the overlapping of at least three distinct problem areas but also the need to use cognitive instruments associated with different disciplines: economic, legal and social sciences.

This is why a multidisciplinary approach has been adopted in this volume, so as to arrive at common conclusions in the definition of policy guidelines. In this respect, the editor wishes to express gratitude to the Institute for International Political Studies (ISPI) that promoted the research programme.

Multidisciplinary work can be an important asset for a book, but it is also a challenge for an editor, given the trade-off between homogeneity in the focus of the volume and the richness – that is means heterogeneity – of its analyses.

Here, given the ex ante chapters' content coordination by the editor, every author was autonomous in choosing their methodological approach and the writing style consistent with his or her own scientific discipline, with the aim of reaching, at the end of the story, common conclusions on policy design.

The volume is organised as follows. Chapter 1 introduces the theme, illustrating how the problem of the presence of offshore centres has gradually emerged, first in combating organised crime and then in combating the financing of terrorism.

Offshore Financial Centres (OFCs) are defined as those countries and territories whose profile of financial and/or fiscal rules has been judged damaging by the major industrial nations and by supranational institutions in terms of defending the integrity of international capital flows and/or correctness in the fiscal and financial competition among countries.

The analysis in Chapter 1 presents the opposition of two viewpoints, which helps to explain why progress is so difficult towards an international design of rules approved by all.

On the one hand there is the dominant viewpoint of the countries we shall call 'onshore', i.e. the more developed nations, which feel that the increasing integration of world banking and financial markets requires the progressively stronger coordination of financial policy decisions – as well as fiscal policy, according to one current of thought – of all countries and territories, none excluded, in accordance with rules defined internationally.

Without this, there is a strong risk that opportunistic conduct on the part of individual countries will negatively influence the dynamics of capital movements, introducing risks for both the integrity and efficiency of the worldwide resource allocation process. In this approach, the financial war on terrorism and organised crime becomes an important step in defining effective rules and deterrent sanctions for those countries that derive the benefits of international financial globalisation without paying the price in terms of compliance.

On the other hand, however, there is also the viewpoint of the offshore countries, which on grounds of legitimacy challenge both the method and the merit of the action of the international institutions, inspired in turn by the intentions of the onshore countries.

The question of legitimacy ultimately raises important questions about the entire architecture of the financial war – which we have defined here in the four postulates – and from a number of approaches: institutional, economic and political.

Thus, there clearly emerges the necessity for diversified analyses, conducted with the methodological instrument of the various disciplines.

Chapter 2 starts with an institutional and legal point of view and then deals with the study of the evolution of international legislation, first against organised crime and then against terrorism. The attention is focused on the centrality assigned by the onshore countries to two themes: on the one hand, the risks associated with the diffusion of terrorist and criminal finance; on the other, the need to reduce these risks by convincing the offshore countries to modify substantively their policies in both the financial field and in taxation. Both of these themes can be examined in parallel from the economic standpoint.

Regarding the financing of terrorism, Chapter 3 analyses the possible characteristics of the financial flows benefiting Islamic fundamentalist organisations, even proposing a preliminary estimate of them based on econometric techniques.

Concerning the policies of the offshore countries, Chapter 4 analyses the policies of financial regulation, while Chapter 5 examines taxation policies.

Both chapters take a careful approach to the indications of both the new political economics and the new comparative economics. They seek to understand the determinants of the choices of economic policy of the offshore countries, starting with an overall examination of the economic, political and geographical characteristics of those countries, alternating theoretical analysis with econometric verification.

The objective of the analysis is to study both the problem of laxity in financial regulation and the problem of harmful tax competition, to achieve better understanding of the objective functions of the various policymakers so as to define what design of international regulation can best reconcile the interests of the onshore countries with those of the offshore countries, so as to obtain a positive-sum game.

Finally, a concrete example of progress achieved in the political attitude of the 'onshores' and 'offshores' toward the rules can already be observed by analysing the path taken by jurisdictions straddling the two shores, the so-called UK territories: Guernsey, Isle of Man, Jersey and Gibraltar. Chapter 6 is devoted to this analysis.

In the end, the parallel study of the economic, institutional and political aspects produces common conclusions both on the model of analysis of the four postulates at the base of the financial war on terrorism and on the desirable characteristics that a policy of prevention and contrast should have in order to combine the quest for efficiency with the protection of integrity in defining the international rules on capital movements. The policy conclusions are presented in the final chapter.

Chapter 1

Overview: Markets, Offshore Sovereignty and Onshore Legitimacy

George Peter Gilligan

Introduction

The world economy and individual national economies are becoming increasingly internationalised and interdependent, and this impacts upon the capability of the vast majority of individual nation states to control how their national economies function within the world economy. This can happen in a number of ways. It may be a matter of a deliberate choice in policy, as in the case of those Member States of the European Union (EU) who adopted the euro as their common currency, thereby reducing their flexibility regarding national monetary policy. In addiction, there are significant effects that may be not a discrete policy initiative but are due rather to the growing influence of more internationalised markets in goods and services, whereby all manner of resources and trading relationships may be transferred in and around global, regional and national markets. Consequently, as economic and political ties between many jurisdictions are deepening, nation states are increasingly playing a mediating role regarding the interests of much business that may be conducted within their spheres of influence. These developments are affecting contemporary understandings of sovereignty, as national political priorities become more intertwined with international politics and the requirements of international business.[1] A major consequence of these developments is that regulatory structures and processes have become more internationalised and a variety of modes of governance are emerging that have a capacity for impacts of broad international scope. These shifts in regulatory power can be manifested in a global sense through bodies such as the Basle Committee on Banking Supervision (BCBS), the International Association of Insurance Supervisors (IAIS), the International Organisation of Securities Commissions (IOSCO), and the World Trade Organisation (WTO). The capacity for international regulation also can be facilitated through networks of specific agreements between professional bodies,

---

[1] These developments are growing in impact and some commentators such as Chayes and Chayes see sovereignty as a form of status with multiple elements. See: A. Chayes and A.H. Chayes, 1995.

between state-sanctioned self-regulatory organisations and between government departments of different jurisdictions. Consequently, agreements can be multi-lateral, through mechanisms such as international treaties and conventions, or bilateral, such as a memorandum of understanding (MOU) between the national securities regulators, or mutual agreements between the taxation authorities of different jurisdictions.[2] Significant motivations for many of these agreements are a desire for higher levels of stability and/or capability in the economic arena, and increased capacity to manage risk.

Inevitably, different national and cultural influences will impact upon both national systems of regulation and on emerging modes of global governance, and in a more international context some of these value systems may conflict. In some situations there can be disagreement about what should constitute prevailing standards of compliance and the repercussions of such disagreements can be substantial. For example, at the time of writing this chapter[3] (February 2003), arguably the most important geopolitical issue is the US-led campaign regarding Iraq and its alleged failures to comply with numerous UN Security Council Resolutions concerning weapons of mass destruction.[4] However, there has been disagreement between different countries not only about how best to evaluate Iraq's levels of compliance with a number of UN Security Council Resolutions but also to decide what recriminations Iraq should face for perceived non-compliance. At the heart of debates about Iraq and the actions of its President Saddam Hussein, are claims and counter-claims about notions and levels of legitimacy. Similar debates regarding interpretations of business norm and compliance standards have been ongoing within the financial services sector between a number of jurisdictions

---

[2] An example of the latter is the US-Switzerland Income Tax Convention. See for example: *Treasury Announces Mutual Agreement with Switzerland Regarding Tax Information Exchange*, 28 January 2003, http://www.ustreas.gov/press/releases/kd3795.htm.

[3] Editor's note: on March 17 President Bush gives Saddam Hussein and his sons 48 hours to leave Iraq; then on March 19 the US bombs Baghdad. On April 9, the Government and military abandon Baghdad and a crowd pulls down a giant Saddam statue. Finally, on May 22, the UN Security Council approves a resolution backing the US-led administration in Iraq and the lifting of economic sanctions

[4] The prospect of armed conflict over these compliance issues is growing and the 2003 State of the Union address by US President George W. Bush has been interpreted widely as a call to wage war against Iraq. For example: M. Wilkinson, 'Bush makes case for war', *The Age*, 30 January, 2003, p.1; and Hartcher, P. (2003), 'Bush vows to go it alone on Iraq', *The Australian Financial Review*, 30 January, p.1.

and various organisations, such as the Organisation for Economic Cooperation and Development (OECD),[5] the Financial Action Task Force (FATF)[6] and the Financial Stability Forum (FSF).[7] In many ways this is not surprising and is

---

[5] The OECD is based in Paris and comprises 30 member countries, with the European Commission as an international organisation member. The 30 member countries are: Australia, Austria, Belgium, Canada, Czech Republic, Denmark, Finland, France, Germany, Greece, Hungary, Iceland, Ireland, Italy, Japan, Korea, Luxembourg, Mexico, Netherlands, New Zealand, Norway, Poland, Portugal, Slovak Republic, Spain, Sweden, Switzerland, Turkey, the United Kingdom (UK) and the United States (US). All members share a stated commitment to democratic government and the market economy. The OECD has active relationships with 70 other countries and seeks to foster good governance in the public service and in corporate activity. For more information regarding the OECD, see: http://www.oecd.org.

[6] The Financial Action Task Force on Money Laundering (FATF) is an inter-governmental organisation that seeks to develop and promote policies at both national and international levels to combat money laundering. The FATF was established following the G7 Summit held in Paris in 1989. G7 members are: Canada, France, Germany, Italy, Japan, the United Kingdom (UK) and the United States (US). Initially, the FATF was convened from the G7 member States, The European Commission (EC) and eight other countries, but it now has a membership of 29 jurisdictions, with the EC and the Gulf Cooperation Council as member international organisations. The 29 member jurisdictions are: Argentina, Australia, Austria, Belgium, Brazil, Canada, Denmark, Finland, France, Germany, Greece, Hong Kong, Iceland, Ireland, Italy, Japan, Luxembourg, Mexico, Netherlands, New Zealand, Norway, Portugal, Singapore, Spain, Sweden, Switzerland, Turkey, the United Kingdom (UK) and the United States (US). The FATF has a small Secretariat that is housed in the headquarters of the OECD in Paris, but the FATF is a separate international body and not part of the OECD. For more background information regarding the FATF, see: http://www.oecd.org/fatf/.

[7] The FSF was established following the meetings in October 1998 in Washington DC and in Bonn in February 1999 of the Finance Ministers and Central Bank Governors of the G7, which commissioned (in Washington), and later accepted (in Bonn), the recommendation of the *Tietmeyer Report*, on *International Co-operation and Co-ordination in the Area of Financial Market Supervision and Surveillance* to establish a Financial Stability Forum. The FSF was convened on 14 April 1999 to promote international financial stability through international co-operation and information exchange in financial supervision and surveillance. The FSF has a total of 40 members comprising: Chairman (1), representatives of National Authorities (25), International Financial Institutions (6), International Regulatory and Supervisory Groupings (6) and Committees of Central Bank Experts (2). Of the National Authority Representatives: the G7 member countries each supply three (from their treasury, central bank and financial supervisory agency); and Australia, Hong Kong, Netherlands and Singapore each supply a single representative. Regarding the International Financial Institutions, representatives are drawn from: International Monetary Fund (2), World Bank (2), Bank for International Settlements (1) and OECD (1). Representatives of the International Regulatory and Supervisory Groupings are: BCBS (2), IOSCO (2) and IAIS (2). The Committee on the Global Payments System (1) and the Committee on Payment and Settlement Systems (1) represent the Committees of Central Bank Experts. The FSF has a small Secretariat housed at the Bank for International Settlements in Basel, Switzerland. For more background information regarding the FSF, see: http://fsforum.org/About/Home.html.

indicative of the difficulties associated with developing an integrated international regulatory response to the phenomenon of the internationalisation of financial capital, much of which is highly liquid and some of which may be controlled by entities that may be incorporated or have some connection in offshore financial centres (OFCs).[8] As we will stress in all the chapters of the book, there are numerous interpretations of what constitutes an OFC. One useful working definition is:

> ...a centre that hosts financial activities that are separated from major regulating units (states) by geography and/or by legislation. This may be a physical separation, as in an island territory, or within a city such as London, the New York International Banking Facilities (IBFs).[9]

The International Monetary Fund (IMF) provides an alternative working definition that focuses on the practices of OFCs:

> a centre where the bulk of financial sector activity is offshore on both sides of the balance sheet (that is the counter parties of the majority of financial institutions' liabilities and assets are non-residents), where the transactions are initiated elsewhere, and where the majority of the institutions involved are controlled by non-residents.[10]

So it should be immediately clear that the generic term OFCs encompasses quite a diverse range of jurisdictions and financial centres with large variances in levels of available resources, and in levels of economic development. It is important to stress that OFCs are not a homogeneous grouping, as is discussed in some detail in this chapter and in Chapter 4.

It is imperative that regulatory initiatives regarding OFCs acknowledge the heterogeneity of OFCs in *meaningful* ways. Almost anywhere can fulfil the functions of an OFC and, in some ways, the label 'offshore' can be somewhat misleading. For example: OFCs can be small islands in the Caribbean, such as Barbados or St Lucia; small islands in the Pacific Ocean, such as the Cook Islands or Western Samoa; small islands in the Indian Ocean, such as Mauritius; small islands around the coast of the British Isles, such as Guernsey, Jersey or the Isle of Man; highly developed economies in Europe, such as the Principality of Liechtenstein or the Principality of Monaco; or specialist enclaves within financial centres, such as in Dublin, Ireland. OFCs that are quite small in physical terms may handle huge totals of financial capital. In 1999, for example, the combined total of funds managed by Jersey, Guernsey and the Isle of Man has been estimated to be

---

[8] For an analysis of the strategic role of OFCs see: M. Hampton, *The Offshore Interface, Tax Havens in the Global Economy*, Macmillan, London, 1996.

[9] M.P. Hampton, 'Treasure islands or fool's gold: Can and should small island economies copy Jersey?' *World Development*, 22, 1994, p. 237.

[10] International Monetary Fund, *Offshore Financial Centres, International Monetary Fund Background Paper*, 23 June 2000, p. 3.

more than US$ 600 billion, and the total has probably increased since then.[11] The IMF estimated that in mid-1999, on-balance sheet OFC cross-border assets comprised US$ 4.6 trillion, or 50 per cent of the world's total cross-border assets.[12]

Capital is intrinsically flexible, and under a market economy paradigm individuals and corporate entities (whether or not they are resident in advanced economies) will logically seek conditions of maximum reward for their capital. This may well include utilisation of the tax and other advantages offered by OFCs. It can be difficult for national regulators to decide whether capital moving through these centres is *clean* or part of some illegal operation such as tax evasion, fraud or money laundering.[13] Some OFCs may survive and thrive precisely because their regulatory structures and processes are either intensely resistant to outside scrutiny or they do not trouble to engage in active supervision of those entities that reside in their territory, but this is not necessarily true for all OFCs. Consequently, OFCs are a tremendous regulatory challenge for advanced economies, which themselves embrace the ideology of free trade and markets but may also be fiercely protective of national interests. The dilemmas associated with these important issues are a major motivation for the essays in this volume.

The aim of this chapter is to examine these debates from a perspective that synthesises a number of theoretical social constructs, in order to develop in the following chapters a multidisciplinary approach to the problem. These constructs are: legitimation and, most especially, social constructions of legitimacy;[14] structuration theory;[15] legal pluralism;[16] and the sociology of censure.[17] This

---

[11] M.P. Hampton and J. Christensen, 'The British Isle Offshore Financial Centres of Jersey, Guernsey, and the Isle of Man: Should the Onshore State Act?' *Tax Notes International*, 11 January 1999, p. 207.

[12] International Monetary Fund, *Offshore Financial Centres, International Monetary Fund Background Paper*, 23 June 2000, p. 9.

[13] One example is the Maxwell scandal, where Robert Maxwell utilised the secrecy provisions of Liechtenstein's regulatory systems to obfuscate ownership of his interlocking networks of trust and corporate holdings. This concealed his activities from UK regulators and facilitated his plundering of the pension fund of Mirror Group Newspapers (MGN) employees. See: R. Greenslade, *Maxwell's Fall*, Simon & Schuster, London, 1992.

[14] See: D. Beetham, *The Legitimation of Power*, Macmillan, London, 1991.

[15] Structuration theory emphasises the interaction between structures and human agency, interaction that may occur in past, present and future contexts. See: A. Giddens, *The Constitution of Society*, Polity Press, Cambridge, 1984.

[16] Legal pluralism is a perspective that emphasises different orders of legal rules and accepts the strength of principles and rules that are produced in a non-state environment. See generally: R. Macdonald, 'Metaphors of multiplicity: civil society, regimes and legal pluralism', *Arizona Journal of International and Comparative Law*, 15, 1998, p. 69; and G. Teubner, 'The two faces of Janus: rethinking legal pluralism', *Cardozo Law Review*, 13, 1992, p. 1443.

[17] A sociology of censure approach emphasises the fundamental importance of prevailing sets of power relations in determining how modes of censure are constructed and applied. See: C.S. Sumner, 'Rethinking deviance: towards a sociology of deviance', in C. Sumner (ed.), *Censure Politics and Criminal Justice*, Open University Press, Milton Keynes, 1990.

particular theoretical mix is especially useful for examining the wide array of forces that impact upon debates about whether and how OFCs might be regulated. Of particular importance for the purposes of this chapter, however, is the construct of legitimacy.

Legitimacy itself can be a complex and elastic concept. Legitimacy affects the character of power relations and can help explain systems of power, not only how power works as an ongoing process, but also how it originates.[18] There are two types of *story* of legitimacy: one is a story of developmental stages and the other is how self-confirming processes are at work within any settled power relations to reproduce and consolidate their legitimacy.[19] This cycle is never perfect or complete and is open to contextual influences, whether those influences reside in arenas as diverse as the domestic political sphere or the international regulatory context.[20] Legitimacy is integral to any system of regulation or body of knowledge, and it can reside in positions of authority or in institutions.[21] It is a complex concept, however, involving not only beliefs, but also legality, judicial determination, and consent, both active and passive. This chapter considers legitimacy regarding OFCs and their regulatory context, rather than as an absolute ideal, or as an abstract concept, because legitimacy and consent are culturally specific matters.[22]

The financial services sector, like most societies or social groupings, functions through legitimacy by expressed consent to existing power relations. Within democracies, people confer legitimacy by voting for preferred candidates or political parties and accepting the overall political framework. Often, however, power does not act in a linear fashion, and sometimes powerful interest groups may manufacture their own rationalisations in order to legitimate their preferred positions. These processes can occur in a global political context, as with recent international debates surrounding Iraq, on a macro scale within a huge industry like financial services, as seen in the recent efforts of international organisations like the OECD, FSF and FATF, or on a micro scale, as Flyvbjerg found in his 15-year study of how power was operationalised in municipal urban planning in Denmark.[23] An example of these regulatory legitimation processes in a national context can be seen in the strenuous consultation efforts of the UK Government

---

[18] D. Beetham, *The Legitimation of Power*, Macmillan, London, 1991, p. 38, and pp. 100-101.

[19] *Ibid*, pp. 98-99.

[20] For analysis of how constructs of legitimacy can impact in international arenas see: T.M. Franck, 'Legitimacy in the international system', *American Journal of International Law*, 82 (4), 1988, pp. 705-759; and T.M. Franck, *The Power of Legitimacy Among Nations*, Oxford University Press, New York, 1990.

[21] T.R. Tyler, *Why People Obey the Law*, Yale University Press, New Haven, 1990, p. 29.

[22] For a critical analysis of how legitimacy issues impact upon the regulatory structures and processes of financial services regulation, especially regarding the UK, see: G.P. Gilligan, *Regulating the Financial Services Sector*, Kluwer Law International, London, 1999.

[23] B. Flyvbjerg, *Rationality and Power: Democracy in Practice*, Chicago University Press, Chicago, 1998.

prior to the Financial Services and Markets Act 2000, as the Labour Government sought to engender significant levels of interest group participation in the developmental stages of the Act.[24]

Regulatory norms and standards can be local, national or international phenomena, and as regulatory space becomes more congested and contested, increasing importance is accorded to those actors perceived as possessing specialist knowledge and professional legitimacy. This professional knowledge may be employed strategically in regulatory disputes between practitioners of regulation, or amongst the regulated, or between groupings such as the OECD and International Tax and Investment Organisation (ITIO).[25]

As we shall analyse in Chapter 5, under contemporary trading conditions, taxation could become a site of dispute between jurisdictions, international organisations and regional groupings as the 21st century progresses.[26] That taxation should be a springboard for, or a source of, conflict, is of course not a new phenomenon. For example, a key trigger in cementing support for the ultimately successful independence struggle of the UK's only contemporary superpower was a taxation protest by American colonial patriots that is celebrated in US folklore as *The Boston Tea Party*, when on 16 December 1773 angry colonial settlers hurled hundreds of crates of tea from three English ships into Boston Harbour.[27] The protest was not sparked by any new tax, indeed the relevant Tea Act actually removed duties and tariffs, but only for the East India Company and its nominated American merchants. So the Boston Tea Party was actually about issues of

---

[24] Examples of Consultation Papers can be accessed at the websites of HM Treasury and the Financial Services Authority. See: http://www.hm-treasury.gov.uk and http://www.fsa.gov.uk.

[25] Members of the ITIO are: Anguilla, Antigua and Barbuda, Bahamas, Barbados, Belize, British Virgin Islands, Cayman Islands, Cook Islands, Malaysia, St Kitts and Nevis, St Lucia, Turks and Caicos and Vanuatu. Organisations that have formal observer status with the ITIO include the CARICOM Secretariat, the Commonwealth Secretariat and the Pacific Islands Forum Secretariat. The disagreements between the OECD and the ITIO have been sparked by the OECD's efforts to eliminate what it sees as harmful tax competition, the effects of which are discussed in more detail below.

[26] An example of this potential for dispute is the ongoing disagreement over a period of some years between various Member States of the EU, the European Commission (EC) and other European jurisdictions, such as Switzerland, concerning the efforts of specific EU Member States to introduce a Savings Tax Directive and/or various forms of a withholding tax with regard to the assets of individuals that may be held in different jurisdictions.

[27] The Boston Tea Party incident was specifically a protest against the preferential treatment given by the British Government to the East India Company (EIC) regarding how the EIC's tea would be sold within the American colonies. More importantly, along with the Sugar Act of 1764, Stamp Act of 1765 and the Townshend Acts of 1767, it was part of a series of taxation initiatives of the Government of King George III that the American colonists saw as *taxation without representation*. For further information see: http://www.bostonteapartyship.com/History.htm; and http://odur.let.rug.nl/~usa/E/teaparty/bostonxx.htm.

inclusion, exclusion, notions of equity and the legitimacy of external bodies, in this case the British Government, to structure markets through regulation.

These issues of inclusion, exclusion, taxation, representation, regulation and legitimation are as intertwined today as they were in the 1760s, and it is the inter-connectedness of these issues as they relate to the regulation of OFCs that is the core focus of this chapter. These issues are applied as a conceptual matrix from which to examine the ramifications of recent regulatory activity by international organisations such as the OECD, FATF and FSF, especially the processes associated with, and the effects of, the so-called blacklists that they have produced.[28] The memberships of the OECD, FATF and FSF are dominated by the more powerful advanced economies, and the vast majority of OFCs are not well represented within these organisations. Some of the critics of the various measures introduced by the OECD, FATF and FSF have highlighted what they perceive as the relative exclusion of the interests and *voice* of the OFCs from the evaluation and blacklisting processes introduced by the OECD, FATF and FSF. Sir Ronald Sanders, Antigua and Barbuda's Chief Negotiator on international financial services, for example, has described the early efforts of the OECD regarding harmful tax competition initiatives as 'high-handed'.[29]

In 2003, in an increasingly global economy, with its increasing number of international, indeed global in many cases, business actors taken with the increasing potential for global, or at least multiple citizenship for individuals, the capacity to levy taxes and subsequently provide services to citizens, both natural and corporate, is central to how political and economic structures will be organised. It is in this context that the role of OFCs and their regulation should be considered, because they have the capacity to upset the *cosy tea party* nature of recent attempts by international organisations and regional groupings to determine what should be the parameters of operation for the provision of financial services on an international or distance basis.

It should be borne in mind at all times that the intensely competitive environment of the financial services sector informs all regulatory developments in the area. In recent years, there have been regulatory initiatives and reports from a number of international organisations including the BCBS,[30] the EU, the FATF, the FSF, the IMF, IOSCO, the OECD and the World Bank. Some of the reports of these organisations have been accepted without rancour by governments and by participants in the financial sector. For example, the BCBS has produced frameworks of standards and voluntary principles that have been adopted by many central banks and other

---

[28] Appendices A-C detail which jurisdictions have been listed by the FATF, the FSF and the OECD, and when those listings occurred. Appendices D-E consolidate the various blacklists produced by these organisations and the effects of these blacklisting processes are discussed throughout this chapter.

[29] 'Antigua queries IMF anti-money laundering methodology', *Tax-News.com*, 3 February 2003, http://www.tax-news.com/asp/story/story.asp?storyname=10711. These issues of representation and legitimation are discussed in more detail throughout this chapter.

[30] Much of the administrative and research function of the BCBS is carried out by the Bank for International Settlements (BIS), which is based in Basel, Switzerland.

regulatory agencies in their supervision of financial institutions.[31] Similarly, IOSCO set out in detail how regulators, issuers, market intermediaries and secondary markets could meet IOSCO's Objectives and Principles of Securities Regulation.[32] However, as is discussed in more detail below, the outputs of other international organisations such as the OECD, FSF and FATF have met with a more mixed reception. There has been considerable discussion in several international fora about blacklists of jurisdictions, whereby, for example, those jurisdictions with bank secrecy regimes that are perceived as obstructive in some quarters might be penalised by the international community in other trade contexts. Any subsequent sanctions could be extremely damaging to smaller jurisdictions and raise issues of legitimacy. This chapter examines in some detail the social and political dimensions of recent international regulatory initiatives that seek to impact upon OFCs, particularly the interpretations put forward by various actors of both the legitimacy of these initiatives and responses to them, interpretations that sometimes may be contradictory. First, however, it would be helpful to consider briefly how and why OFCs have emerged, and their role within the contemporary financial sector.

OFCs, International Financial Markets and Regulatory Competition: The Legitimacy Challenge

Banking has always had a tradition of confidentiality, but the codification of specific bank secrecy laws is more recent, originating in Switzerland in the 1930s.[33] This was largely a response to the efforts of many German Jews seeking to repatriate their assets in Switzerland outside the reach of the Third Reich regime that was persecuting them. The new law and Switzerland's subsequent reputation for bank secrecy proved a boon to its financial sector, and Switzerland has become 'the world's third-largest financial power'.[34]

Unsurprisingly, and as will be empirically demonstrated in Chapter 4, many other jurisdictions around the world, especially those that are smaller, lack much in the way of natural resources and are less wealthy, have been impressed by the Switzerland experience and subsequently have sought to replicate it to some extent. They have seen how a small jurisdiction like Switzerland, by providing an environment that is attractive to incoming capital, can compete effectively in the enormously lucrative markets for provision of financial services and products. The

---

[31] Examples of BCBS work include: *Principles for the Supervision of Banks' Foreign Establishments*, Basel, May 1983; *Minimum Standards for the Supervision of International Banking Groups and Their Cross-Border Establishments*, Basel, July 1992; and *The Core Principles for Effective Banking Supervision*, Basel, September 1997.

[32] See: www.iosco.org/docs-public/1998-objectives-document04.html; and www.iosco.org/docs-public/1998-objectives-document05.html.

[33] The Federal Law Relating to Banks and Savings Banks 1934.

[34] G.J. Moscarino and M.R. Shumaker, 'Beating the shell game: bank secrecy laws and their impact on civil recovery in international fraud actions', *The Company Lawyer*, 18, 1997, p. 177.

net result is an increasing number of jurisdictions entering the financial services sector, with many of these new entrants seeking to establish themselves as OFCs.

It seems perfectly reasonable and legitimate that jurisdictions large and small should take this path, as they seek to generate wealth and other public goods for their local communities. However, some OFCs have been accused of facilitating money laundering, tax evasion and other external costs to other members of the international financial community, and it is these effects that have prompted criticism and prospective punitive measures from the OECD, FATF and others.

Nevertheless, despite the blacklists produced by these organizations in recent years, it is hard to be definitive about the regulatory issues regarding OFCs. There can be multiple interpretations for the actions and regulatory infrastructures of OFCs, and this is perhaps not so surprising when one considers that, for some time, the specific place of OFCs in the lower hierarchies of international financial capital has been described as 'quite murky – even confused'.[35] What is reasonably clear, and what might surprise some observers, is that OFCs have been around for a considerable length of time. The Netherlands Antilles, for example, has been an OFC since 1940. But the rapid growth of contemporary OFCs probably is best signalled by the emergence in the 1960s of a number of small island economies, such as Barbados, the Bahamas, the British Virgin Islands and the Cayman Islands, as OFCs. Many of the small OFCs are UK territories or independent states that are former UK colonies.[36] These jurisdictions have tended to be relatively stable politically and have a common law tradition. This mix, which is empirically investigated in Chapter 4, seems to lend itself to achieving the appropriate standards of trust that are essential within the participating networks of offshore exchange.

The single most important factor in the emergence of a greater number of OFCs in recent years, however, has arguably been the rapid development of information technology in the area. It is almost impossible to overstate the impact of the technological innovations of late-modernity on global financial markets in general, and on OFCs in particular. These technological innovations have facilitated the specific processes of trading in financial markets, allowing an enormous expansion in the numbers of actors involved in the provision of financial services around the world.

However, they have been especially helpful in the development of smaller OFCs, permitting their integration into the international financial sector *without* significant capital outlays. Even a tiny jurisdiction can now be a base to large numbers of global trades that can be made in a matter of seconds. Simultaneously, developments in information technology have opened up a huge pool of potential clients for the services that OFCs might provide, by massively enlarging the pools of investment opportunities, especially in international markets.

---

[35] S.C. Cobb, 'Global finance and the growth of offshore financial centers: the Manx experience', *Geoforum*, 29, 1998, p. 8.

[36] M.P. Hampton and M. Levi, 'Fast spinning into oblivion? Recent developments in money-laundering policies and offshore finance centres', *Third World Quarterly*, 20, 1999, p. 651.

These new features of financial markets are symptomatic of the broader characteristics of modernity that inevitably involve some disembedding of social relations from their traditional contexts and: 'in respect of the consequences of at least some disembedding mechanisms, no one can "opt out" of the transformations brought about by modernity'.[37] This disembedding of social relations can be seen in the reduced influence of religion, cultural traditions and place-based community pressures on human agents and social structures under conditions of late-modern market economy.

In financial services, these disembedding mechanisms have included: increased velocity and complexity in markets; an increasing disruption of existing forms of regulation, which is accompanied in turn by a continuing and increasing reliance upon co-operative international agreements for cohesion in national and international markets (a key driver for the FATF, FSF and OECD blacklisting processes); dismantling of the barriers separating professional groups; and increased competition between those professional groups, between financial centres and between regulators. There has been a significant process of disintermediation as restrictive practices in securities markets have been removed, commission rates have fallen, financial institutions have consolidated and the pools of both investment capital and clients hungry for financial services products and providers have expanded rapidly.

Certainly, most OFCs can be seen as definitely *opting-in* to the influences of the modern market economy, in order to derive some of the benefits offered by a rapidly globalising financial services sector. OFCs seek to service the growing numbers of investors who now can access many of the world's trading systems, resulting in: cheaper executions costs; increased competitive pressure on markets and greater flexibility for investors.

These developments do not come free of danger however and, in an increasingly uncertain world, strategies of personal and institutional risk management, and the importance of notions of trust to the success of these strategies, assume premium importance. In late-modern society, these sociologies of trust are being extended continually across time, space, information systems and anonymous commercial networks, which significantly enlarge the zones of risk. Regarding financial services, additional zones of risk are constantly being formed through the development of large numbers of new financial instruments and market participants. These are the products of an industry that is moving increasingly towards market-based, rather than relationship-based, financial intermediation. The growing numbers of finance centres mean that jurisdictions that may be very different in a whole host of ways are now interdependent players in the matrix of trust that underpins the world of finance. OFCs are increasingly being integrated into this new paradigm and are likely to remain a feature of the financial landscape for the foreseeable future.

These various expansions of risk place the trust networks of the financial services sector under increasing strain, however, as numerous forms of white-collar crime can be hidden more easily within the millions of electronic impulses that represent the complex trading of modern financial markets across a myriad of jurisdictions. It is the

---

[37] A. Giddens, *Modernity and Self Identity, Self and Society in the Late Modern Age,* Polity Press, Cambridge, 1991, p. 22.

role allegedly played by OFCs around the world in this expansion of crime risk that has become an increasing concern for international organisations such as the FATF, FSF and OECD in recent times. The growth prospects for the types of services provided by OFCs seem quite rosy in an era of late-modern market economy.

What is not so clear, however, is whether it will be the smaller OFCs or longer-established finance centres that will largely meet these needs in the future. At the most basic level, on grounds of equity and natural justice alone, it is hard to argue against the legitimate right of a jurisdiction to attempt to function as an OFC, but under what rules? Who, or what, should construct the regulatory frameworks for international financial services and how should they be policed in order to protect the legitimate interests of affected actors, such as preservation of the tax base of other jurisdictions? As always in life, it seems the devil is in the detail. Consequently, it is a core contention of this chapter that international efforts to shape the regulatory regimes and business activities of OFCs should be inclusive and holistic in their approaches. In particular, they should be transparent and honest about the realities of how commercial and regulatory competition impact upon emerging multilateral regulatory processes in the financial sector.

Overarching all the debates about the pros and cons of various regulatory models, processes and initiatives is the fundamental importance of competition amongst financial centres. Every jurisdiction, large or small, advanced or less-developed, onshore or offshore or both, seems to desire as large a market share and/or available revenues as possible.

There is increasing competition amongst various nation states and amongst financial centres for market share in the financial sector, and this competition is sure to become more intense as they seek to promote their individual versions of leading-edge business environments and associated regulatory infrastructures.

In recent years, for example, financial sector reform has been a high-profile issue in the United States, accompanied by intense political lobbying and public debate. Ed Yingling, the chief lobbyist for the American Bankers Association, has described banking reform as '...the most heavily lobbied, most expensive issue to come before congress in a generation'.[38] During 1997 and 1998 alone, the banking, insurance and securities industries are reported to have '...donated $87 million in so-called soft money to the political parties, and they reported spending $163 million in additional lobbying expenses'.[39] These large sums of money spent in order to nurture specific legislative change indicate how intense the pressures for seeking *internationally competitive regulation* can be, as financial centres and financial institutions seek to maintain or increase market share.

---

[38] There was wide media coverage of these issues, for a summary article see: J. Brinkley, 'Behind the Banking Bill, Years of Intense Lobbying', *The New York Times*, 23 October 1999.

[39] *Ibid.*

Such pressure can produce results, though, and the US Congress eventually passed the so-called Financial Modernization Bill.[40]

The net effect was the most significant overhaul of US financial services legislation since the *New Deal* era in the early 1930s. The reforms were described by President Clinton as a 'potentially historic agreement' and by then US Treasury Secretary Lawrence Summers as 'legislative foundation for a 21st century financial system'.[41]

The US reforms are symptomatic of the ongoing competitive regulatory change that permeates both the internal politics and practice of regulation in most jurisdictions around the world, and also the organisation of international arenas of competition in financial services. This is the economic and political reality that can act as a constraint or a stimulus to prevailing levels of regulatory action, or indeed in some instances, regulatory inaction.

Private, corporate and state forces are continually at work in the world of financial services regulation, which functions within more flexible and ill-defined parameters than many other areas of law. There is constant interaction between state and private influences, and between the regulators and regulated. It is inevitable that regulators respond to the market forces of their industry, and regulatory control is a reciprocal arrangement, shaped by negotiated and symbiotic relationships. It is not a static phenomenon, but rather a process of continuing political adaptation within a regulatory setting, in which actors can erode existing regulation, lobby for change and take advantage of competition between different regulatory regimes.

Like other legal arenas such as company law, financial services regulation is a social and political process, not a value-neutral and automatic system. A great deal of financial services regulation is expressed in broad standards and its mobilisation depends upon:

> a vast inter-organizational network of stock issuers, brokers, independent gatekeepers (lawyers, accountants, and the like), regulators, and investors who transcend the form and content of their constituent agencies to create a shared, albeit temporary and contingent, "regulatory authority".[42]

These disparate yet interdependent agents actually give shape and effect to these broad standards, thereby in effect *manufacturing regulatory law*. Of course major players such as the Stock Exchanges of London or New York, or a G7-backed

---

[40] The official title as introduced was: 'To enhance competition in the financial services industry by providing a prudential framework for the affiliation of banks, securities firms, and other financial services providers, and for other purposes'. The short titles as passed the House were: ATM Reform Act of 1999; Financial Services Act of 1999; and Federal Home Loan Bank System Modernization Act of 1999.

[41] S. Labaton, 'Agreement Reached on Overhaul of U.S. Financial System', *The New York Times*, 23 October 1999.

[42] N. Reichman, 'Moving Backstage, Uncovering the Role of Compliance Practices in Shaping Regulatory Policy' in K. Schlegel and D. Weisburd (eds), *White Collar Crime Reconsidered*, Northeastern University Press, Boston, 1992, p. 246.

organisation like the FATF, possess greater regulatory authority and therefore more capacity to set the rules or change the parameters of the regulation game than do smaller players.[43]

Financial regulation and other legal contexts, such as tax law, are not *givens* but a basis for negotiation for some major players.[44] In Chapters 4 and 5 the endogeneity of financial and tax policies are discussed. Professional groups, established institutional and social structures, interdependent relationships between markets, and national political priorities are some of the most powerful influences in the production of regulation.

Certainly these forces have been present in the regulatory changes that have accompanied recent trends in globalisation. Many of those individuals, organisations and governments contributing views to debates on how to best organise either their own domestic, or international, markets in financial products and services, may seek to justify their positions as in the public interest. However, what is the public good and what are and/or should be its parameters? The issues associated with these questions are fundamental to the organisation of any human interaction, whether that interaction takes place in a social, political or economic context, or indeed any combination of these contexts. The question of the public good is debated at all strata of all societies, and a universal definition is probably impossible to achieve. The public good might be described as the issue of collectives telling individuals '...what is good for them...' and labelling this 'the public interest'.[45] This 'alchemy of social construction of the public good' emerges in different forms in different societies as a component of the political economy.[46] As such, it is virtually impossible to eliminate political influences from decision-making in any regulatory forum, whether that forum is a global one like the United Nations, international like the OECD, or a small local council.

As with notions of the public good, there are very real problems of definition associated with regulation. In the context of the financial services sector, examples of regulation include provisions against insider trading and market manipulation, disclosure requirements, and compulsory probity standards for financial professionals.[47] The central element of regulation is interference, what I have termed elsewhere as '...the busybody model of the public interest'.[48] The extent of this

---

[43] E. Meidinger, 'Regulatory Culture A theoretical outline', *Law and Policy*, 9, 1987, p. 357.

[44] Y. Dezelay, 'Professional Competition and the Social Construction of Transnational Regulatory Expertise', in J. McCahery, S. Picciotto and C. Scott (eds), *Corporate Control and Accountability*, Clarendon Press, Oxford, 1993, p. 207.

[45] G.R. Underhill, 'The Public Good Versus Private Interests in the Global Monetary and Financial System', *International and Comparative Corporate Law Journal*, 2, 2000, p. 335.

[46] *Ibid*, p. 336.

[47] N. Poser, *International Securities Regulation – London's Big Bang and the European Securities Markets*, Little, Brown & Co., Boston, 1991, p.2.

[48] G.P. Gilligan, 'International trends in the regulation of the financial services sector', *Australian Journal of Corporate Law*, 14, 2002, p. 69.

interference, however, can be extremely difficult to measure precisely.[49] This notion of regulation as interference that is primarily conducted under the aegis of the state is an explanation that is accepted by most social scientists, lawyers and economists. Therefore, a reasonable working definition of regulation is:

> ...a means of coping with technological change: specialized enforcement agencies have been invented to get to grips with the problem of order in complex societies... [in which] ...some notion of the public good is to take precedence over narrow economic interests.[50]

So it is important to remember that regulation, like notions of the public interest, is fermented in the cauldrons of social construction that prevail at any time, in any society or other setting, and may be subject to multiple interpretations. But whose interpretations should be accepted and to what extent? A key concept in discerning and classifying these multiple interpretations is legitimacy. As international organisations such as the FATF, the FSF and the OECD assume a higher profile in how international regulatory financial infrastructures are constructed, there is an increasing emphasis on the legitimacy of the specific processes involved. This is especially the case regarding who actually participates in the relevant decision-making and their relative levels of influence on the decisions that are made. Indeed, in the cut and thrust of debates on any subject, whether football teams, political discourses or appropriate models and processes of regulation, it is by claiming legitimacy for a particular view of the world, or of specific phenomena, that a party will try to persuade others to support their position. This is very much the case for recent regulatory initiatives that can impact upon the activities of OFCs.

Legitimacy can be a culturally specific matter and play a key role in struggles for ideological and cultural dominance. As such it may be difficult to apply standards of legitimacy regarding systems of financial regulation that may be prevalent in wealthy large jurisdictions, such as the UK and the US, in much poorer jurisdictions, such as the Cook Islands and Nauru. It may be equally difficult to justify such standards in places such as Liechtenstein and Monaco, which are relatively wealthy small jurisdictions but are heavily dependent upon financial services for a significant proportion of their GDP.[51]

It is an economic fact of life in an increasingly competitive sector, for example, that the levels of secrecy that a jurisdiction can offer client investors may be related to the totals of capital flows routed through that jurisdiction, and subsequently the levels

---

[49] B.M. Mitnick, *The Political Economy of Regulation*, Columbia University Press, New York, 1980, pp. 2-7.

[50] K. Hawkins, Environment and Enforcement: Regulation and the Social Definition of Pollution, Clarendon Press, Oxford, 1984, p. 16.

[51] For example, 30 per cent of Liechtenstein's state revenues are generated by fees levied on holding companies, (sometimes called 'letter box' or 'shelf' companies), which have only a nominal presence in Liechtenstein. See: Bureau for International Narcotics and Law Enforcement Affairs, *International Narcotics Control Strategy Report 1999*, http://www.state.gov./www/global/narcotics_law/1999_narc_report/ml_country99. html, p. 80.

of fees and other associated incoming revenues that are generated by these flows. Self-interest is sure to be a powerful influence in such scenarios.

Some critics have contended that the major motivation for advanced economies attacking the banking regimes of OFCs via organisations such as the OECD is a concern for losses of revenue due to the tax management strategies of high net worth individuals or companies. Certainly in 2000 this was the argument of Sir James Mitchell, Prime Minister of St Vincent and the Grenadines, in his reaction to international initiatives regarding tax competition:

> Let it be clear that harmful tax competition has nothing to do with drug money or money laundering. We are doing nothing that is illegal or immoral. Tax competition is really about whose treasury gets the money. The international financial community urges competition and open markets but when we succeed they declare it unfair.[52]

Sir James Mitchell seems to be adopting an *Orwellian* perspective, in the sense that it might appear that all financial centres are equal in that they can access a globalising financial sector, but some are more equal than others. Levels of confidentiality in a jurisdiction's financial sector can be an intrinsically political issue fuelled by socio-political concerns and perceived as a fundamentally legitimate avenue of economic development.

It is important to remember that different jurisdictions have different perceptions about what their respective legitimate interests are. Some are increasing the levels of their bank secrecy provisions, whilst others are pursuing increased transparency in their financial systems. The political, social and economic implications of this asymmetry are apparent, as is the need for compromise on how appropriate levels of transparency in financial systems might be achieved. Statutory legislation alone may not be sufficient, and in many cases it may be the combined effects of both the supporting regulatory infrastructures and prevailing levels of commitment to specific standards of behaviour within both the political and business environments that are the key factors.

Normative issues are crucial, therefore, when seeking to understand issues of compliance, whether at the local, national or international level. Franck, in his efforts to produce a general theory of compliance, stressed that levels of compliance are shaped substantially by how legitimate the relevant rules are considered to be by those communities supposedly subject to them.[53]

Indeed, there is growing empirical evidence of '...a linear relationship between legitimacy and compliance, as legitimacy increases, so does compliance'.[54] Tyler found that issues of procedural justice are a crucial mediating factor in deciding

---

[52] Press release 87/2000, Address delivered by Sir James Mitchell, Prime Minister of St Vincent and the Grenadines, at the Opening Ceremony of the 21st Meeting of the Conference of Heads of Government of the Caribbean Community (CARICOM), Canouan,   St   Vincent   and   the   Grenadines,   2   July   2000, http://www.caricom.org/pres87_00.htm, July 2000.

[53] T.M. Franck, 'Legitimacy in the international system', *American Journal of International Law*, 82, 1988, p. 706.

[54] T.R. Tyler, *Why People Obey The Law*, Yale University Press, New Haven, 1990, p. 57.

whether people perceive legal processes as legitimate, and they can provide a valuable cushion for law enforcement agencies when they hand down unfavourable outcomes.[55]

There is every reason to believe that similar forces operate in the financial services sector and could even be more influential, given the symbiotic nature of its regulation and the less secure mandate that regulatory agencies and international organisations possess in comparison to the vast majority of local police forces and courts. Most people believe that laws should be obeyed, and it is this broader normative commitment to compliance as a general principle amongst those regulated that is perhaps the greatest asset that regulators and international organisations can access. This broader normative commitment is crucial for the development of national and international crime prevention strategies in the financial services sector, and is relevant for all financial centres, be they huge centres of international finance or small islands acting as OFCs.

There is an urgent need to understand better the political economy of the discourses surrounding the rules of financial markets and services in different jurisdictions and how these discourses impact upon the regulation at the national, regional and international levels. The following chapters – in particular Chapters 4 to 6 – directly tackle all these issues.

Increasingly, national models of financial and tax regulation are like company law and many other systems of regulation, in that at least in part they are elements of the competition between different jurisdictions to attract capital.[56]

The need to construct legal systems and processes attuned to the requirements of investment capital is a major justification for much regulatory reform, whether in finance, employment law or in other areas. This is not a novel position.

It has long been a commonly held assumption, for example, that company law possesses social utility because it is the vehicle of market economy.[57] This notion of the social utility of law and regulation is a key issue in the growing contemporary debates on *social capital*. Putnam views social capital as the norms, networks and typologies of trust that societies share in order to achieve common objectives.[58] Similarly, Fukuyama sees social capital as the resource of shared values that a society has.[59]

Financial regulation is but one piece of the social capital jigsaw, as it seeks through its structures and processes to facilitate entrepreneurial activity for the benefit

---

[55] *Ibid*, pp. 104-107.

[56] Since 1997, for example, there has been sharp disagreement amongst some Member States of the European Union regarding a Draft Directive on the Taxation of Savings Income and issues of tax competition, especially regarding the issue about introducing a withholding tax. For some discussion of these issues, see: S. Sieker, 'Offshore Financial Centers and "Harmful Tax Competition": The Year 2000 in Review', *Tax Notes International*, 29 January 2001, pp. 557-573.

[57] D. Wishart, *Company Law in Context*, Oxford University Press, 1994, p. 167.

[58] R. Putnam, 'The Strange Disappearance of Civil America', *Policy (Autumn)*, 1996, pp. 3-15.

[59] F. Fukuyama, 'The Great Disruption', *The Atlantic Monthly*, 283, 1999, pp. 55-80.

of affected individuals, entities and society in general. Different jurisdictions will seek to produce social capital for themselves in different ways, and establishing themselves as OFCs to some degree in order to generate further social capital is one possible alternative now open to many states and territories, both large and small.

The more players there are in the OFC marketplace, the more likely it will be that regulatory competition between different financial centres will intensify as they seek to maintain or increase their levels of market share. These competitive pressures inevitably affect the decisions that OFCs make about their regulatory infrastructures and the standards that they set for business conducted through their jurisdiction.

Given the economic motivations that may exist under certain conditions for less onerous regulatory regimes in the financial sector, and the uncertainty about how best to promote regulatory compliance, what should the appropriate regulatory norms be for governments and law enforcement agencies, whether in New York, London, Moscow, or virtually any small Caribbean jurisdiction one could care to name? Uniform and readily transferable standards are difficult to produce, so what processes of harmonisation or convergence are feasible? Can we expect to see systematic transferable standards across cultures and jurisdictions? How much more complex is the situation, when one considers – notwithstanding the ongoing financial blurring process – the overriding cultural and religious norms, and traditional financial arrangements, that apply in certain countries and cultures?

Examples include underground banking systems such as the Hawalah system, which is most closely associated with the South Asia region, particularly India and Pakistan, or the Fei Chien (sometimes called Chit or Chop), a system which has been affiliated with both expatriate and mainland Chinese communities for centuries.[60] These alternative financial systems play crucial strategic roles in their host business cultures and are difficult, if not impossible, for conventional financial regulatory regimes to supervise. The low public profile of underground banking in western countries contrasts with the increasingly high priority that governments, financial regulators and law enforcement agencies are giving to efforts to counter the facilitative role that underground banking may play in the activities of money launderers, terrorist groups, organised crime and tax evaders, as Chapters 2 and 3 will point out.[61]

Law enforcement strategies in this area are increasingly international in their character (at both formal and informal levels), like many of the behaviours that they

---

[60] The physical exchange of cash can be a feature of both the Hawalah and Fei Chien systems, but more commonly they rely on symbolic tokens of any form, such as tickets, stamps or, as was traditionally common under the Fei Chien system, a small wooden carving. Virtually anything can be remitted, whether through symbolic tokens or a verbal commitment, for example: goods, debt, credit, services or currency. For more information on underground banking systems see: G.P. Gilligan, 'Going Underground – The Not So New Way to Bank?' *Journal of Financial Crime*, 9, 2001, pp. 105-108.

[61] The effects of underground banking systems, for example, are one of the concerns amongst US legislators regarding money laundering that have prompted a flurry of legislative activity in recent times, such as S.1371 the Money Laundering Abatement Act, introduced in the US Senate in August 2001.

are seeking to combat.[62] It should not be assumed, however, that there is an exclusively dependent relationship between OFCs and money laundering or other forms of white-collar crime. Both offshore and onshore centres facilitate money laundering. Some OFCs resent some of the criticism that they receive and argue that most financial crimes, such as money laundering, are endemic within the major onshore centres such as London and New York. There is some truth in this assertion, simply because of the scale of the major onshore centres and the nature of financial markets.

Indeed the Director of the UK Serious Fraud Office (SFO) notes that because more than $1,000 billion a day is exchanged in the foreign currency markets of the City of London, it has been reported that there are perceptions in some quarters of the US that 'London had become the money laundering capital of the world'.[63] It is more likely, in fact, that far greater totals of dirty money are washed through those finance centres with the highest reputations, such as London and New York, than through OFCs.

In 1999, for example, Walker estimated that of the total amount of money laundered globally the US was the origin of more than 46 per cent and the destination of more than 18 per cent.[64] So it is not surprising that those smaller jurisdictions with a reputation for secrecy, which derive a significant portion of their GDP from the financial sector, would want to defend those interests. It is probable that the provision of financial products and services in an offshore context will remain a growth industry and that more and more jurisdictions will aggressively pursue market share. In the past, this pursuit of market share has resulted in some offshore jurisdictions being regulated in the loosest of fashions, and this is still the situation in certain cases. It is significant, however, that many jurisdictions are making strenuous efforts to rid themselves of the stigma of being labelled facilitators of money laundering or as tax havens.

This can be seen in various ways, such as public statements by local politicians and regulators, the willingness of many jurisdictions to submit letters of commitment to the OECD regarding the elimination of harmful tax practices, and many OFCs agreeing to inspection visits by teams from the IMF.

There is a growing awareness that any finance centre seeking long-term success should establish information sharing and other co-operative processes with other national regulators and with international organisations. The change in attitude in much of the offshore finance sector – which Chapter 6 analyses in the case of UK

---

[62] Examples of these international strategies include: Mutual Legal Assistance Treaties (MLATs); multilateral treaties such as the Council of Europe Money Laundering Convention; policy initiatives such as the Financial Action Task Force (FATF) Ad Hoc Group on Non-cooperative Countries and Territories (NCCT) and the Financial Stability Forum (FSF) Working Group on Offshore Financial Centres; and asset freezing orders such as 'mareva' injunctions.

[63] R. Wright, 'Keynote Address to the 17th International Cambridge Symposium on Economic Crime', *Journal of Financial Crime*, 7, 2000, p. 305.

[64] J. Walker, 'How Big is Global Money Laundering?', *Journal of Money Laundering Control*, 3, 1999, p. 33.

territories – can be explained partially as a response to pressure from international organisations such as the FATF, FSF and OECD and their processes of blacklisting.

Another significant factor in changing attitudes is the growing and widespread concern around the world of the threats posed by terrorism.

The Effects of Terrorism and Organised Crime on Regulation of the Financial Sector

The devastating terrorist attacks in New York and Washington DC on 11 September 2001 and their aftermath have become a powerful factor in all political discourses around the world.

Of particular relevance for this volume is the political reality that the response to the various threats of terrorism is now a key driver of regulatory developments in the financial sector, especially in relation to issues associated with the financing of the activities of terrorism.

The effects of terrorism and organised crime on the regulation trends are discussed in Chapter 2, while the financial side of terrorism is analysed in Chapter 3.

Here, from a mere descriptive point of view, and in order to introduce the issues, it is probably fair to say that for many years in most developed economies, such as the US, money laundering, OFCs and underground banking systems have not been prominent in the public consciousness, and few American citizens were worried about how much money was being laundered through New York. That position has changed dramatically, and probably irrevocably, since 11 September 2001, simply because of concerns about the funding of terrorist organisations and their operations.

There had been initiatives targeting terrorist financing prior to the September 11 attacks, such as the International Convention for the Suppression of the Financing of Terrorism[65] and, in the US, the activities of The National Commission on Terrorism.[66] Following the horrors of 11 September, however, and the very real fears of similar atrocities being committed in the future, there has been a glut of initiatives in both national and international environments seeking to counter terrorism and particularly to obstruct, expose and seize the finances associated with terrorism.

These initiatives include the establishment within the White House on 8 October 2001 of the Office of Homeland Security in the US, which has since issued its first National Strategy for Homeland Security.[67] Also in the US there has been Executive Order 13224, 23 September 2001 (with updates), issued by the US Treasury,[68] and also what is likely to be the most significant legislative response to the terrorist attacks of 11 September: the Uniting and Strengthening America by

---

[65] Convention 54/109, 9 December 1999, http://untreaty.un.org/English/Terrorism.asp.

[66] http://www.state.gov/www/global/terrorism/000605_natl_com_terror.html.

[67] http://www.whitehouse.gov/homeland/book/index.html.

[68] http://www.ustreas.gov/terrorism.html.

Providing Appropriate Tools Required to Intercept and Obstruct Terrorism (USA PATRIOT) Act of 2001.[69]

Various provisions of The PATRIOT Act 2001 not only broaden and deepen the mandatory compliance requirements for financial institutions operating within the US or holding assets within the US, but also acknowledge the commitment of the US to the outputs and recommendations of those international organisations such as the OECD and the FATF in which the US participates.[70] Other examples of a national response include the Anti-Terrorism Crime and Security Act 2001 in the UK.

On a regional basis, the European Union has responded through the Council of the European Union, with Council Decision (EC) No. 2580/2001.[71] Broader international responses have included the UN Security Council Resolutions on Terrorism.[72] On 31 October 2001, the FATF issued its Special Recommendations on Terrorist Financing, which stressed the need for jurisdictions and/or financial institutions to: ratify and implement relevant UN instruments; criminalise the financing of terrorism and associated money laundering; freeze and confiscate terrorist assets; report suspicious transactions relating to terrorism; increase levels of international co-operation; license or register alternative remittance systems; increase supervision over wire transfers; and improve supervision of non-profit organisations.[73]

On 24 April 2002 the FATF issued further guidance for financial institutions in detecting terrorist financing which offered specific advice regarding the characteristics and sources of terrorist funding.[74] As time goes on, these various specific national, regional and international responses to the attacks of 11 September will have increasingly substantial impacts upon how the international financial sector functions. These developments will affect not only how many OFCs may emerge in the future but also in what forms current and future OFCs might structure their operational activities, and their regulatory structures and processes.

Despite these specific regulatory and statutory initiatives, and also a renewed urgency and increase in the activities of law enforcement and intelligence communities against terrorism, there remains a dearth of information concerning the activities of some terrorist groups. These difficulties are compounded by the fact that, in certain quarters, there may be some ambiguity regarding the goals and legitimacy of such groups.

---

[69] The Uniting and Strengthening America by Providing Appropriate Tools Required to Intercept and Obstruct Terrorism (USA PATRIOT) Act of 2001 (Public Law 107-56; 115 Stat. 357).

[70] For example, Section 356 of the USA PATRIOT Act mandates more stringent reporting rules regarding suspicious transactions.

[71] http://europa.eu.int/eur-lex/en/index.html.

[72] http://www.un.org/terrorism/sc.htm.

[73] http://www.fatf-gafi.org/SRecsTF_en.htm.

[74] http://www.fatf-gafi.org/pdf/GuidFITF01_en.pdf.

To an extent, similar ambiguities are true for the activities of certain organised crime groupings and law enforcement efforts against them. Historically, this has presented distinct difficulties to agencies of law enforcement as they seek to counter the activities of organised crime.

Another very significant practical imperative affecting the law enforcement response to organised crime is the fact that much organised crime actually provides services, or meets market needs. This in many ways is the greatest pragmatic difficulty facing law enforcement, because it is attempting the daunting task of seemingly bucking the needs of the market. The US experience with the prohibition of alcohol in the 1920s, and contemporary law enforcement problems with drugs markets (which are flexible, irregular and largely open), are clear examples of this phenomenon. As the flexibility and scale of the global financial services sector continues to grow and the number of players increases, there is a sense that, to some extent, international organisations such as the FATF, the OECD and relevant law enforcement agencies may be facing similar problems as they seek to counter the activities of organised crime in OFCs.

As was discussed earlier, as well as in Chapter 4, most OFCs are politically stable. This is an important consideration for both legal and illegal entrepreneurs using their services, because the relationships between OFCs and their clients (including organised crime groupings) tend to be characterised by distance and place a high premium on trust and stability.

In addition, as we will see again in Chapter 4, some of the OFCs that may facilitate money laundering may be relatively poor, smaller jurisdictions that consequently do not offer many profitable opportunities for organised crime. The result of these factors is that, in contrast to many more wealthy advanced economies, the infrastructures of civil society of OFCs tend not to be threatened substantially by the activities of organised crime.

OFCs therefore are able to externalise the costs usually associated with organised crime and yet may derive the benefits of fees, taxes or other charges associated with the provision of financial services, even though others, such as international organisations or foreign law enforcement agencies, might classify some of these servicing activities as money laundering or facilitating tax evasion.

This tends to be something of a 'double whammy' to the regulatory efforts of international organisations like the FATF, FSF and OECD, because the motivation levels may not be high enough for some OFCs to exclude organised crime groupings from utilising their financial services capabilities. Increasing the levels of motivation of OFCs to counter organised crime is one of the strategic objectives of initiatives promoted in recent years by organisations such as the FATF, FSF and OECD, as part of their efforts to protect the integrity of the financial sector and counter activities such as money laundering and tax evasion.

International Regulatory Initiatives and OFCs

This section focuses on specific listing initiatives – analysed in depth from an economic point of view in Chapters 4 and 5 – taken separately by the FATF, FSF and OECD since 2000, as those organisations have focused on their separate priorities.

These listing initiatives have become widely referred to as blacklists because, in the main, they have highlighted what the FATF, FSF or OECD have seen as problematic, or non-co-operative, jurisdictions that are currently operating in global financial markets, some of which are classified as OFCs.

Regarding the listing processes, the FATF has as its main priority preventing money laundering, while for the FSF it is protecting the integrity of the financial system and for the OECD it is countering harmful tax practices. Although these lists are issued separately, however, they do have combined and cumulative effects, as some jurisdictions have been named on multiple occasions in multiple lists. It is almost impossible to measure accurately the specific effects of being listed, and there has been little research that seeks to throw light on the impacts of multiple listing. For these reasons, Chapters 4 and 5 exploit specific economic and political analyses.

What I have done in Appendices A-C is produce tables that show which jurisdictions have been listed, by whom and when (Appendix A = FATF, Appendix B = FSF and Appendix C = OECD). In constructing these tables, I have assigned a score to each listing that a jurisdiction receives from the FATF, FSF or OECD and ranked the jurisdictions according to the points they have accumulated through single or multiple listings. In Appendix D, I have consolidated the scores of all jurisdictions that appear in any of the FATF, FSF or OECD blacklists and ranked the jurisdictions according to points accumulated. In Appendix E, I reproduce this consolidation and ranking process with respect to all blacklists of the FATF, FSF and OECD, but only for those jurisdictions that were classified as OFCs by the FSF in May 2000.

I acknowledge that the scoring process I have applied is value-laden and has statistical deficiencies. I ranked the overall effects of blacklisting by the FATF and OECD to be roughly similar, even though the FATF has produced six different lists and the OECD only two. Consequently, I accorded three points to each separate listing by the FATF, so that a period of continuing appearance in the first list of June 2000 through to the sixth list of February 2003 would attract 18 points. The first OECD blacklist of May 2000 classified 34 jurisdictions as tax havens, and the April 2002 blacklist accorded the more pejorative classification of non-co-operative tax haven status to seven jurisdictions. I then applied six points for an appearance in the OECD list of May 2000 and 12 points for an appearance in the April 2002 list. As a result, any jurisdiction that has been blacklisted continuously by the OECD received 18 points, equal for ranking purposes to continuous classification by the FATF.

As discussed in more detail below, the FSF has adopted a gentler approach than either the FATF or the OECD, and their listing processes seem to have had less impact, and should therefore attract a lower maximum score than the FATF or the OECD. Nevertheless, the FSF did differentiate quite sharply between the quality of supervision and regulatory co-operation exhibited by the various OFCs, and I felt that this should be reflected in any scoring and ranking process. Consequently, those OFCs accorded Group I status by the FSF attracted one point, those in Group II six points and those in Group III twelve points.

Once again I acknowledge that this is an imperfect exercise, and many strong arguments could be advanced for alternative scoring mechanisms and indeed for the futility of any scoring and ranking exercise at all.

I maintain that it is a valuable exercise, however, because it helps to illustrate the cumulative effects of multiple listing and identify which jurisdictions are considered in an unfavourable light by one or more of the FATF, FSF or OECD. The ranking exercise also helps in identifying the characteristics of jurisdictions operating in the global financial sector that are held to be problematic by international regulatory organisations. If the internationalisation of regulation in the financial sector continues to gather momentum, and most indicators signal that this is likely, then the importance of processes such as these that identify and classify difference is also likely to increase, if relative stability and integrity in the finance sector are to be maintained.

In terms of affecting the activities of OFCs, the starting point of significant regulatory activism by international organisations is probably The Forty Recommendations of the FATF first produced in 1990[75] and subsequently revised in 1996 and 2003.[76]

The Forty Recommendations stress the roles that national legal systems, the financial system and international co-operation may play in combating money laundering. In particular, the Forty Recommendations offer guidance on issues such as the scope of the criminal offence of money laundering, confiscation measures, customer identification and other diligence issues, administrative co-operation, and improved mutual assistance and extradition procedures.[77]

Since 1990, the FATF has been one of the lead actors in helping to evaluate what the prevailing desirable norms and standards in the financial sector should be, producing several reports on money laundering typologies.[78] In this regard, the FATF has, to an extent, complemented the ongoing work of other international organisations such as IOSCO and the BCBS. Recent 'naming and shaming' initiatives by the FATF, FSF and OECD,[79] however, which have significant capacity to stigmatise those jurisdictions that are labelled in such a manner, raise issues of accountability, legitimacy and representation.

Who should decide the economic, political and intellectual criteria that supposedly legitimate the methodologies that subsequently underpin decision-making processes to produce blacklists, which in turn might well penalise various finance centres?

---

[75] Financial Action Task Force on Money Laundering, *The Forty Recommendations*, Paris. 1990.

[76] Financial Action Task Force on Money Laundering, *The Forty Recommendations*, Paris. 1996 and 2003.

[77] *Ibid.*

[78] See for example: Financial Action Task Force on Money Laundering, *1997-1998 Report on Money Laundering Typologies*, 1998, Paris.

[79] See Appendices 1.A-1.E.

The FATF has led the way on this issue with its development of mutual evaluation procedures that seek to monitor how effectively jurisdictions implement national and international conventions against money laundering.[80] The FATF processes are predicated on the principles of equal treatment of all participating jurisdictions and field evaluation visits.[81] The FATF has maintained this methodological approach and sought to review its own operations in this regard.[82]

Increasingly, the FATF has moved towards the classification of specific jurisdictions (the so-called blacklists), according to the levels of bank secrecy, cooperation with national and international regulatory organisations and the regulatory standards that they exhibit.[83] In June 2000, the FATF named 15 jurisdictions as having: '…serious systemic problems…' in their anti-money-laundering systems. The 15 labelled by the FATF as '…non-co-operative countries and territories...' (NCCTs) were: the Bahamas, the Cayman Islands, the Cook Islands, Dominica, Israel, Lebanon, Liechtenstein, the Marshall Islands, Nauru, Niue, Panama, Philippines, Russia, St Kitts and Nevis, and St Vincent and the Grenadines.[84]

The FATF recommended that with regard to these 15 NCCTs, '…financial institutions should give special attention to business relations and transactions with persons, including companies and financial institutions'.[85] Since then the FATF has produced a series of reviews of those jurisdictions around the world that it classifies as NCCTs and, as one might expect, there has been some movement onto and off the FATF's blacklists.

In June 2001, the FATF removed the Bahamas, the Cayman Islands, Liechtenstein and Panama from the list of NCCTs, noted the progress of the Cook Islands, Dominica, Israel, Lebanon, the Marshall Islands, Niue, and St Kitts and Nevis, was critical of the lack of progress of Nauru, the Philippines and Russia, and added six new countries (Egypt, Guatemala, Hungary, Indonesia, Myanmar and Nigeria) to the list of NCCTs.[86]

---

[80] Financial Action Task Force on Money Laundering, *Report on Money Laundering Typologies 1999-2000*, 2000, Paris.

[81] For a discussion of these FATF initiatives see: R. Sansonetti, 'The Mutual Evaluation Process: A Methodology of Increasing Importance at International Level', *Journal of Financial Crime*, 7, 1999, pp. 218-226.

[82] Financial Action Task Force on Money Laundering, *Review of Anti-Money Laundering Systems and Mutual Evaluation Procedures 1992-1999*, 2001, Paris.

[83] Financial Action Task Force on Money Laundering, *Report on Non-Cooperative Countries and Territories*, 2000, Paris.

[84] See Appendix 1.A.

[85] Financial Action Task Force on Money Laundering, Review to Identify Non-Cooperative Countries or Territories: Increasing the Worldwide Effectiveness of Anti-Money Laundering Measures, June 2000, Paris, p. 13.

[86] Financial Action Task Force on Money Laundering, *Review to Identify Non-Cooperative Countries or Territories: Increasing the Worldwide Effectiveness of Anti-Money Laundering Measures*, June 2001, Paris, p. 3.

In September 2001, there were no deletions and Grenada and Ukraine were added to the list of NCCTs.[87] There were no admissions or deletions to the list following the FATF plenary meeting in Hong Kong in February 2002.[88] In June 2002, the FATF published its third NCCT Review, in it which removed Hungary, Israel, Lebanon and St Kitts and Nevis from the blacklist and made no additions.[89] In October 2002, the FATF removed Dominica, Marshall Islands, Niue and Russia from the blacklist.[90] In February 2003, as part of its ongoing monitoring programme, the FATF removed Grenada from its latest blacklist. The countries and territories labelled by the FATF as non-co-operative are: the Cook Islands, Egypt, Guatemala, Indonesia, Myanmar, Nauru, Nigeria, Philippines, St Vincent and the Grenadines, Ukraine.[91] From June 2000 to February 2003, the Cook Islands, Nauru and St. Vincent were ever present in the blacklists.

The FATF blacklisting processes are ongoing and some of the world's OFCs, but by no means the majority, have appeared in the lists to date.[92] Similarly, the FSF and the OECD Project on Harmful Tax Practices (OECDPHTP) have produced their own blacklists in recent times.

In April 2000, the FSF released the Report of its Working Group on Offshore Finance Centres, which set out the FSF's priorities regarding market integrity concerns on OFCs.[93] In May 2000, the FSF augmented that report by releasing its grouping of OFCs to assist in setting priorities for assessment. The FSF grouped those jurisdictions it considered to have significant offshore financial activities into three

---

[87] Financial Action Task Force on Money Laundering, *Developments in Non-Cooperative Countries and Territories*, http://www1.oecd.org/fatf/pdf/PR-20010907_en.pdf, September 2001, Paris.

[88] Financial Action Task Force on Money Laundering, *FATF acts against terrorist financing, money laundering and non-cooperative jurisdictions*, http://www1.oecd.org/fatf/pdf/PR-20020201_en.pdf, 1 February 2002.

[89] Financial Action Task Force on Money Laundering, *Review to Identify Non-Cooperative Countries or Territories: Increasing the Worldwide Effectiveness of Anti-Money Laundering Measures*, June 2002b, Paris.

[90] Financial Action Task Force on Money Laundering, *Russia, Dominica, Niue and Marshall Islands removed from FATF's list of non-cooperative countries and territories.* http://www1.oecd.org/fatf/pdf/PR-20021011_en.pdf, 11 October 2002.

[91] Financial Action Task Force on Money Laundering, *FATF withdraws counter-measures with respect to Ukraine and decides on date for counter-measures to Philippines*, http://www1.oecd.org/fatf/pdf/PR-20030214_en.pdf, 14 February 2003. Editor note: on 20 June 2003 the FAFT published the following updated list of non – cooperative countries and territories: the Cook Islands, Egypt, Guatemala, Indonesia, Myanmar, Nauru, Nigeria, Philippines, Ukraine.

[92] If one accepts the FSF list of OFCs issued in March 2000 as the most definitive listing of OFCs, then 11 of the 42 jurisdictions to appear in that FSF list have been blacklisted by the FATF between June 2000 and February 2003.

[93] Financial Stability Forum, *Report of the Working Group on Offshore Centres*, http://www.fsforum.org/Reports/RepOFC.html, 5 April 2000.

categories, based on perceptions of their quality of supervision and degree of regulatory co-operation.[94] The FSF stated that:

> ...it would be in the public interest to release the grouping of OFCs based on the results of the survey. It is hoped that its publication, combined with the assessment process being put in place, will encourage all OFCs to take appropriate steps to raise the quality of their supervision and their degree of co-operation as quickly as possible.

Group I

The jurisdictions in this category are generally perceived as having legal infrastructures and supervisory practices, and/or a level of resources devoted to supervision and co-operation relative to the size of their financial activities, and/or a level of co-operation that are largely of a good quality and better than in other OFCs. These jurisdictions are Hong Kong SAR, Luxembourg, Singapore, and Switzerland. Dublin (Ireland), Guernsey, Isle of Man, and Jersey are also generally viewed in the same light, though continuing efforts to improve the quality of supervision and co-operation should be encouraged in these jurisdictions.

Group II

The jurisdictions in this category are generally perceived as having legal infrastructures and supervisory practices, and/or a level of resources devoted to supervision and co-operation relative to the size of their financial activities, and/or a level of co-operation that are largely of a higher quality than Group III, but lower than Group I. These jurisdictions are Andorra, Bahrain, Barbados, Bermuda, Gibraltar, Labuan (Malaysia), Macau SAR, Malta, and Monaco.

Group III

The jurisdictions in this category are generally perceived as having legal infrastructures and supervisory practices, and/or a level of resources devoted to supervision and co-operation relative to the size of their activity, and/or a level of co-operation that are largely of a lower quality than in Group II. These jurisdictions are Anguilla, Antigua and Barbuda, Aruba, Belize, British Virgin Islands, Cayman Islands, Cook Islands, Costa Rica, Cyprus, Lebanon, Liechtenstein, Marshall Islands, Mauritius, Nauru, Netherlands Antilles, Niue, Panama, St. Kitts and Nevis, St. Lucia, St. Vincent and the Grenadines, Samoa, Seychelles, The Bahamas, Turks and Caicos, and Vanuatu.[95]

The FSF has not produced specific updated lists since 2000 as the FATF has done with regard to NCCTs, but it has indicated that it will establish a table on its website detailing the progress of OFCs regarding the IMF's assessment program.[96] The FSF has maintained an ongoing review role over OFCs: '...drawing on

---

[94] Financial Stability Forum, Financial Stability Forum Releases Grouping of Offshore Financial Centres (OFCs) to Assist in Setting Priorities for Assessment, http://www.fsforum.org/Press/Home.html, May 2000.

[95] *Ibid.* p. 2.

[96] This table will be posted at some point on: http://www.fsforum.org but the results of IMF assessments of some OFC jurisdictions are available at www.imf.org.

supervisory experiences gathered through contact meetings, IMF assessment
results publicly disclosed by OFCs and periodic updates by the IMF'.[97]

Although it has not produced revised lists, the FSF has encouraged all
jurisdictions it named in its May 2000 listing to agree to an IMF assessment by the
end of 2003. At the time of the seventh meeting of the FSF, held in Hong Kong in
March 2002, those jurisdictions listed that had not yet agreed to an IMF assessment
were: Antigua and Barbuda; Barbados, Malta, Nauru, Niue, St Kitts and Nevis, St
Lucia, and St Vincent and the Grenadines.[98] At its eighth meeting, held in Toronto
in September 2002, the FSF noted with regret that Nauru and Niue had not yet
requested an IMF module 2 assessment.[99]

The FSF will review the effectiveness of its initiative once the IMF has
completed its assessment programme in 2003. Until then, the approach of the FSF
will likely remain as it has been to date, somewhat gentler than that of the FATF,
and also gentler than that of the OECDPHTP, as we shall see below.

In another 'naming and shaming' initiative in 2000, the OECDPHTP classified
most of the jurisdictions listed in May 2000 by the FSF in Group III as also being
in a group of jurisdictions that met the OECD technical criteria as tax havens.
Those classified by OECD as tax havens were: Andorra, Anguilla, Antigua and
Barbuda, Aruba, Bahamas, Bahrain, Barbados, Belize, British Virgin Islands, Cook
Islands, Dominica, Gibraltar, Grenada, Guernsey/Sark/Alderney, Isle of Man,
Jersey, Liechtenstein, Liberia, Maldives, Marshall Islands, Monaco, Montserrat,
Nauru, Netherlands Antilles, Niue, Panama, Samoa, Seychelles, St Lucia, St
Christopher & Nevis, St Vincent and the Grenadines, Tonga, Turks and Caicos, US
Virgin Islands and Vanuatu.[100] In April 2002, the OECDPHTP published its second
blacklist and classified Andorra, Liberia, Liechtenstein, Marshall Islands, Monaco,
Nauru, and Vanuatu as '...non co-operative Tax Havens'.[101]

Many of the jurisdictions named in these lists have complained in the media
and other public fora about being categorised in such a manner. Many of the
jurisdictions that are members of the Caribbean Community (CARICOM), for
example, have been strongly critical of the actions of the FSF, FATF and OECD:

> Heads of Government of the Caribbean Community, meeting in Canouan, St Vincent and
> the Grenadines, expressed grave concern at a recent series of orchestrated activities by the
> G7, through three organisations of its creation. These activities, which are unilateral and

---

[97] *Seventh Meeting of the FSF* (Hong Kong, 25-26 March 2002), http://www.fsforum.
org/Press/P20020326.pdf, p. 1.

[98] *Ibid*, p.2.

[99] *Eighth Meeting of the FSF* (Toronto, 3-4 September 2002), http://www.fsforum.
org/press/press_releases_44.html, p. 5.

[100] Organisation for Economic Co-operation and Development, Towards Global Tax Co-
operation, Report to the 2000 Ministerial Council Meeting and Recommendations by the
Committee on Fiscal Affairs, Progress in Identifying and Eliminating Harmful Tax
Practices, 2000, Paris.

[101] Organisation for Economic Co-operation and Development, *The OECD Issues The List
of Unco-operative Tax Havens*, http://www.oecd.org/EN/document/0, EN-document-
103-nodirectorate-no-12-28534-22,00.html, 18 April 2002, Paris.

inconsistent with international practice, are designed to impair the competitive capacity of Caribbean jurisdictions in the provision of global financial services....

Heads of Government took note that each of the reports,[102] was prepared by bodies in which the Caribbean has no representation and was based on incomplete information and on standards set unilaterally by these bodies. They deplored the fact that the lists were published with the objective of tainting jurisdictions in the eyes of the investment community and the international financial market. They condemned the actions of the OECD in particular as contrary to the tenets of a global market economy promoted by G7 countries. They reiterated that the proposed OECD actions have no basis in international law and are alien to the practice of inter-state relations.[103]

Mr Owen Arthur, Prime Minister and Finance Minister of Barbados, was scathing of what he saw as the OECD's: 'institutional imperialism' and its 'use of crude threats and stigmas'.[104] The basis of the arguments of these critics is to attack the legitimacy, and therefore the credibility, of the initiatives of the OECD, FATF and FSF.

It is a clear example of competing social constructions of legitimacy being used to explain differing perspectives and evaluations of the same social phenomena.

The FATF initiative received similar criticism. The Hon George McCarthy, at the time Financial Secretary of the Cayman Islands and a former President of the Caribbean Financial Action Task Force (CFATF), was critical of the FATF assessment procedures and 'astonished' that the Cayman Islands should be categorised by the FATF as a 'non-co-operative jurisdiction in the international fight against money laundering'.[105] The President of the Cayman Islands Bankers Association, Mr Eduardo D'Angelo Silva, was more strident in his condemnation of the FATF classification process, describing it as '...outrageous and ridiculous...'.[106]

The lack of support for the listing processes by many of those listed is not surprising and typifies what some legitimacy theorists might refer to as 'a lack of compliance pull'.

Under this construct of compliance pull, the more legitimate a rule, initiative or regulatory framework is perceived to be by those who are subject to its effects, the greater the level of compliance they will be accorded. Similarly, the lower the levels of legitimacy accorded to specific rules, the lower will be the levels of compliance accorded. Interestingly, the compliance pull–legitimacy relationship is an interactive one, so that increasing levels of compliance pull will strengthen the

---

[102] The FSF, FATF and OECD reports discussed above.

[103] Press release 91/2000, Communiqué Issued on the Conclusion of the 21st meeting of the Conference of Heads of Government of the Caribbean Community (CARICOM), Canouan, St Vincent and the Grenadines, 2-5 July 2000, http://www.caricom.org/pres91_00.htm, pp. 8-9.

[104] *The Tribune*, 6 June 2000.

[105] 'Government of the Grand Cayman Islands Designation Announced By Financial Action Task Force Astonishing and Contradictory', http://www.prnewswire.com, 22 June 2000.

[106] 'Caymans leaders head to U.S. for money talks', http://www.reuters.com/news, 5 July 2000.

legitimacy and compliance levels achieved by rules/initiatives etc, and decreasing levels of compliance pull will have the opposite effect.[107]

The interactive compliance pull–legitimacy relationship is important with respect to the FATF, FSF and OECD initiatives and will be crucial to their ultimate success. Since 2000, the FATF and OECD in particular have been adopting the classic 'stick-and-carrot approach'.

The 'carrot approach' is seen in their increased interaction with critics of the initiatives, and the 'stick approach' is clear in the numerous signals regarding the threat of punitive measures against problem jurisdictions. Both approaches aim to increase the levels of compliance with their preferred standards and to raise the legitimacy of the initiatives themselves amongst those most subject to their effects.

The commitment to the stick approach can be seen in the fact that, despite the fierce criticism they have received from some quarters, the OECD and FATF seem committed to this strategy of 'outing' those jurisdictions they perceive as not acting in accordance with accepted international standards.[108] In addition, on numerous occasions, both the FATF and the OECD have flagged their willingness to promote punitive measures against jurisdictions that they perceive as recalcitrant.

Examples: the FATF decided in December 2001 to impose measures against Nauru;[109] in December 2002 the FATF imposed counter-measures on Ukraine and decided not to impose counter-measures on Nigeria;[110] and then in February 2003, the FATF lifted its counter-measures against Ukraine and decided to apply counter-measures against the Philippines.[111]

These ebbs and flows in the level of the punitive stance the FATF has taken towards specific jurisdictions, such as Nauru, Nigeria and the Ukraine, are evidence of the compliance pull–legitimacy relationship, as different jurisdictions attribute different levels of legitimacy, compliance and commitments to the standards demanded by the FATF, then the FATF responds in kind.

If one examines the movements on and off the blacklists (as represented in Appendix 1.A), the FATF could claim some reasonable levels of success to date

---

[107] For a discussion of the compliance pull–legitimacy interaction see K. Raustalia and A.M. Slaughter, 'International law. International relations and compliance', in W. Carlsnaes, T. Risse, B. Simmons and T. Risse-Kappen (eds), *Handbook of International Relations*, Sage Publications, London, 2002, pp. 538-558 at p. 541.

[108] This approach to law enforcement is not uncommon in countries such as Japan, which have a long tradition of shaming offenders. For a discussion of the potential of shaming as a law enforcement strategy see: J. Braithwaite, Crime, Shame and Reintegration, Cambridge University Press, Cambridge, 1989.

[109] Financial Action Task Force on Money Laundering, *FATF decides to impose counter-measures on Nauru*, http://www1.oecd.org/fatf/pdf/PR-20011205_en.pdf, 5 December 2001, Paris.

[110] Financial Action Task Force on Money Laundering, *FATF decides to impose counter-measures on Ukraine: no counter-measures to apply against Nigeria at this time*, http://www1.oecd.org/fatf/pdf/PR-20021220_en.pdf, 26 December 2002, Paris.

[111] Financial Action Task Force on Money Laundering, *FATF withdraws counter-measures with respect to Ukraine and decides on date for counter-measures to Philippines*, http://www1.oecd.org/fatf/pdf/PR-20021220_en.pdf, 14 February 2003, Paris.

regarding the FATF initiatives on NCCTs, both in a general sense and particularly regarding the carrot-and-stick approach.

What the NCCTs initiative demonstrates is that compliance is best viewed as a continuum in which regulatory frameworks, especially those that seek to operate in an international context with all the myriad pressures that come with such a broad environment and constituency, need to be sufficiently flexible to cope with varying degrees of non-compliance in order to generate sufficient positive momentum in the legitimacy–compliance pull relationship.

Indeed, if one examines Appendix C, the experience of the OECDPHTP also presents some evidence that such strategies will produce positive results, as only seven of the original 34 jurisdictions classified as tax havens in May 2000 were blacklisted as non-co-operative tax havens in April 2002. Since May 2000, the OECD has been making strenuous efforts to sway the original 34 to commit to the elimination of those tax practices that the OECD considers harmful.

For example, in November 2001, the OECD reported success for its strategies when it listed Aruba, Bahrain, the Isle of Man, the Netherlands Antilles and the Seychelles as now being 'jurisdictions committed' to the elimination of harmful tax practices. In addition, it stated that due to recent legislative and administrative changes Tonga would 'not be considered for inclusion in any list of non-co-operative jurisdictions'.[112] Since then there have been further letters or other forms of commitment from Barbados,[113] Antigua and Barbuda,[114] Grenada and St Vincent and the Grenadines,[115] Guernsey and Jersey,[116] St Lucia,[117] Dominica,[118] Anguilla and Turks and Caicos Islands,[119] US Virgin Islands,[120] the Bahamas,[121] Belize,[122]

---

[112] Organisation for Economic Co-operation and Development, *The OECD's Project on Harmful Tax Practices: The 2001 Progress Report*, November 2001, Paris, p.9.

[113] Organisation for Economic Co-operation and Development, *OECD Says Barbados Will not Appear on its Forthcoming List of Uncooperative Tax Havens*, http://www.oecd.org, 31 January 2002, Paris.

[114] Organisation for Economic Co-operation and Development, *Antigua and Barbuda commit to Co-operate with OECD to Address Harmful Tax Practices*, http://www.oecd.org, 20 February 2002, Paris.

[115] Organisation for Economic Co-operation and Development, *Grenada and St Vincent and the Grenadines commit to Co-operate with OECD to Address Harmful Tax Practices*, http://www.oecd.org, 27 February 2002, Paris.

[116] Organisation for Economic Co-operation and Development, *Guernsey and Jersey commit to Co-operate with OECD to address Harmful Tax Practices*, http://www.oecd.org, 27 February 2002, Paris.

[117] Organisation for Economic Co-operation and Development, *St Lucia Commits to the Principles of Transparency and effective Exchange of Information*, http://www.oecd.org, 5 March 2002, Paris.

[118] Organisation for Economic Co-operation and Development, *Dominica Commits to the Principles of Transparency and effective Exchange of Information*, http://www.oecd.org, 6 March 2002, Paris.

[119] Organisation for Economic Co-operation and Development, *Anguilla and Turks and Caicos Islands Commit to Co-operate with OECD to Address Harmful Tax Practices*, http://www.oecd.org, 8 March 2002, Paris.

the Cook Islands,[123] the British Virgin Islands,[124] Niue,[125] Panama,[126] and Samoa.[127]

The OECD regards the commitments by various jurisdictions as indicators of the success of its strategies regarding harmful tax competition. There has been substantial opposition to the activities of the OECDPHTP from different sources, however, and alternative social constructions have been put forward in relation to both the levels of success achieved by the OECD to date, and the legitimacy of the Project on Harmful Tax Practices itself.

Lobby groups such as the National Taxpayers Union (NTU),[128] and the Center for Freedom and Prosperity (CFP),[129] for example, have emerged to play a high profile role in the debates on tax competition. The NTU has helped to organise international coalitions to oppose the efforts of the EU and OECD on harmful tax competition, including *The Saint Louis Declaration*, which denounces the efforts of the EU and OECD in this area as oppressive.[130]

The CFP, like the NTU and so many other lobby groups, is based (unsurprisingly) in Washington DC, and it has argued fiercely against the overall legitimacy of the

---

[120] Organisation for Economic Co-operation and Development, *US Virgin Islands Commits to Co-operate with OECD to Address Harmful Tax Practices*, http://www.oecd.org, 11 March 2002, Paris.

[121] Organisation for Economic Co-operation and Development, *The Bahamas Commits to Co-operate with OECD to Address Harmful Tax Practices*, http://www.oecd.org, 18 March 2002, Paris.

[122] Organisation for Economic Co-operation and Development, *Belize Commits to Co-operate with OECD to Address Harmful Tax Practices*, http://www.oecd.org, 20 March 2002, Paris.

[123] Organisation for Economic Co-operation and Development, *Cook Islands Commits to Co-operate with OECD to Address Harmful Tax Practices*, http://www.oecd.org, 27 March 2002, Paris.

[124] Organisation for Economic Co-operation and Development, *British Virgin Islands Commits to Co-operate with OECD to Address Harmful Tax Practices*, http://www.oecd.org, 3 April 2002, Paris.

[125] Organisation for Economic Co-operation and Development, *Niue Commits to Co-operate with OECD to Address Harmful Tax Practices*, http://www.oecd.org, 15 April 2002, Paris.

[126] Organisation for Economic Co-operation and Development, *Panama Commits to Co-operate with OECD to Address Harmful Tax Practices*, http://www.oecd.org, 17 April 2002, Paris.

[127] Organisation for Economic Co-operation and Development, *Samoa Commits to Co-operate with OECD to Address Harmful Tax Practices*, http://www.oecd.org, 18 April 2002, Paris.

[128] The National Taxpayers Union was founded in the US in 1969 and has 335,000 members. It is an influential lobby group in the US and is a founding member of the World Taxpayers Association. The NTU produces regular newsletters and other information on taxation matters. See: http://www.ntu.org.

[129] The Centre produces regular newsletters and articles on these issues. See: http://www.freedomandprosperity.org.

[130] National Taxpayers Union, *Taxpayers of the World Unite: 33 Groups across the Globe Denounce EU/OECD Tax Cartel Scheme*, http://www.ntu.org.

OECDPHTP. Similar to the NTU, the CFP has portrayed the OECDPHTP as inimical to notions of individual freedom, harmful to concepts of free trade and therefore against the national interest of the US.[131] The CFP has made much of the political reality that there has been a Republican president, rather than a Democrat, in the US since January 2001 and that this seems to have had a slowing and emasculating effect on the momentum and timetables of the OECDPHTP.

The CFP, for example, has persistently iterated its alternative social construction regarding many of the letters of commitment that the OECD had received from a number of jurisdictions that included several OFCs:

> ...almost all of the commitment letters sent to the Paris-based bureaucracy included level playing field clauses, stating that the jurisdiction would not implement bad tax policy unless all OECD member nations agreed to abide by the same misguided rules.[132]

Now the foregoing language describing the so-called Isle of Man clause is more pejorative than the actual language in the relevant letters of commitment from the jurisdictions concerned, but it highlights the challenge to the legitimacy of the OECD's interpretations of the progress of the OECDPHTP.[133]

More recently, the CFP has predicted that in 2003 the OECDPHTP will 'remain stalled' and that '...many low-tax jurisdictions will disavow their commitment letters.'[134] How accurately the CFP reads the political runes will be revealed in due course, but such disagreement and alternative social constructions of legitimacy are to be expected on an issue such as tax competition, which is a game of very high stakes to the players involved.

It should also be pointed out that the OECD itself admits that even amongst its own members there are sharply differing views about elements of the OECDPHTP. Belgium and Portugal, for example, abstained from the 2001 Progress Report; Luxembourg recalled its abstention to the OECD's 1998 *Report Harmful Tax*

---

[131] The CFP has produced a large number of strategic memoranda and other publications on these issues. For example: *CFP Halls of Fame and Shame, May 23 Edition*, http://www.freedomandprosperity.org/hall/hall.shtml; and D.J. Mitchell, *CFP Strategic Memo, June 16 2001, To: Leaders of Low-Tax Jurisdictions and Supporters of Tax Competition, Financial Privacy, and Fiscal Sovereignty*, http://www.freedom andprosperity.org/Papers/m06-16-01/m06-16-01.shtml.

[132] D. Mitchell, *Death of the EU Savings Tax Directive*, Center for Freedom and Prosperity Strategic Memorandum, 26 August 2002, http://www.freedomandprosperity. org/memos/m08-26-02/m08-26-02.shtml, p. 1.

[133] The Isle of Man was the first jurisdiction to insist in its commitment letter to the OECD that its commitment to the OECDPHTP was dependent on all OECD member jurisdictions adopting similar levels of commitment on issues of tax competition. Since then many of the other jurisdictions that subsequently signed letters of commitment to the OECDPHTP have inserted this 'Isle of Man Clause' as a condition of their own commitment.

[134] D.J. Mitchell, *CFP Strategic Memo, January 6, 2003, To: Supporters of Tax Competition: Analysis of 2002 and Prospects for 2003*, http://www.freedom andprosperity.org/memos/m01-06-03/m01-06-03.shtml.

Competition: An Emerging Global Issue and applied that abstention to the 2001 Progress Report; and Switzerland applied its 1998 abstention to any follow-up work undertaken since 1998.[135]

So it is manifestly clear that there is no unanimity within the OECD on its strategies in this area, and this inevitably undermines to some extent the legitimacy and subsequent impact of its actions. This uncertainty within the ranks of the OECD membership has been noted by some of those jurisdictions that have felt threatened by the initiatives of various international organizations, such as those of the OECD.

Lynette Eastmond, Director of the ITIO Secretariat, for example, has publicly questioned whether OECD members and other developed economies are 'prepared explicitly to confirm their intention of abiding by the standards demanded of small and developing economies'.[136] Ms Eastmond's comments focused on the positions of Belgium, Luxembourg and Portugal in particular and were made following the release of the OECD's 2001 Progress Report regarding its project on Harmful Tax Practices.[137]

This, of course, is the key question from a legitimacy perspective in a debate in which some critics argue that the tax revenue-gathering priorities of a number of member jurisdictions, in particular France and Germany, seem to be driving the general taxation competition policy of the OECD and EU.[138]

The ITIO emerged from the activities of the Joint-Working Group on Cross-Border Tax Matters, which itself was an initiative to mediate growing tensions between the OECD and many small and developing economies (SDEs) that operated as OFCs, and which felt threatened by the increasingly interventionist activities of the OECD and certain other international organisations. The ITIO has received support from the Commonwealth Secretariat, which itself has been critical of some aspects of the OECD approach.

Example: 'While the OECD has called for transparent and open tax regimes from OFCs, its own process for seeking international co-operation has been less than transparent and inclusive. Multilateralisation of this process would be

---

[135] Organisation for Economic Co-operation and Development, *The OECD's Project on Harmful Tax Practices: The 2001 Progress Report*, November 2001, Paris, p. 4. .

[136] 'Offshore Jurisdictions Give Guarded Welcome To OECD Report', *Tax-News.com*, 16 November 2001, http://www.tax-news.com.

[137] Organisation for Economic Co-operation and Development, *The OECD's Project on Harmful Tax Practices: The 2001 Progress Report*, November 2001, Paris.

[138] G. Parker, 'France and Germany call for EU tax accord', *New York Times*, 1 December 2002, http://www.nytimes.com/financialtimes/international/FT1037872455975.html?pagewanted=print&position=bottom.

desirable.'[139] The OECD has been more open about the OECDPHTP since 2000, as evidenced by the activities of the OECD Global Forum on Taxation.[140]

The ITIO continues to stress, however, that 'non-OECD countries, including members of the ITIO, have long objected to being asked to implement standards that OECD states themselves refuse to accept'.[141] The ITIO has been reported as complaining in particular about what it sees as '...a lack of a level playing field in the whole process...' which has been the OECD's campaign against perceived harmful tax practices.[142] The ITIO has been active in its campaign to legitimate the activities of its members and eager to present more positive alternative constructions of how OFCs function in the contemporary financial services sector, rather than the more negative images stimulated by the OECD, FSF and FATF blacklists.

As part of this campaign, the ITIO, in conjunction with the Society of Trust and Estate Practitioners (STEP),[143] commissioned the international law firm Stikeman Elliott to produce a critique of the review procedures followed by the OECD regarding some of their international initiatives.[144]

There are sure to be many more sharp exchanges and ongoing ebbs and flows in debates on tax competition and money laundering as political and economic conditions change in the future. It is interesting to note, however, that all the specific jurisdictions that are members of the ITIO are listed as OFCs by the FSF, and many have been blacklisted by both the OECD and the FATF, as shown by their scores in Appendices A-C, and their rankings in Appendices D and E.

---

[139] Commonwealth Secretariat, *The Implications of the OECD Harmful Tax Competition Initiative for Offshore Finance Centres*, London, 2000, p. 9, http://www.thecommonwealth.org/.

[140] The Global Forum has sought to bring together in a more cohesive way the OECD, certain OECD members and many of those jurisdictions likely to be affected by the OECDPHTP. Its most recent meeting was held in the Cayman Islands from 28 October – 11 November 2002, http://www.oecd.org/EN/document/0,,EN-document-103-nodirectorate-no-12-36128-22,00.html.

[141] ITIO, *ITIO seeks OECD commitment to level playing field*, 12 February 2002, http://www.itio.org/news.html.

[142] A. Banks, 'ITIO accuses OECD of double standards', *Tax-News.com*, 15 February 2002, http://www.tax-news.com/asp/story/story_print.asp?storyname=7327.

[143] STEP has branches in 26 jurisdictions and more than 8,000 members drawn largely from the legal, accountancy, corporate trust, banking, insurance and related professions.

[144] E. Stikeman, *Towards A Level Playing Field – Regulating Corporate Vehicles in Cross-Border Transactions*, ITIO and STEP, London, 2000.

Table 1.1 The ITIO membership, FATF, FSF and OECD blacklists

Jurisdiction	FATF score	FSF score	OECD score	Points Total	Appendix D Ranking	Appendix E Ranking
Cook Islands	18	12	6	36	$3^{rd} =$	$3^{rd} =$
St Vincent and Gren.	18	12	6	36	$3^{rd} =$	$3^{rd} =$
Niue	12	12	6	30	$6^{th} =$	$6^{th} =$
Vanuatu		12	18	30	$6^{th} =$	$6^{th} =$
St Kitts and Nevis	9	12	6	27	8th	8th
Bahamas	3	12	6	21	$11^{th} =$	$11^{th} =$
Anguilla		12	6	18	$14^{th} =$	$14^{th} =$
Antigua - Barbuda		12	6	18	$14^{th} =$	$14^{th} =$
Belize		12	6	18	$14^{th} =$	$14^{th} =$
British Virgin Isl.		12	6	18	$14^{th} =$	$14^{th} =$
St Lucia		12	6	18	$14^{th} =$	$14^{th} =$
Turks & Caicos Isl.		12	6	18	$14^{th} =$	$14^{th} =$
Cayman Islands	3	12		15	$27^{th} =$	$24^{th} =$
Barbados		6	6	12	$33^{rd} =$	$25^{th} =$
Malaysia (Labuan)		6		6	$46^{th} =$	$34^{th} =$

Looking at Table 1.1, 12 of the 15 jurisdictions that are members of the ITIO are ranked 14th or higher in the consolidated rankings (Appendices D and E). All of the ITIO members other than Malaysia (through Labuan) are very small jurisdictions with a substantial proportion of their GDP dependent upon the provision of financial services and tourism, and most fit the stereotype of the small island in the Caribbean or the Pacific that is supposed to be problematic in terms of money laundering and/or tax evasion.

It is not surprising that many of these smaller, and to an extent more marginalized, OFCs should seek to consolidate in order to press their view, and thereby present a stronger voice for the interests of smaller OFCs. Individual OFCs and their representatives, however, are still more than prepared to be critical of the OECDPHTP.

Sir Ronald Sanders, High Commissioner to the UK for Antigua and Barbuda, for example, accuses the OECD of not only double standards and being highly selective in its listing processes but also of seeking to coerce certain non-OECD members into adopting tax systems that would be detrimental to their own national interest but would benefit the interests of OECD members:

Throughout this initiative, the OECD is seeking to curb the rights of sovereign small states and autonomous jurisdictions, defying the norms of international rules and practice ... It is noteworthy for instance that Hong Kong was never named as a tax haven, yet by every criteria that the OECD has established, Hong Kong should have been a prime target. Was

Hong Kong's omission an indication that the OECD did not want to offend the People's Republic of China?[145]

Unsurprisingly the OECD sees things a little differently:

The real success of the project so far is that we have received commitments from 31 jurisdictions to the OECD's principles of transparency and effective exchange of information ... We have gone a long way towards achieving a level playing field as a result of having a very large number of on and offshore financial centres commit to the same principles.[146]

In the future, there are sure to be many other critical and often competing perspectives on the legitimacy of the positions of both the OECDPHTP and those jurisdictions that are most affected by it.

Nevertheless, whatever vested interests may be involved in the future in different areas, it is likely that the orientation and methodological models adopted by the OECD, FATF, FSF and IMF will remain a feature within the financial sector in general, as international organisations and the governments and regulatory agencies of certain nation states seek to increase their levels of regulatory oversight in the international arena. The emphasis is likely to be on monitoring and accreditation standards, which have the potential to be operated in a manner similar to contemporary credit ratings systems. Under the latter, jurisdictions derive both economic and political benefits from having a high credit rating.

A similar economic rationale may well prove to be the greatest motivation to promoting increased transparency and probity in financial services. In addiction, like the financial services sector they seek to regulate, the corresponding legislative frameworks, regulatory agencies and regulatory practices must have an increasing capacity for global strategies and action in ways that foster co-operation between the offshore and onshore sectors and represent the legitimate interests of all parties.

Conclusion

It is abundantly clear that, in an increasingly internationalising world economy, the problem of how to increase transparency in financial services and financial markets is a global one.

This global character is being strengthened constantly by developments in information technology that are transforming the economic system in general, and

---

[145] R. Sanders, The Fight Against Fiscal Colonialism: The OECD and Small Jurisdictions, *The Commonwealth Journal of International Affairs*, 365, London, 2002, http://www.antigua-barbuda.com.

[146] OECD, *The OECD List of Unco-operative Tax Havens - A statement by the Chair of the OECD's Committee on Fiscal Affairs, Gabriel Makhlouf*, 18 April 2002, Paris, http://www.oecd.org/EN/document/0,,EN-document-22-nodirectorate-no-12-28549-22,00.html.

the financial sector in particular, into networks of computer mediated information. Initiatives regarding financial services and financial markets will have to be global in their outlook and effect, responsive to changes in technological development, and sensitive to the legitimate needs of those jurisdictions affected by them.

Such initiatives in general, and those affecting OFCs in particular, are likely to be multilateral and based on international conventions and treaties, with an emphasis on enabling frameworks rather than a reliance on mandatory technical requirements.

In all of this discussion of the social and political influences that may shape the present and future regulation of OFCs, one should not forget the powerful influence of Adam Smith's *Invisible Hand*,[147] that is to say, market forces themselves and, in particular, the decisions and choices of the consumers of the services of OFCs.

Investors and other consumers of the services of OFCs are likely to engage in some forum shopping between jurisdictions, but under-regulation may be just as unattractive for some investors as over-regulation.

Some investors may prefer more costly financial centres precisely because some may have a better reputation for stability, investor protection and transparent regulatory standards.[148] Other investors may select financial centres that have less onerous regulatory regimes, lower costs or stronger secrecy provisions. Under this paradigm of regulatory arbitrage, exchanges and financial centres understandably exploit what they perceive as their cost or other structural advantages, such as a particular jurisdiction's system of company law, or levels of bank secrecy, in order to gain competitive advantage.

There is an urgent and growing need for more and continuing empirical research on the general role of OFCs within global markets for financial services and products, and also on the efficacy of international regulatory initiatives such as those of the OECD, FATF and FSF. The empirical studies in Chapters 4 and 5 are in these directions.

Permeating specific research studies and more general debates, however, is perhaps the key philosophical, political and economic issue for both theoretical and pragmatic decision-making on international regulatory competition: how far should regulatory competition go? Or to pose the same issue in a slightly different way, how far should international organisations such as the FATF, FSF, OECD or IMF dictate the levels of regulatory competition regarding OFCs, tax or indeed any other trade-related area?

The elusive holy grail of successful international regulation is at heart an issue of balance. Increased regulatory competition is not bad, but competition itself has to be tempered with appropriate checks and balances. Undeniably, substantial amounts of resources that are owed or due to national tax authorities are being

---

[147] A. Smith, *The Wealth of Nations*, T. Nelson and Sons, London, 1884.

[148] This has been brought home to me on many of the occasions when I have been in contact with regulators of a number of different OFCs. Most have stressed to me that they want to be perceived as *Premier League OFCs* and do not want *dirty money* passing through their jurisdictions.

lost/concealed/invested in international financial markets. Reconciling the competing claims of nation states for tax revenues, financial centres for market access and financial institutions for freedom to operate is a substantial challenge.

The roles of financial institutions as stakeholders in the regulation of a globalising economy are evolving continually. Increasingly, financial institutions are bearing the costs of regulatory monitoring, and this trend seems inexorable, as the private sector is likely to assume increasing responsibility for the governance of financial services. This can be seen around the world in the evolving systems of anti-money laundering regimes and risk-based approaches to regulation.

These political, social, economic and technological realities must be acknowledged, so that issues of national sovereignty will be factored heavily into the development of international initiatives, and the input of affected jurisdictions sought in an inclusive manner, in order that multilateral regulatory efforts may have a realistic hope of success. On this point of view, the analysis on the UK territories developed in Chapter 6 is particularly interesting.

It should therefore be clear, from the preceding discussion, that the political context is powerful and omnipresent in regulatory praxis. Criteria of legitimacy and normative codes of conduct fluctuate as social, economic and political conditions change, and this inevitably affects how regulatory systems function, and subsequent levels of law enforcement at local, national and international levels.

Nevertheless, although its constituent elements may vary, the importance of moral issues in regulatory compliance remains central. In many ways, this moral element is the 'master card' for the promotion of meaningful crime prevention strategies by international organisations, and within business organisations and cultures.

It is important to remember the potential power of this moral context, along with the fact that a synergy exists between the agendas of various agencies of law enforcement, national ministries of both justice and international development portfolio, international organisations such as the FATF, FSF and OECD, and international conduits for aid such as the IMF and the World Bank. The trick, of course, is to construct meaningful, effective regulatory and aid programmes on the basis of that synergy.

Such synergy will only be achieved by initiatives that can clearly demonstrate their intrinsic legitimacy. The 'war on drugs' in the US and elsewhere is failing because of the legitimacy deficits of its general emphasis on supply side strategies that stress law enforcement, rather than the intrinsically more legitimate demand side strategies that emphasise drugs as a social health issue.

The regulation of OFCs is a similar 'legitimacy story'. As Chapters 4 and 5 will demonstrate, there are dangers associated with the strategy of naming and shaming jurisdictions. It may be a dangerous game, as it may inhibit innovation in a sector where reputation is a valuable asset. In addition, it may have a signalling effect, as even more capital, especially from the illegitimate and/or black economy, may be attracted to those financial centres that are named and shamed.

There is also the potential of the 'dual regulation hypothesis', in that too much anti-money laundering regulatory action could makes the bad worse and the good better. The objective for all regarding the regulation of OFCs is to strive for an optimum balance in the compliance pull–legitimacy interaction in ways that take account of the legitimate interests of all affected parties.

The many competing interpretations regarding the initiatives of the FATF, FSF and OECD point to the need for much more data in these areas. It would seem a reasonable proposition, however, that those international initiatives likely to stand a greater chance of success in the future will be those that adopt fundamentally more legitimate demand side strategies.

These demand side strategies will be based on incentive models that will seek simultaneously:

- not only to decrease taxation burdens in all countries, while at the same time ensuring that all countries have functional taxation systems targeting optimal levels of social capital creation;
- but also to foster meaningful development in less developed jurisdictions and effective integration of all jurisdictions into the global and regional economies.

As stated earlier, the Boston Tea Party protest of 1773 centred on notions of inclusion, exclusion and the regulatory intervention of external actors in matters of taxation and commerce, and more than 200 years later these issues are centre stage regarding the regulatory regimes of OFCs.

The lessons of Boston in the 18th century still have purchase in the 21st century. If regulatory initiatives are truly inclusive and representative, and perhaps most importantly, perceived as legitimate by those who are affected by them, then there is a much greater prospect that OFCs, indeed an increased likelihood that all jurisdictions, will accept the invitation of organisations such as the FATF, FSF and OECD to their 'regulatory tea parties'. More tea anyone?

Methodology of the Ranking Tables in Appendices 1.A-1.E

- Appendices A-C list those jurisdictions that have been listed by the FATF (Appendix A), the FSF (Appendix B) and the OECD (Appendix C).
- Appendix D consolidates the scores of all jurisdictions that appear in any of the FATF, FSF or OECD blacklists and ranks the jurisdictions according to cumulative points.
- Appendix E reproduces this consolidation and ranking process with respect to all blacklists of the FATF, FSF and OECD, but only for those jurisdictions that were classified as OFCs by the FSF in May 2000.
- I have ranked the overall effects of blacklisting by the FATF and OECD to be roughly similar. However, the FATF has produced six different lists and the OECD only two. Consequently, I accorded three points for each separate listing by the FATF, so that a period of continuing appearance in the first list of June 2000 through to the sixth list of February 2003 would attract 18 points. The first OECD blacklist of May 2000 classified 34 jurisdictions as tax havens, and the April 2002 blacklist accorded non-co-operative tax haven status to seven

jurisdictions. So I applied six points for an appearance in the OECD list of May 2000 and 12 points for an appearance in the April 2002 list. As a result, any jurisdiction that has been blacklisted continuously by the OECD received 18 points and therefore an equal effect, for ranking purposes, to continuous classification by the FATF.

- The FSF has adopted a gentler approach than either the FATF or the OECD, and seems to have had less impact and therefore should attract a lower maximum score than the FATF or the OECD. Nevertheless, the FSF did differentiate quite sharply between the quality of supervision and regulatory co-operation exhibited by the various OFCs, and I felt that this should be reflected in any scoring and ranking process. Consequently, those OFCs accorded Group I status by the FSF attracted one point, those in Group II six points and those in Group III 12 points.

Appendix 1.A FATF Blacklists of Non-Co-operative Countries and Territories (NCCTs)

For purposes of ranking, each appearance in a FATF NCCT blacklist attracts 3 points

Ranking	Jurisdiction	Jun. 2000	Jun. 2001	Sep. 2001	Jun. 2002	Oct. 2002	Feb. 2003	Points Total
1st	Cook Islands	X	X	X	X	X	X	18
1st	Nauru	X	X	X	X	X	X	18
1st	Philippines	X	X	X	X	X	X	18
1st	St Vincent and Gren.	X	X	X	X	X	X	18
5th	Egypt		X	X	X	X	X	15
5th	Guatemala		X	X	X	X	X	15
5th	Indonesia		X	X	X	X	X	15
5th	Myanmar		X	X	X	X	X	15
5th	Nigeria		X	X	X	X	X	15
10th	Dominica	X	X	X	X			12
10th	Marshall Islands	X	X	X	X			12
10th	Niue	X	X	X	X			12
10th	Russia	X	X	X	X			12
10th	Ukraine			X	X	X	X	12
15th	Grenada			X	X	X		9
15th	Israel	X	X	X				9
15th	Lebanon	X	X	X				9
15th	St Kitts and Nevis	X	X	X				9
19th	Hungary		X	X				6
20th	Bahamas	X						3
20th	Cayman Islands	X						3
20th	Liechtenstein	X						3
20th	Panama	X						3

Appendix 1.B FSF List of Offshore Finance Centres (May 2000)

For purposes of ranking:

Group I = good quality supervision and co-operation   = 1 point
Group II = regulatory infrastructure in place but below Group I standard   = 6 points
Group III= lower quality regulatory infrastructure than Group II standard =12 points

Ranking	Jurisdiction	FSF Group	Points Total
1st	Anguilla	III	12
1st	Antigua and Barbuda	III	12
1st	Aruba	III	12
1st	Bahamas	III	12
1st	Belize	III	12
1st	British Virgin Islands	III	12
1st	Cayman Islands	III	12
1st	Cook Islands	III	12
1st	Costa Rica	III	12
1st	Cyprus	III	12
1st	Lebanon	III	12
1st	Liechtenstein	III	12
1st	Marshall Islands	III	12
1st	Mauritius	III	12
1st	Nauru	III	12
1st	Netherlands Antilles	III	12
1st	Niue	III	12
1st	Panama	III	12
1st	Samoa	III	12
1st	Seychelles	III	12
1st	St Kitts and Nevis	III	12
1st	St Lucia	III	12
1st	St Vincent and Gren.	III	12
1st	Turks and Caicos Islands	III	12
1st	Vanuatu	III	12
26th	Andorra	II	6
26th	Bahrain	II	6
26th	Barbados	II	6
26th	Bermuda	II	6
26th	Gibraltar	II	6
26th	Labuan (Malaysia)	II	6
26th	Macau SAR	II	6
26th	Malta	II	6
26th	Monaco	II	6
35th	Dublin (Ireland)	I	1
35th	Guernsey/Sark/Alderney	I	1

Appendix 1.B (continued)

35th	Hong Kong SAR	I	1
35th	Isle of Man	I	1
35th	Jersey	I	1
35th	Luxembourg	I	1
35th	Singapore	I	1
35th	Switzerland	I	1

Appendix 1.C OECD Project on Harmful Tax Practies – Blacklists of Tax Havens

For purposes of ranking:
May 2000   = classified as Tax Haven Status   =6 points
April 2002   = classified as Non-co-operative Tax Haven Status   =12 points

Ranking	Jurisdiction	May 2000	April 2002	Points Total
1st	Andorra	X	X	18
1st	Liberia	X	X	18
1st	Liechtenstein	X	X	18
1st	Marshall Islands	X	X	18
1st	Monaco	X	X	18
1st	Nauru	X	X	18
1st	Vanuatu	X	X	18
8th	Anguilla	X		6
8th	Antigua and Barbuda	X		6
8th	Aruba	X		6
8th	Bahamas	X		6
8th	Bahrain	X		6
8th	Barbados	X		6
8th	Belize	X		6
8th	British Virgin Islands	X		6
8th	Cook Islands	X		6
8th	Dominica	X		6
8th	Gibraltar	X		6
8th	Guernsey/Sark/Alderney	X		6
8th	Isle of Man	X		6
8th	Jersey	X		6
8th	Maldives	X		6
8th	Montserrat	X		6
8th	Netherlands Antilles	X		6
8th	Niue	X		6
8th	Panama	X		6
8th	Samoa	X		6
8th	Seychelles	X		6
8th	St Kitts and Nevis	X		6
8th	St Lucia	X		6
8th	St Vincent and Gren.	X		6
8th	Tonga	X		6
8th	Turks and Caicos Islands	X		6
8th	US Virgin Islands	X		6

Appendix 1.D Consolidated Table of scores of all Jurisdictions that appear in any of the FATF, FSF & OECD blacklists (as at 19 February 2003)

Please refer back to Appendices A-C for specific scores for each jurisdiction as for each separate list of the FATF, FSF or OECD, but for purposes of ranking in this Table:

Each appearance in a FATF NCCT blacklist (3 points)

FSF Group I	= good quality supervision and co-operation (1 point)
FSF Group II	= regulatory infrastructure in place but below Group I standard (6 points)
FSF Group III	= lower quality regulatory infrastructure than Group II standard (12 points)
OECD May 2000	=classified as Tax Haven Status (6 points)
OECD April 2002	=classified as Non-co-operative Tax Haven Status (12 points)

Ranking	Jurisdiction	FATF score	FSF score	OECD score	Points Total
1st	Nauru	18	12	18	48
2nd	Marshall Islands	12	12	18	42
3rd	Cook Islands	18	12	6	36
3rd	St Vincent and Gren.	18	12	6	36
5th	Liechtenstein	3	12	18	33
6th	Niue	12	12	6	30
6th	Vanuatu		12	18	30
8th	St Kitts & Nevis	9	12	6	27
9th	Andorra		6	18	24
9th	Monaco		6	18	24
11th	Bahamas	3	12	6	21
11th	Lebanon	9	12		21
11th	Panama	3	12	6	21
14th	Anguilla		12	6	18
14th	Antigua and Barbuda		12	6	18
14th	Aruba		12	6	18
14th	Belize		12	6	18
14th	British Virgin Islands		12	6	18
14th	Dominica	12		6	18
14th	Liberia			18	18
14th	Netherlands Antilles		12	6	18
14th	Philippines	18			18
14th	Samoa		12	6	18
14th	Seychelles		12	6	18

Appendix 1.D (continued)

14th	St Lucia		12	6	18
14th	Turks and Caicos Isl.		12	6	18
27th	Cayman Islands	3	12		15
27th	Egypt	15			15
27th	Guatemala	15			15
27th	Indonesia	15			15
27th	Myanmar	15			15
27th	Nigeria	15			15
33rd	Bahrain		6	6	12
33rd	Barbados		6	6	12
33rd	Costa Rica		12		12
33rd	Cyprus		12		12
33rd	Gibraltar		6	6	12
33rd	Mauritius		12		12
33rd	Russia	12			12
33rd	Ukraine	12			12
41st	Grenada	9			9
41st	Israel	9			9
43rd	Guernsey/Sark/Aderney		1	6	7
43rd	Isle of Man		1	6	7
43rd	Jersey		1	6	7
46th	Bermuda		6		6
46th	Hungary	6			6
46th	Labuan (Malaysia)		6		6
46th	Macau SAR		6		6
46th	Maldives			6	6
46th	Malta		6		6
46th	Montserrat			6	6
46th	Tonga			6	6
46th	US Virgin Islands			6	6
55th	Dublin (Ireland)		1		1
55th	Hong Kong SAR		1		1
55th	Luxembourg		1		1
55th	Singapore		1		1
55th	Switzerland		1		1

Appendix 1.E Consolidated Table of OFCs Listed by the FSF in March 2000 that Appear in any of the FATF, FSF and OECD Blacklists (as at 19 February 2003)

Please refer back to Appendices A-C for specific scores for each jurisdiction as for each separate list of the FATF, FSF or OECD; but for purposes of ranking in this table:

Each appearance in a FATF NCCT blacklist (3 points)

FSF Group I	= good quality supervision and co-operation (1 point)
FSF Group II	= regulatory infrastructure in place but below Group I standard (6 points)
FSF Group III	= lower quality regulatory infrastructure than Group II standard (12 points)
OECD May 2000	= classified as Tax Haven Status (6 points)
OECD April 2002	= classified as Non-co-operative Tax Haven Status (12 points)

Ranking	Jurisdiction	FATF score	FSF score	OECD score	Points Total
1st	Nauru	18	12	18	48
2nd	Marshall Islands	12	12	18	42
3rd	Cook Islands	18	12	6	36
3rd	St Vincent and Gren.	18	12	6	36
5th	Liechtenstein	3	12	18	33
6th	Niue	12	12	6	30
6th	Vanuatu		12	18	30
8th	St Kitts and Nevis	9	12	6	27
9th	Andorra		6	18	24
9th	Monaco		6	18	24
11th	Bahamas	3	12	6	21
11th	Lebanon	9	12		21
11th	Panama	3	12	6	21
14th	Anguilla		12	6	18
14th	Antigua and Barbuda		12	6	18
14th	Aruba		12	6	18
14th	Belize		12	6	18
14th	British Virgin Islands		12	6	18
14th	Netherlands Antilles		12	6	18
14th	Samoa		12	6	18
14th	Seychelles		12	6	18
14th	St Lucia		12	6	18
14th	Turks and Caicos Isl.		12	6	18
24th	Cayman Islands	3	12		15
25th	Bahrain		6	6	12

Appendix 1.E (continued)

25th	Barbados		6	6	12
25th	Costa Rica		12		12
25th	Cyprus		12		12
25th	Gibraltar		6	6	12
25th	Mauritius		12		12
31st	Guernsey/Sark/ Alderney		1	6	7
31st	Isle of Man		1	6	7
31st	Jersey		1	6	7
34th	Bermuda		6		6
34th	Labuan (Malaysia)		6		6
34th	Macau SAR		6		6
34th	Malta		6		6
38th	Dublin (Ireland)		1		1
38th	Hong Kong SAR		1		1
38th	Luxembourg		1		1
38th	Singapore		1		1
38th	Switzerland		1		1

References

Banks, A. (2002), ITIO Accuses OECD Of Double Standards, *Tax-News.com*, 15 February.

Beetham,D. (1991), *The Legitimation of Power*, Macmillan, London.

Braithwaite, J. (1989), *Crime, Shame and Reintegration*, Cambridge University Press, Cambridge.

Brauner, Y. (2002), *An International Tax Regime in Crystallization – Realities, Experiences and Opportunities*, NYU Law School, Public Law Research Paper No. 43, New York.

Brinkley, J. (1999), Behind the Banking Bill, Years of Intense Lobbying, *The New York Times*, 23 October.

Chayes, A. and Chayes, A.H. (1995), *The New Sovereignty: Compliance with International Agreements*, Harvard University Press, Cambridge, MA.

Cobb, S.C. (1998), Global Finance and the Growth of Offshore Financial Centers: The Manx Experience, *Geoforum*, Vol.29, No.1.

Commonwealth Secretariat (2000), *The Implications of the OECD Harmful Tax Competition Initiative for Offshore Finance Centres*, London, 2000.

Dezelay, Y. (1993), Professional Competition and the Social Construction of Transnational Regulatory Expertise in *Corporate Control and Accountability*, J. McCahery, S. Picciotto and C. Scott (eds), Clarendon Press, Oxford.

Financial Action Task Force on Money Laundering (2003a), *The Forty Recommendations*, Paris.

Financial Action Task Force on Money Laundering (2003b), *FATF withdraws counter-measures with respect to Ukraine and decides on date for counter-measures to Philippines*, 14 February.

Financial Action Task Force on Money Laundering (2002a), *FATF acts against terrorist financing, money laundering and non-cooperative jurisdictions*, 1 February.

Financial Action Task Force on Money Laundering (2002b), *Review to Identify Non-Cooperative Countries or Territories: Increasing the Worldwide Effectiveness of Anti-Money Laundering Measures*, June, Paris.

Financial Action Task Force on Money Laundering (2002c), *FATF decides to impose counter-measures on Ukraine: no counter-measures to apply against Nigeria at this time*, 26 December, Paris.

Financial Action Task Force on Money Laundering (2002d), *Russia, Dominica, Niue and Marshall Islands removed from FATF's list of non-cooperative countries and territories*, 11 October.

Financial Action Task Force on Money Laundering (2001a), *FATF decides to impose counter-measures on Nauru*, Paris.

Financial Action Task Force on Money Laundering (2001b), *Review to Identify Non-Cooperative Countries or Territories: Increasing the Worldwide Effectiveness of Anti-Money Laundering Measures*, June, Paris.

Financial Action Task Force on Money Laundering (2001c), *Developments in Non-Cooperative Countries and Territories*, September, Paris.

Financial Action Task Force on Money Laundering (2001d), *Review of Anti-Money Laundering Systems and Mutual Evaluation Procedures 1992-1999*, Paris.

Financial Action Task Force on Money Laundering (2000a), *Review to Identify Non-Cooperative Countries or Territories: Increasing the Worldwide Effectiveness of Anti-Money Laundering Measures*, June, Paris.

Financial Action Task Force on Money Laundering (2000b), *Report on Non-Cooperative Countries and Territories*, Paris.

Financial Action Task Force on Money Laundering (2000c), *Report on Money Laundering Typologies 1999-2000*, Paris.

Financial Action Task Force on Money Laundering (1998), *1997-1998 Report on Money Laundering Typologies*, Paris.

Financial Action Task Force on Money Laundering (1996), *The Forty Recommendations*, Paris.

Financial Action Task Force on Money Laundering (1990), *The Forty Recommendations*, Paris.

Financial Stability Forum (2000), *Report of the Working Group on Offshore Centres*, 5 April.

Financial Stability Forum (2000), *Financial Stability Forum Releases Grouping of Offshore Financial Centres (OFCs) to Assist in Setting Priorities for Assessment*, May.

Flyvbjerg, B. (1998), *Rationality and Power: Democracy in Practice*, Chicago University Press, Chicago.

Franck, T.M. (1990), *The Power of Legitimacy Among Nations*, Oxford University Press, New York.

Franck, T.M. (1988), Legitimacy in the International System, *American Journal of International Law*, 82 (4).

Fukuyama, F. (1999), The Great Disruption, *The Atlantic Monthly*, 283.

Giddens, A. (1991), *Modernity and Self Identity, Self and Society in the Late Modern Age,* Polity Press, Cambridge.

Giddens, A. (1984), *The Constitution of Society*, Polity Press, Cambridge.

Gilligan, G.P. (2002), International trends in the regulation of the financial services sector, *Australian Journal of Corporate Law*, 14.

Gilligan, G.P. (2001), Going Underground – The Not So New Way to Bank?, *Journal of Financial Crime*, Vol.9, No.2.

Gilligan, G.P. (1999), *Regulating the Financial Services Sector*, Kluwer Law International, London.

Greenslade, R. (1992), *Maxwell's Fall*, Simon & Schuster, London.

Hampton, H.M. and Levi, M. (1999), Fast spinning into oblivion? Recent developments in money-laundering policies and offshore finance centres, *Third World Quarterly*, Vol.20, No.3.

Hampton, M.P. and Christensen, J. (1999), The British Isle Offshore Finance Centers of Jersey, Guernsey, and the Isle of Man: Should the Onshore State Act?, *Tax Notes International*, January 11.

Hampton, M. (1996), *The Offshore Interface, Tax Havens in the Global Economy*, Macmillan, London.

Hampton, M.P. (1994), Treasure islands or fool's gold: Can and should small island economies copy Jersey?, *World Development*, 22.

Hartcher, P. (2003), 'Bush vows to go it alone on Iraq', *The Australian Financial Review*, 30 January.

Hawkins, K. (1984), *Environment and Enforcement: Regulation and the Social Definition of Pollution*, Clarendon Press, Oxford.

International Monetary Fund, (2000), *Offshore Finance Centers, International Monetary Fund Background Paper*, June 23 2000.

Janeba, E. and Schjelderup, G. (2002), *Why Europe Should Love Tax Competition – and the U.S. Even More So, NBER Working Paper No. 9334*, Cambridge MA.

Johnson, J. and Desmond Lim, Y.C. (2002), Money Laundering: Has the Financial Action Task Force Made a Difference?, *Journal of Financial Crime*, Vol.10, No.1.

Labaton, S. (1999), Agreement Reached on Overhaul of U.S. Financial System, *The New York Times*, 23 October.

Macdonald, R. (1998), Metaphors of Multiplicity: Civil Society, Regimes and Legal Pluralism, 15 *Arizona Journal of International and Comparative Law*.

Masciandaro, D. and Portolano, A. (2003)., It takes two to tango: international financial regulation and off-shore centres, *Journal of Money Laundering Control*, Vol. 6, Num. 4, pp 311-330.

Meidinger, E. (1987), Regulatory Culture: A Theoretical Outline, 9, *Law and Policy*.

Mitchell, D. (2002), *Death of the EU Savings Tax Directive*, Center for Freedom and Prosperity Strategic Memorandum, August 26.

Mitnick, B.M. (1980), *The Political Economy of Regulation*, Columbia University Press, New York7.

Moscarino, G.J. and Shumaker, M.R. (1997), Beating the shell game: bank secrecy laws and their impact on civil recovery in international fraud actions, *The Company Lawyer*, Vol.18, No.6.

Organisation for Economic Co-operation and Development (2002a), *OECD Says Barbados Will not Appear on its Forthcoming List of Uncooperative Tax Havens*, 31 January, Paris.

Organisation for Economic Co-operation and Development (2002b), *Antigua and Barbuda commit to Co-operate with OECD to Address Harmful Tax Practices*, 20 February, Paris.

Organisation for Economic Co-operation and Development (2002v), *Grenada and St Vincent and the Grenadines commit to Co-operate with OECD to Address Harmful Tax Practices*, 27 February, Paris.

Organisation for Economic Co-operation and Development (2002d), *Guernsey and Jersey commit to Co-operate with OECD to address Harmful Tax Practices*, 27 February, Paris.

Organisation for Economic Co-operation and Development (2002e), *St Lucia Commits to the Principles of Transparency and effective Exchange of Information*, 5 March, Paris.

Organisation for Economic Co-operation and Development (2002f), *Dominica Commits to the Principles of Transparency and effective Exchange of Information*, 6 March, Paris.

Organisation for Economic Co-operation and Development (2002g), *Anguilla and Turks and Caicos Islands Commit to Co-operate with OECD to Address Harmful Tax Practices*, 8 March, Paris.

Organisation for Economic Co-operation and Development (2002h), *US Virgin Islands Commits to Co-operate with OECD to Address Harmful Tax Practices*, 11 March, Paris.

Organisation for Economic Co-operation and Development (2002i), *The Bahamas Commits to Co-operate with OECD to Address Harmful Tax Practices*, 18 March, Paris.

Organisation for Economic Co-operation and Development (2002j), *Belize Commits to Co-operate with OECD to Address Harmful Tax Practices*, 20 March, Paris.

Organisation for Economic Co-operation and Development (2002k), *Cook Islands Commits to Co-operate with OECD to Address Harmful Tax Practices*, 27 March, Paris.

Organisation for Economic Co-operation and Development (2002l), *British Virgin Islands Commits to Co-operate with OECD to Address Harmful Tax Practices*, 3 April, Paris.

Organisation for Economic Co-operation and Development (2002m), *Niue Commits to Co-operate with OECD to Address Harmful Tax Practices*, 15 April, Paris.

Organisation for Economic Co-operation and Development (2002n), *Panama Commits to Co-operate with OECD to Address Harmful Tax Practices*, 17 April, Paris.

Organisation for Economic Co-operation and Development (2002o), *Samoa Commits to Co-operate with OECD to Address Harmful Tax Practices*, 18 April, Paris.

Organisation for Economic Co-operation and Development (2002p), *The OECD Issues The List of Unco-operative Tax Havens*, 18 April, Paris.

Organisation for Economic Co-operation and Development (2001), *The OECD's Project on Harmful Tax Practices: The 2001 Progress Report*, November, Paris.

Organisation for Economic Co-operation and Development (2000), *Towards Global Tax Co-operation, Report to the 2000 Ministerial Council Meeting and Recommendations by the Committee on Fiscal Affairs, Progress in Identifying and Eliminating Harmful Tax Practices*, Paris.

Parker, G. (2002), France and Germany call for EU tax accord, *New York Times*, 1 December.

Poser, N. (1991), *International Securities Regulation - London's 'Big Bang' and the European Securities Markets*, Little, Brown & Co., Boston.

Putnam, R. (1996),The Strange Disappearance of Civil America, *Policy (Autumn)*.

Raustalia, K. and Slaughter, A.M. (2002), International Law. International Relations and Compliance, in W. Carlsnaes, T. Risse, B. Simmons and T. Risse-Kappen (eds), *Handbook of International Relations*, Sage Publications, London.

Reichman, N. (1992), Moving Backstage, Uncovering the Role of Compliance Practices in Shaping Regulatory Policy in *White Collar Crime Reconsidered*, K. Schlegel and D. Weisburd (eds), Northeastern University Press, Boston.

Sanders, R. (2002), The Fight Against Fiscal Colonialism: The OECD and Small Jurisdictions, *The Commonwealth Journal of International Affairs*, 365, London.

Sansonetti, R. (1999), The Mutual Evaluation Process: A Methodology of Increasing Importance at International Level, *Journal of Financial Crime* Vol.7, No.3.

Sieker, S. (2001), Offshore Financial Centers and "Harmful Tax Competition": The Year 2000 in Review, *Tax Notes International*, 29 January.

Smith, A. (1884), *The Wealth of Nations*, T. Nelson and Sons, London.

Sorensen, P.B. (2001), *International Tax Coordination: Regionalism Versus Globalism*, *CESifo Working Paper No.483*, Munich.

Stikeman, E. (2000), *Towards A Level Playing Field – Regulating Corporate Vehicles in Cross-Border Transactions*, ITIO and STEP, London.

Sumner, C.S. (1990), Rethinking deviance: towards a sociology of deviance, in C. Sumner (ed), *Censure politics and criminal justice*, Open University Press, Milton Keynes.

Teubner, G. (1992), The Two Faces of Janus: Rethinking Legal Pluralism, 13 *Cardozo Law Review*.

Tyler, T.R. (1990), *Why People Obey the Law*, Yale University Press, New Haven.

Underhill, G.R. (2000), The Public Good Versus Private Interests in the Global Monetary and Financial System', *International and Comparative Corporate Law Journal*, Vol.2, No.3.

Walker, J. (1999), How Big is Global Money Laundering? *Journal of Money Laundering Control*, Vol.3, No.1.

Wilkinson, M. (2003), 'Bush makes case for war', *The Age*, 30 January.

Wishart, D. (1994), *Company Law in Context*, Oxford University Press.

Wright, R. (2000), Keynote Address to the 17th International Cambridge Symposium on Economic Crime, *Journal of Financial Crime*, Vol.7 No.4.

Chapter 2

Law: The War on Terror and Crime and the Offshore Centres: The 'New' Perspective?

Barry A.K. Rider

Introduction

For the last 20 or so years, one of the principal strategies in fighting serious crime, particularly criminal activity that is motivated by economic gain, has been to attack the proceeds of crime through a number of legal devices.

Associated with this strategy is the concern to impede the laundering of wealth, which places a hurdle in front of those seeking to attribute wealth to a particular criminal act or course of crime. At the same time, far more attention has been given, for a variety of reasons, to the financial aspects of crime and, in particular, the development of financial intelligence.

The horrific attack against the United States on 11 September 2001 justified and mandated an extreme response. In part that response – the so-called 'War on Terrorism' – has involved far more attention being given by traditional and non-traditional law enforcement agencies to the role of OFCs in the funding of terrorist organisations.

It was perhaps understandable that the now considerable experience that has been developed in a number of countries around the world in attempting to interdict the assets of organised crime should be deployed against the threat of international terrorism. Indeed, if the 'War on Drugs' has been fought, at least in part, through the banking and financial system, why not the 'War on Terror'?

There are several problems with this approach. Firstly, the success that law enforcement agencies have had around the world in 'taking the profit out of crime' is very limited and does not commend itself as a particularly efficient strategy in the fight against terrorists. Secondly, there are very important differences between property in the hands of criminal organisations and those who can be considered terrorists, at least in some jurisdictions.

While the US and UK authorities have had some success in freezing funds associated with the Taliban and groups identified in previous criminal investigations as being 'involved' in supporting terrorist outrages, it remains to be seen whether sufficient resources will be committed over a period to enable this strategy to reap the benefits that President George Bush, among others, contemplates.

Disrupting the funding of terrorist organisations is not a new strategy. Indeed, the expertise, such as it is, that has been deployed in fighting organised crime was first developed in the 1960s by the intelligence and security community to disrupt the activities of subversive organisations. To some extent, it was the freeing up of these resources, and their deployment in traditional law enforcement, that led to the dramatic realisation that organised crime does present such a threat to security and stability.

The UK government, from the early 1980s to rather recently, had achieved some degree of success in disrupting the funding of terrorist organisations in Northern Ireland. The German and Italian authorities have also adopted a similar strategy in regard to their own problems. Other jurisdictions, including Hong Kong and South Africa, have developed financial intelligence to assist them in ensuring relative stability during periods of transition.

The United Nations and other inter-governmental organisations have also been concerned with the funding of terror. The International Convention for the Suppression of Financing Terrorism[1] was opened for signature at the UN, in New York, on 10 January 2000. Few countries considered this a priority[2] until Mr Bush's 'crusade'. Having said this, the UK government must be commended, as the Terrorism Act 2000 goes somewhat further than the requirements of the UN Convention, and the Anti-Terrorism Crime and Security Act 2001 goes much further!

Accepting that much has changed since 11 September 2001, let us examine – focusing on law and institutions – the experience that we have had now over many years in pursuing the proceeds of crime and disrupting criminal and subversive enterprises. This examination may well lead us to extract some lessons on the relationship between the war on terror and crime and the role of OFCs, and furthermore to take, the view that, as with the 'War on Drugs', we will still be counting the costs of terror for some years to come.

Economically Motivated Crime

The acquisition of, and control over, wealth is the motivation for most serious crimes involving premeditation. This is all the more true when the criminal activity resembles an enterprise that inevitably requires capital to operate and with which to lubricate its aspirations. Money, or rather wealth, in its disposable form, is therefore not only the goal of criminal enterprises but also the lifeblood of the enterprise.

---

[1] *Convention 54/109* 19 December 1999.
[2] Before the 11 September 2001 the only signatories were the UK, Botswana, Sri Lanka and Uzbekistan!

Therefore, until the profits of crime are taken away from subversive and criminal factions, we stand little chance of effectively discouraging criminal and abusive conduct that produces great wealth or allows power and prestige to be acquired through its profits. As soon as the state devises methods for tracing and seizing such funds, there is an obvious and compelling incentive for criminals to hide the source of their ill-gotten gains – in other words to engage in money laundering.

Like most social evils, let alone economic evils, money laundering is nothing new. It is as old as is the need to hide one's wealth from prying eyes and jealous hands, and concern about the uses and misuses of hidden money is not just an issue in our century.

Of course, modern money launderers will no doubt adopt rather more sophisticated techniques than the gem carriers of India or the Knights Templar, but their objectives and essential modus operandi will be the same. The objectives will be to obscure the source, and thus the nature, of the wealth in question, and the modus operandi will inevitably involve resort to transactions, real or imagined, designed to confuse the onlooker and confound the inquirer. In recent years, the organisation and management of extremely profitable criminal enterprises have given greater emphasis to strategies designed to ensure crime does not pay.

When the time comes to look back at the last two decades of the 20th Century, a future historian would be forgiven for thinking we were almost obsessed with organised crime, corruption and money laundering. Of course, when one considers the ignominious fall from favour of so many world leaders, in circumstances where serious corruption was at least alleged, if not self-evident, the exposure of rampant financial malpractice in inter-governmental organisations, the penetration of entire economic and political structures by what, for want of a better notion, we describe as organised crime, then perhaps our historian's impression might not be too far from the truth.

Although the odd comment can be found in international meetings about the serious implications of economic crime and the like, before the 1980s these were few and far between,[3] and mostly related to complaints from developing countries about the unwillingness of developed countries to assist in the enforcement of exchange control laws.

---

[3] For example, *Communiqué of the Commonwealth Law Ministers' Meeting*, Winnipeg, Canada, 1977 and the ICPO – Interpol General Assembly, Accra, Ghana, 1976.

In fact, it was not until November 1980 that the Commonwealth, an organisation – or rather association – of states whose justification has increasingly been based on its ability to recognise and address problems related to small and relatively fragile economies, began to concern itself at the governmental level with the implications of what appeared to be a growth in serious economic abuse.[4]

In those days, there was little talk about the threat of organised crime, even in such organisations as ICPO-Interpol. Terrorism, whether by individuals or by state agencies, was then considered to be a matter almost beyond the remit of traditional law enforcement agencies. It was much later that most came to recognise that organised crime and terrorist organisations might well be one and the same.

Some have argued that organised crime is a problem of the last quarter of the 20th Century and, in the case of most states, it is a new phenomenon. Of course, so much depends upon what is meant by 'organised crime'.

Groups of individuals, formed and managed to perpetrate acts against the law is nothing new. Nor is it novel that the primary motivation of such enterprises is economic gain – spurred on by 'plain old-fashioned' greed and corruption. What has changed is the criminals' ability to operate beyond the reach of the domestic legal system and therefore be able to conduct an enterprise in crime that is not so amenable to the traditional criminal justice system and its agents.

Of course, in truth, thinking criminals have always sought to place themselves beyond the reach of the law, and it was not just a matter of having a faster horse! The corruption of officials and the patronage of powerful individuals whose interests, for whatever reason, might be at variance with those of the state are tried and tested tools. It has always been recognised that even though, in theory, jurisdiction was unfettered, the practicalities were such as to render enforcement parochial.

Thus, when Henry II of England was asked towards the end of the 12th Century how far his writ ran, he responded: 'as far as my arrows reach'. While developments in ballistic technology might render this a relatively useful approach to dealing with the international criminal, in the vast majority of cases the criminal law on its application or at least administration will be confined within domestic borders. Developments in technology, communications, travel and the liberalisation of movement, whether of persons, things or wealth, have all combined to give the criminal enterprise of today the same ability as any other business to move from one jurisdiction to another, or involve two or more different jurisdictions in a single act.

---

[4] For example, *Communiqué of the Commonwealth Law Ministers' Meeting*, Barbados, May 1980. See also B. Rider, *The Promotion and Development of International Co-operation to Combat Commercial and Economic Crime*, Memoranda, Meeting of Commonwealth Law Ministers, Barbados, Commonwealth Secretariat London, 1980; B. Rider, 'Combating International Commercial Crime – a Commonwealth Perspective, *Lloyds Maritime and Commercial Law Quarterly*, 6, p. 217, 1985, and A. Shipman and B. Rider, 'Organised Crime International', *Security and Defence Reference Book*, 9, 1987, Cornhill Publications, London.

In addition to these factors, which criminals have exploited no less imaginatively than legitimate businessmen, there is another and perhaps crucial consideration. This is the profitability of smuggling and, in particular, the illicit trade in drugs, psychotropic substances and other narcotics. The enterprise of smuggling is a natural and predictable consequence of the imposition of restrictions or other costs on the supply of a commodity for which there is a greater market. History records that highly developed illicit operations developed not just to evade the imposition of taxes but also to avoid tariffs and other market controls. Indeed, by creating situations where otherwise law-abiding members of society see advantage in resorting to secret and illicit suppliers of goods or services, we foster the existence and long-term viability of criminal and subversive structures.

The horrendous trade that has developed in immigrant 'workers' and 'refugees' has also enabled organised crime to retain influence and control over these poor men and women whom it has placed in, or assisted in finding, work. Although the illicit trade in weapons and cultural and heritage property is vast, it is the illicit market in drugs that has given organised crime its almost incomprehensible resources and capital.

Unlike arms and works of art, the illicit drugs trade has a commodity that can be relatively easily smuggled and for which there is a more or less uniform, discreet and insatiable market. In the early days of what might be termed the modern trade, those areas of the world in a position to supply the raw material were not particularly amenable to external supervision, let alone control. To what extent some of the states that became 'victims' of this cancerous trade almost facilitated the existence and growth of the criminal enterprises that subsequently took advantage of these opportunities is a matter for debate.

It is true, or at least reasonably well documented, that some criminal groups that had been almost suppressed prior to and during the Second World War were 'allowed' to revive, and even strengthen themselves, as a bulwark against the threat of communism. It is said that such a strategy was defensible on the basis that these organisations tended to have local concerns and were not, at the time, a viable threat to other societies. An allegation of naivety is always easier to assert with the privilege of hindsight, and perhaps the 'planners' really did believe that the Sicilian gangs thought drugs were immoral!

On the other hand, we should not forget the consistent inability of those that inform and advise the 'planners' to predict even quite fundamental changes. The developments in technology and mobility, to which we have already referred, were much more profound and quicker than perhaps were anticipated. Furthermore, even the most alarmist predictions of the growth of the illicit market and trade in drugs and narcotics proved to be conservative. During the 1970s drugs became just far too profitable and easy a trade for even traditional and 'conservative' organised crime groups to ignore. Within a decade, even terrorist groups that conventional wisdom considered unwilling to risk the taint of drugs entered the market, and by so doing became virtually indistinguishable from 'ordinary' organised crime.

Secret Money Demand: Similarities and Differences between Terrorism and Organised Crime

The reasons why an individual, not to mention an organisation, would wish to hide the source of money, or transmit it in a manner that obscures its ownership or character, are legion.

While a great deal of attention has been given to the vast profits that are being generated by the illicit trade in narcotics, it is dangerously misconceived to assume that the processes involved in money laundering cannot be, and are not, deployed just as effectively to cleanse and covertly transfer funds produced by other types of crime, or even activities that would not be generally considered criminal but to which a certain amount of opprobrium might attach.

There are pressing needs for 'secret money' not only in the underworld of organised and syndicated crime but also to service intelligence and security networks and to facilitate commercial and banking transactions that if not 'ordinary' are not necessarily abusive. There are needs for 'unaccountable funds' in many situations, and the processes involved in laundering money can be, and are, efficiently employed to create hidden reserves or secret money and are then utilised to service and transmit the funds in accordance with the requirements of those who desire them.

It must also be remembered that the purposes for which money is required will also influence, if not dictate, the transactions used to hide its true nature and the way it is permitted to move.[5]

Those who facilitate the flow of capital from developing nations, in violation of currency and fiscal controls, for example, may be able to operate with impunity and no embarrassment in other jurisdictions – especially those receiving the money in question. Therefore, there will be little need to ensure that the money surfaces covertly, and there will be no requirement that the money should appear to have a legitimate origin. Indeed, when the money is escaping from a country which is seeking to expropriate wealth, whether pursuant to a programme of so called 'in-digitisation' or otherwise, those involved in such financial operations may even be held in high esteem by those whom they service and those outside the country in question.

Furthermore, it must also be remembered that although an economic embargo may well be considered an appropriate device to employ against a country that is considered to be in breach of its international obligations, the perception in that country may be very different. State-endorsed, and even state-employed, 'sanction busters', of Mr Ian Smith's Rhodesia, or 'Apartheid South Africa', let alone of Saddam Hussein's Iraq, employ all the techniques of the money launderer.

Where the funds are the result of criminal activity, however, it will be necessary to ensure that each material element in the laundering process is covert and the money must appear to be clean when it finally emerges from the pipeline.

---

[5] See generally B. Rider and C. Nakajima, *Money Laundering*, Loose Leaf Service, 1999, Sweet & Maxwell, London, Chapter 1.

The purpose to which such funds are to be applied will also influence the processes involved to some degree. If money is to be reinvested in other criminal or subversive operations, the transactions that establish it must not be referable to other risk activity, but the money need not appear to be from a legitimate source to those who receive it.

Where the money is being used to penetrate an institution or organisation, however, then it must be not only unconnected to the activity which generated it but also apparently acceptable to those in control of the relevant body. It should be obvious that the somewhat simplistic notions of money laundering that have been preferred in a number of recent reports and publications presuppose a clarity and simplicity of purpose that rarely exist.

While many appear to have assumed, often without much thought, that terrorist organisations will inevitably adopt the modus operandi of organised crime in laundering their funds to create secret money, there are important differences between terrorists and conventional criminals.[6]

We have already emphasised that the laundering process will be determined by the needs of those seeking to hide or disassociated the wealth in question. Of course, many terrorist organisations are almost indistinguishable from organised crime and, in recent years, there has been a tendency to label terrorists as almost a sub-species of organised crime. Terrorists have stooped to ordinary crime to raise funds and secure their objectives and, of course, most terror networks would have the characteristics of a 'continuing criminal enterprise'.

While the objectives of most terrorists can be stigmatised as criminal, however, they are generally not acquisitive – at least in the proprietary sense.

Furthermore, a significant proportion of terrorist funding may not necessarily be derived from specific criminal activity. Donations and contributions from a diverse spectrum of supporters may, to a greater or lesser extent, provide a significant proportion of a particular group's funds. While the giving of property for the purpose of committing serious criminal acts might effectively 'criminalise' the property in question, it is not necessarily of illicit, and thus tainted, origin. It will often be quite clean, in the sense that we use that concept in the context of money laundering control. As we have seen, the creation of secret money is not of itself objectionable, let alone criminal.

The situation is rather similar to that of flight capital. The very act of transmitting wealth in violation of exchange control, or evading some other form of fiscal or tax control, arguably 'criminalises' wealth, which would otherwise be perfectly legitimate. There is also the problem of those who support terrorist organisations as seemingly bona fide political groups, without any desire to promote violence and perhaps in ignorance as to what their contributions will be used for. Religious charities,[7] not only within Islam, have been drawn into funding organisations that manifestly do not practise what they preach!

---

[6] See in particular FATF, *Report on Money Laundering Typologies 2001-2002*, 2002, Paris.

[7] See for example *UN General Assembly Resolution 51/210*, 17 December 1996, referring to charities being used as trusts for terrorist activities and, in particular, fundraising.

Where terrorist organisations secure their funding from criminal activity, whether it be trafficking in drugs or running extortion rackets, they will have the same needs, in regard to the proceeds of their crime, as traditional organised crime groups. They will wish to disassociate their wealth from crime and all that might befall them as ordinary criminals. It might well be necessary, depending on the nature of their business, to facilitate the investment of their illicit wealth back into their continuing criminal enterprises. Terrorist organisations have similar needs to ordinary criminals in securing the instruments of their crime.

However, their need for security and secrecy is probably more compelling in most cases, since the stakes are somewhat higher. Perhaps to a greater extent than most forms of organised crime, terrorists with a political objective will require funds for a wider agenda. They will wish to maintain individuals and perhaps their families and networks, even when they are not directly pertinent to the prosecution of terror. They will also need to create secret money that can be easily accessed by operational units.

Consequently, it would be rash to suppose that the expertise, such as it is, that we have developed in pursuing the proceeds of drug trafficking and serious fraud is necessarily applicable or even relevant to pursuing and interdicting the funds of terrorist organisations. Indeed, as Chapter 1 remembered, and as we shall see later, terrorist organisations will often seek to operate in large measure outside the formal financial and banking systems – through informal and underground systems.

Secret Money Supply: The Offshore Dimension in the 'New' Regulatory View

It is not uncommon for politicians, law enforcement officers and the media to indict those thought to be involved in money laundering. It may well be a useful device for those engaged in fighting serious crime to persuade at least those whose job it is to handle other people's wealth that those prepared to assist criminals and terrorists to retain their ill-gotten gains and further their illicit enterprises are no better than the crooks they serve.

Of course, when the money is the product of drug trafficking or even a bank robbery, then the opprobrium that can attach to those who assist in the laundering process is justly deserved. It is important to remember, however, that those most actively involved in providing such services may never transgress the law, and in many cases the laundering may well involve funds that are not referable to a crime or other forms of misconduct.

The popular press has been wont to ignore this when criticising the apparent failure of regulatory authorities to take effective steps to interdict what are assumed to be money-laundering operations. Whether it was appreciated that the Bank of Credit and Commerce International and its various offshoots were engaged in laundering moneys which were not necessarily the proceeds of serious criminal offences or not will, in all probability, remain a matter of debate.[8]

However, it is often forgotten that the relevant authorities, even if they had such information in a reliable form, would have been hard-pressed to curtail such operations through legal and coercive processes. Laundering the proceeds of drug trafficking is one thing, but merely assisting the leader of a developing country to retain his wealth on a confidential basis outside his country may be a very different issue.

To say that even knowingly facilitating such an individual's acquisition of wealth by covert movements of substantial amounts of wealth, where no specific crime is involved, is an unsound banking practice is a statement that few central bankers would be prepared to support. Responsible banking is a vague concept, even in a wholly domestic environment. In an international context it is nebulous and an entirely different issue than that of soundness.

What is of more concern, perhaps, is when government agencies condone or 'turn a blind eye to' criminal conduct that they are aware of. In February 1980, for example, the Commissioner of Banking for Hong Kong entered into an agreement with the Government under which he was authorised not to report offences under the banking laws to the Attorney General, save where, in the Commissioner's view, they were deliberate or for some other reason he felt he should do so. In other words, the Commissioner was relieved from the general 'duty' to report offences for prosecution.

The Commissioner justified this on the basis that '…bearing in mind our aim to protect depositors, we are really more concerned in getting things put right in the bank or deposit-taking company than in considering a prosecution, which could, and probably would, lead to a loss of public confidence in the bank or deposit taking company, and could even start a run on that institution which might spread to others'. While no one could argue with the need for sensitivity in administering the relevant laws and regulations, and this approach was by no means confined to Hong Kong, it is a dangerous precedent to relieve regulators of their basic responsibility to inform the Attorney General that crimes have been committed. Although there is no evidence that this agreement was abused in Hong Kong, similar arrangements or understandings have led to extraordinary states of affairs in other countries. Nor is it confined to the banking sector. In one instance in Britain, for example, the relevant authority was accused of permitting an investment company, which was known to be engaged in fraudulent activity, to continue to operate so that it could earn money to pay its tax bills! In all these cases, however, we are not talking about corruption on the part of officials, at least in the conventional sense. Their conduct is dictated by what they consider to be in the greater public interest.

Some countries have courted money and wealth on the basis that their legal systems will throw over their owners and their transactions a cloak of secrecy

---

[8] See generally The Rt. Hon. Lord Justice Bingham *Inquiry into the Supervision of the Bank of Credit and Commerce International*, 22 October 1992, House of Commons, HMSO.

thicker and rather more impenetrable than the traditional rules relating to professional confidentiality.[9]

In some instances, an assurance of absolute secrecy has been marketed as a privilege that can be bought for either a relatively small registration fee or for the cost of opening a deposit account. The original justifications for laws that extend the more traditional privilege between a banker and his customer were no doubt acceptable. It is hard to find fault with any attempt to protect those who are being slaughtered by an oppressive and evil regime.

Other countries, however, have not been slow to perceive the benefits of becoming a depository for not only fugitive and flight capital but also dirty money. Countries in and around Africa, Latin America, and increasingly Southeast Asia and the Pacific, have been prepared to extend the privilege of secrecy not only to their oppressed but also to their very rich neighbours. It is easy to criticise the naivety and worse of such countries, but prostitution says rather more about the state of society and its values than the morality of the prostitute.

There are countries that have become so isolated from conventional sources of development finance that their leaders, even assuming them to be men of honour and integrity, have little alternative to seeking funds from those who require discretion. Chapter 4 empirically demonstrates this issue.

The laundering of money, in varying states of cleanliness, through national treasuries and government-sponsored projects is nothing new. Some, such as the Government of the Seychelles, would appear to have made a decision to do much more than just 'stand on street corners'. Others have imposed additional legal devices that effectively block all inquiries from overseas, or for that matter even domestic regulators and agencies.

While the provision of tax efficient services is unobjectionable,[10] and there is justification for many of the facilities offered on an 'offshore' basis, there can be no doubt that too many of these jurisdictions have become complicit, or at least involved, in money laundering activities. In some, ministers and senior officials have been corrupted with serious consequences for the integrity of their governments. While these problems were recognised by the late 1970s,[11] and

---

[9] See B. Rider, 'The Practical and Legal Aspects of Interdicting the Flow of Dirty Money', *Journal of Financial Crime*, 3, 1996, pp. 234-236, and generally R. Blum, *Offshore Haven Banks, Trusts and Companies: The Business of Crime in the Euromarket*, Praeger, New York, 1984.

[10] See Grundy's Tax Havens, *Offshore Business Centres: A World Survey*, Sweet & Maxwell, London, 1993. In *Inland Revenue* v *Duke of Westminster* (1936) HL (E) 1, Lord Tamlin observed 'Every man is entitled, if he can, to order his affairs so that the tax attaching under the appropriate Acts is less than it otherwise would be. If he succeeds in ordering them so as to secure this result, then, however, unappreciative the Commissioner of Inland Revenue or his fellow taxpayers may be of his ingenuity, he cannot be compelled to pay in increased tax.'

[11] See B. Rider *supra* at note 4.

discussed in many international meetings during the 1980s,[12] only recently has significant pressure been brought to bear upon these states to 'clean up their acts'.[13]

Of course, many have made determined, genuine efforts themselves to improve their laws and their administration, in an attempt to discourage bad business and dirty money.[14] In this respect, Chapter 6 discusses the case of UK territories.

Others, however, have not been so willing, or perhaps able, to take responsibility. As was pointed out in Chapter 1, the suggestion that such states should be 'cold shouldered' by the international financial community is not new,[15] albeit now being much more seriously considered by international organisations.[16] The problem with such a policy is that it is susceptible to political considerations that can render the process apparently partisan.[17] Furthermore, it remains to be seen whether it is practical to place a jurisdiction in a state of Purdah. Developments in technology require rather more for an effective blockade than a few 'gunboats'. It

---

[12] See for example, B. Rider, *Commercial Crime Co-operation in the Commonwealth,* Proceedings and Papers of the 7th Commonwealth Law Conference, Hong Kong, 18-23 September 1983.

[13] Note, for example, the Notice to financial institutions issued by the UK Treasury warning about the deficiencies in the anti-money laundering system in Antigua, 19 April 1999. Commenting on the notice, the Economic Secretary at the Treasury, Ms Patricia Hewitt MP stated: 'The UK is determined to take a global approach to combat money laundering. As part of the G7 initiative on financial crime, we have signalled our willingness to identify jurisdictions that fail to meet minimum standards. In so doing, we also help protect UK financial institutions from corruption by criminal money, as well as help to address the insidious influence of global organised crime'. Reference should also be made to UNDCP Report, *Financial Havens, Banking Secrecy and Money Laundering,* Vienna, May 1998.

[14] See generally A. Edwards, *Review of Financial Regulation in the Crown Dependencies,* UK Home Office, London, 1998 and UNDCP, *Financial Havens, Banking Secrecy and Money laundering,* Vienna, 1998 and by way of example, D. Harris and S. Hellman, 'Cayman Islands; Anti-Money Laundering Legislation – the Proceeds of Criminal Conduct Law 1996', *Journal of Money Laundering Control,* 1, 1997, p. 104 and M.L. Alberga, 'Cayman Islands: Privacy – A Balancing Act in Changing Times', *Journal of Financial Crime,* 6, 1998, p. 176.

[15] See, for example, the statement of Mr Saul Froomkin QC, Attorney General of Bermuda, at *The White House Conference for a Drug Free America,* Washington DC, 3 March 1988.

[16] See Financial Action Task Force on Money Laundering, *Review to Identify Non-Cooperative Countries and Territories: Increasing the Worldwide Effectiveness of Anti-Money Laundering Measures,* Paris, 22 June 2001. The 'blacklisting' of jurisdictions by the OECD on the basis of their having internationally 'harmful tax regimes' is at least conceptually a different initiative from that of the FATF in regard to money laundering. But see also Council of Europe, *International Co-operation in the Fight Against Corruption and Offshore Financial Centres: Obstacles and Solutions,* 4th European Conference of Services Specialized in the Fight Against Corruption, Limassol (Cyprus), 1999 and in particular OECD Steering Group on Corporate Governance, *Report on the Misuse of Corporate Vehicles for Illicit Purposes,* Paris, 2001.

[17] See generally K. Alexander, 'Trafficking in Confiscated Cuban Property: Lender Liability Under the Helms-Burton Act', *Journal of Financial Crime,* 5, 1998, p. 207.

must also be remembered that it is not just Caribbean and South Sea islands that offer the services that those so concerned with these issues consider objectionable.[18] In the modern world, physical location is becoming increasingly irrelevant.

The pressure consistently applied to those jurisdictions offering 'offshore' facilities has significantly increased since 11 September 2001.

Before the outrage, it was rumoured that the Bush Administration was nowhere near as sanguine as the Clinton Government in supporting the OECD's initiative against those jurisdictions considered to engage in 'harmful tax practises'.

However, 11 September changed this dramatically. The tragedy swept away any sympathy for secrecy and coyness in financial transparency, and the collapse of Enron exorcised even the 'ghost' of apology. The potential impact of the new US legislation on the future of financial and commercial activity could be profound.

While the name of the new US statute may be somewhat contrived, its reach and impact may be rather more subtle. The 'Uniting and Strengthening America by Providing Appropriate Tools Required to Intercept and Obstruct Terrorism (USA PATRIOT Act of 2001)', while wholly understandable in its concerns and acceptable in its objectives, has the potential for significantly changing the way in which the world conducts business. The provisions contained in Title 111 enhancing the obligations on those who handle other peoples' wealth in the USA are more or less in line with what we will soon have as the 'standard' in Europe. The difference, as always, is that in the USA the rules will be enforced!

Whereas in Britain organisations such as the Financial Services Authority speak in terms of 'setting standards', the US agencies articulate their objectives rather more robustly! Of great significance is the extension of the regime to foreign financial institutions with assets in the USA, as a pre-condition for doing any business in the USA. Previously, most of these businesses were not directly under the yoke of US law.

The statute also goes far further than even the OECD was contemplating in its offensive against jurisdictions that had 'unfriendly' (to the developed nations, that is) tax systems. All correspondent accounts for 'foreign shell banks' are outlawed. Additional 'due diligence' and enhanced 'know your customer' procedures will be required for US private banking and correspondent banking accounts that involve foreign persons, foreign offshore banks and, perhaps most significantly, correspondent banking accounts of foreign banks in jurisdictions designated as 'non-co-operative' by intergovernmental organisations in which the US Government participates.

Thus, those countries on both the FATF and OECD's blacklists will be included in these new provisions. This has serious implications for a number of jurisdictions whose failure to enact and implement appropriate law is not entirely the result of apathy or irresponsibility.

---

[18] See for another perspective M. Findlay, 'Crime as a Force in Globalisation', *Journal of Financial Crime*, 6, 1998, p. 103.

The Act also empowers the US Treasury to initiate measures requiring far greater inquiry and surveillance over accounts from suspect foreign jurisdictions and by foreigners. The application of the general US law relating to money laundering has also been greatly increased by providing that the US courts will have jurisdiction if any part of a money laundering transaction occurs in the US or if the foreign person is a financial institution with a bank account at a financial institution in the US. While certain circuits in the US have been sympathetic to applying the US law on a more or less extra-territorial basis, this new statute puts the issue beyond doubt.

The Act also requires foreign institutions to co-operate and facilitate co-operation in investigations and enforcement actions. It is also worthy of note, given that the debate over the control of corruption is taking place in many jurisdictions, that the statute makes it clear that laundering the proceeds of foreign corrupt practices is within the reach of the US law.

The PATRIOT Act will have a considerable impact on the level and depth of compliance required not only by those operating in the US but by any institution or intermediary that deals with the US or effectively transacts its business in US currency. Consequently, the US requirements will become the international norm – whether we like it or not.

The extent of the present US Government's change of attitude on such matters as financial privacy and the 'legitimacy' of offshore 'tax efficient' activities has been profound, after the atrocities of 11 September. While, in many areas of the legal system, we are used to legislation being little more than a reaction to an event, such as a scandal that has outraged public sentiment, the magnitude of the impact on our lives of some laws now being enacted in the wake of the attack on the USA has perhaps not been appreciated.

The danger is that a good deal of nonsensical law, which may even produce counter-productive results, may be swept into the statute book on the crest of a wave of genuine concern to deal with a dangerous and despicable group of people. The cost to us all of the outrage in the USA may be far greater than many suppose.

The new US legislation and the measures to follow – at least in the developed economies – will have a serious impact on those jurisdictions that have been regarded, appropriately or otherwise, as 'non-co-operative'. Indeed, their financial institutions may well find themselves practically excluded from the international markets. US intermediaries and other international players may simply conclude that the costs of compliance and regulatory risks are just too great. The international economic, political and social implications of excluding those who do not 'measure up' from the international banking and financial system may not have been adequately considered in the rush to address the fight against terrorist property.

When many Western and socially responsible governments, including the UK government, are addressing problems of social exclusion resulting, in part, from a lack of access to banking and related services, it seems strange that we should be contemplating the de facto exclusion of whole continents. Of course, the issues are complex and the appropriateness of particular initiatives differ from country to country and society to society. What is clear, however, is that there is a very real danger we will do far greater long term and systemic damage to our financial and corporate world than Osama Bin Laden would ever have dreamed possible.

Beyond the Offshore Dimension. The Laundering Cycle

Let us now return to the topic of money laundering. The wish to hide a source of wealth is nothing new, or necessarily objectionable.[19] The desire to sever the product of an activity from the enterprise that produced it is perhaps of more recent origin.

Secrecy about one's financial affairs may be justified on a number of grounds, some socially and morally more justified than others. The contention that strict bank secrecy was introduced to provide a safe haven for those subject to Nazi oppression has some merit, although perhaps less, in the light of experience, than it did.[20]

The general view in most developed jurisdictions, until recently, was that it was perfectly acceptable for individuals and even business organisations to order their affairs as they chose and that the state of their finances was a matter for them to decide, provided they remained within the law.[21] If they wished to keep their finances hidden under the bed or in the name of a nominee, that was their business. Indeed, the law of trusts even aided discretion in the holding of property.[22]

There is, of course, a variety of legal obligations to reveal at least the quantity of wealth, such as in insolvency and matrimonial proceedings, or in certain cases under tax law. Furthermore, when exchange control was far more common, controls were also imposed on the actual location of wealth. Now such laws are rare and becoming rarer. Although in most common law countries secrecy of financial information is not protected by specific statutes, as it is in most civil law countries, the general law of confidentiality has been well used to provide a significant degree of protection, albeit through the civil law.[23]

Indeed, such is the protection afforded to banking information by the common law that some have wondered what possible justification there can be for common law jurisdictions, such as Singapore, Malaysia and some of the Caribbean countries, to reinforce their law by enacting specific secrecy provisions. Somewhat

---

[19] See B. Rider, 'The Practical and Legal Aspects of Interdicting the Flow of Dirty Money', *Journal of Financial Crime*, 4, 1996, p. 234. See also D. Campbell, *International Bank Secrecy*, Sweet & Maxwell, London, 1992, p. vii.

[20] See T. Bower, *Blood Money: The Swiss, the Nazis and the Looted Billions*, Pan Macmillan, London, 1997, p. 46.

[21] B. Rider and H. L. French, *The Regulation of Insider Trading*, Macmillan, London, 1979, p. 420; H.P. Friedrich, 'The Anonymous Bank Account in Switzerland', *Journal of Business Law*, 15, 1962 and see also R.T. Nayler, *Hot Money and the Politics of Debt* , Unwin, London, 1987.

[22] See, for example, M.S. Kenny, 'The Penetration of Asset Protection Trusts', *Journal of Financial Crime*, 6, 1998, p. 111.

[23] See generally T.M. Ashe and B. Rider, *International Tracing of Assets*, Vol. 1, Sweet & Maxwell, London, 1998.

paradoxically at a time when many seem to advocate greater transparency as almost a universal cure to our social and moral ills, there is increasing concern, at least in Britain, to protect privacy, including that of financial and business information, as a human right.

It is also sadly the case that, as in the past, the world for many is not, and will not in their lifetime, be a safe place. Without the ability to protect their wealth, particularly that which is more liquid, they and their loved ones will remain even more at risk from greedy dictators, corrupt tyrants and racist thugs masquerading as governments.

This is not the place to enter upon a discussion of the economics, let alone the morality, of secret money in all its manifestations. Such may, with confidence, be left to the economists and theologians.

Instead, we seek here to discuss only dirty money, where the issues are relatively clear, although far from settled. Dirty money is money, or some other form of wealth, derived from a crime or other wrongdoing. Of course, even such a simple definition opens a Pandora's box.

Firstly, even if we can determine a reasonably clear definition of money, the notion of wealth is much wider. It is not difficult to perceive the ramifications of a concept of wealth broad and ingenious enough to encompass the various products and derivations which may, in a certain place and a particular time, have a peculiar value of their own, or at least signify such a value to specific individuals.

There have been cases, for example, where inside information was used as a valuable commodity, within what was, in essence, a money laundering operation, to purchase cocaine. Those who have encountered the various underground banking systems, which will be referred to later as well as in Chapter 4, will be aware that tokens, ranging from simple passwords to coloured sugar lumps and marked bank notes, can be used to facilitate the transfer of money. Such tokens, at the relevant time, within the processes of the particular 'banking' systems, will often represent, and for all intents and purposes be, great wealth.

Perhaps from a lawyer's standpoint, not to mention a policeman's, an even more vexing issue is when is an item of wealth, presupposing that it is capable of being satisfactorily itemised or appropriated to a particular transaction, the product of an act or series of acts, or even, in the case of some generous legal systems, a continuing enterprise? To some degree the issue is not just one of tracing but rather referencing.

The wealth in question may not necessarily be produced by the relevant conduct or crime. It may be sufficient that it is associated with such conduct to acquire the sufficient degree of taint. The legal process will generally require a much higher standard of relationship than might be acceptable at the level, for example, of an intelligence operation. Even if we pass over this very difficult matter of relationship and causation, we must enter into an even more controversial area: determining what sort of conduct will be sufficient to justify describing the money as 'dirty'. Moral values are not necessarily uniform, and attitudes will vary from one society to another.

It might well be that the conduct giving rise to the funds is regarded as a criminal offence in the country concerned, while the same conduct would not be regarded as even improper elsewhere, and certainly not in the country where the money comes to rest. It is hardly necessary to seek examples, as a moment's thought will prompt scenarios of religious and racial activities that amount to criminal offences in a particular state but would not necessarily be considered improper in other jurisdictions.

The importance of this issue should be obvious when one considers the vast amounts of money earned by Cosa Nostra during Prohibition in the United States. If such laws existed today in the US, and such funds were transferred to foreign banks, would this amount to laundering 'dirty' money? Perhaps viewed from the perspective of the US legal system the answer would be yes, but a different view would surely be taken in most other countries.

Even when the wealth in question is the proceeds of what might be considered an ordinary criminal offence, is it appropriate to designate it as dirty in all cases? And if so, for how long and to what state of derivation? Common sense, no matter what the economists, yea the moralists, might argue, indicates there must come a point in time when the taint that attaches to the money loses its relevance.

Even when those responsible for the crime that created the profits, or those who are charged with laundering it, are unsuccessful in giving it an aura of legitimacy, there must come a time when longevity, or the complexity of its history, accords de facto legitimacy.

Indeed, given the vast sums of money that we are told are passing through the laundering pipeline at any point in time, it is perhaps good for society that most criminals, and certainly those with greater sophistication, evidently yearn to become legitimate, or at least appear to be, and thus support our own value system and financial structures.

While wealth can, to some extent, assume respectability, there is an obvious incentive for those desiring such status to bring 'dirty money' back into the conventional and lawful economy. It can therefore be argued that procedures and laws that inhibit this repatriation of wealth to the lawful economy by perpetuating the taint that attaches to the proceeds of crime are disadvantageous.

The simple definition we have adopted for 'dirty money' is broad enough to encompass money that is, in some way, referable to a civil wrong. It is true that proceeds of every imaginable civil wrong could not be considered 'dirty'. Such money may be 'hot', to use another epithet, but it will not be considered dirty.

There are situations, however, where the proceeds of a civil wrong can and should be regarded as dirty. While it is difficult to be specific, it is submitted that it is appropriate to regard funds that are the proceeds of a civil wrong involving a degree of dishonesty as worthy of attracting the designation 'dirty'. It is not in every such case that the conduct would amount to a criminal offence. Where the funds have been created by conduct lacking probity, however, it would not seem unjustified to regard them as dirty.

Although perhaps little other than institutional attitudes are influenced by such designations, there are practical considerations in not distinguishing too sharply between the proceeds of a specific crime and something that may only give rise to a claim in the civil courts.

So far we have avoided attempting to set out what money laundering involves. We have spoken often in the same breath of money laundering, secret money and dirty money, without attempting to establish the interface between the process and the product.

Definitions of money laundering range from the authoritative language of statutes to the punchy comments of the judges. For our present purposes, and at the risk of adding yet another definition to the lists, it amounts to a process that obscures the origin of money and its source. Of course, this is a wide approach, which would encompass transactions designed to hide money as well as wash dirty money into clean. It is the processes of transfer and misrepresentation, which constitutes the modus operandi of laundering and secreting wealth.

Unfortunately, because of the attention that has been given, understandably, to the fight against drug cartels, the topic of money laundering has become linked to, if not captured by, the debate on tracing and confiscating the profits from the illicit narcotics trade. Consequently, most discussions of money laundering focus almost exclusively on this and ignore the wider issues.

The author has deliberately attempted to avoid placing emphasis on the drug-related aspects of the subject, although from the standpoint of statutory law and in particular systems for international co-operation, it is in this area that most, if not all, significant steps have been taken.

Discussion of the processes involved in money laundering has been limited and essentially derivative, outside the USA. Few have recognised that even the now traditional process of laundering involves a series of actions and not a seamless process. Perhaps this is understandable, given our experience in Britain with regard to other areas of asset recovery and tracing. While establishing the derivation of property pursuant to a tracing claim is nothing exceptional, such cases rarely involve the structuring of transactions solely for the purpose of avoiding investigation. Obviously, there are cases in which considerable care has been taken to frustrate inquiry, particularly where the funds in question have been created or diverted by systematic fraud.

In Britain, however, at least until comparatively recently, the need to examine deliberate and sophisticated attempts to obscure ownership and control were rarely encountered by lawyers, or for that matter policemen. Thus, we still tend to a somewhat simplistic notion of the laundering process, even in the case of narcotics trafficking. Laundering will involve a series of stages, and different legal enforcement considerations will naturally be applicable to each.

Many forms of crime and misappropriation will produce quantities of cash in relatively low denominations. This will need to be consolidated into a form of wealth that can be more easily transported, particularly out of the jurisdiction. The methods of achieving this are limited only by the ingenuity of the launderer.

Of course, enterprises with high turnover and relatively low investment, which can be used to facilitate such a process, will be especially attractive, particularly if they are outside the conventional banking system. Those involved in consolidating cash at this stage of the laundering cycle will be most concerned to avoid the creation of any external record that could be used to initiate an audit or paper trail leading to subsequent stages or layers of the operation.

Once the money has been converted into a form that can be transferred or smuggled, it will often be moved offshore. This offers a number of practical advantages. Firstly, it will often place the funds beyond the legal reach of the authorities in the jurisdiction where the profit-generating activity occurred. Even if the relevant laws were capable of application on an extra-territorial basis, and very few are, involving another jurisdiction places significant practical barriers in the path of investigators in obtaining and securing evidence admissible in court.

As has already been mentioned, certain jurisdictions are willing to offer banking and other facilities on the basis that secrecy will be assured. Sadly, there are countries that have been prepared to facilitate the receipt of money no matter what its source. Once the money has been taken offshore, it can then enter into the conventional banking system, either directly, or more likely, indirectly. Obviously, the more discreet this process is, the better for the launderer. Hence the attraction of jurisdictions that offer secrecy or in which the level of corruption is sufficient to ensure effective non-co-operation with foreign agencies.

What is important to stress is that the offshore dimension just concerns the stages involved in the money laundering cycle.

Once the money has entered the conventional banking system it can move through usual channels. The launderer's objective will be to create a web of transactions, often involving a multitude of parties, with various legal statuses in as many different jurisdictions as possible, through which the money will be washed on a wave of spurious or misleading transactions.

The purpose of this is to confuse even the most dedicated and well-resourced investigators and to defeat any attempt to reconstruct a money trail. Given the ease with which companies and other legal entities may be created in countries throughout the world, the launderer's only constraint is likely to be financial or the time at his disposal.

On the other hand, it must be remembered that the laundering of money is a cost, and both the launder and his principals will only wish to expend what is necessary and prudent to ensure the relevant funds remain beyond the reach of law enforcement agencies or others interested in locating them.

Obviously, the amount of effort and expense required for laundering, for example, the profits of a major drugs operation, would be rather more than that required for frustrating a regulatory authority investigating a case of suspected insider dealing. It must also be remembered that while the money is in the pipeline it is unlikely to be fully usable. Consequently, most launderers are not only mindful of the costs involved in the actual process, but the length of time that will be required to launder the money.

Given the importance of ensuring that the records on which an audit train can be based are unreliable or, preferably, unavailable, there is an increasing tendency for those involved in money laundering to resort to the old practice of cash transfers and bulk movement of currency.

Containerisation has provided launderers with a relatively cheap and statistically reliable means of moving large amounts of money around the world without having to risk the creation of conventional records.

Thus, the circumstances will to some extent influence the extent of the laundering process and its sophistication. Laundering operations will range from the simplest manipulation of accounts to structures involving hundreds of companies with thousands of bank accounts.

However it must always be remembered that the larger the organisation employed to launder the money, the greater the costs and the higher the risk of detection or of something going wrong. In this context it should not be forgotten that developments in information and transaction technology have been of considerable assistance to launderers.

The transactions used to obscure the source of the relevant funds will be structured in such a manner as to render it almost impossible to obtain admissible evidence that would allow a court to establish the derivation of the money. Law enforcement agencies often refer to this process as layering, but this rather implies that with diligence the true facts may be uncovered through a progressive investigation. While there have been cases where dedicated, extremely lucky, and well-resourced investigators have been able to peel-off a series of layers to reveal what in fact took place, in the case of the more sophisticated structure, the concept of layering is too simplistic.

Certain operations are structured in a manner that resembles a mosaic or kaleidoscope rather than a layer-cake. Transactions will not be progressive – but parallel, establishing mutual obligations which can be married or crossed, often on a contingent basis, and which would not be substantiated to the satisfaction of a court applying conventional legal rules.

It is true, however, that as the notion of layering is often used to conjure up a picture of a stone gradually dropping to the bottom of a pond, the longer money remains in the system the more difficult it is to follow and identify it. Furthermore, such an analogy makes the important point that money in flight will be most noticeable when it first 'splashes' into the pool. It is at this point of entry into the conventional banking system that regulations designed to create an 'audit trail' are likely to be most effective.

In recent years there has been much discussion about the impact of technology on the processes of money laundering. There can be little doubt that criminal organisations have been and are as well placed as anyone to take full advantage of developments in technology, and in particular communications technology.

The advent of cellular telephones with the capacity to reach around the world afford to criminal organisations a communications system that few a decade ago could have dreamed would exist today. Added to this, the development of electronic systems that facilitate and accelerate transactions, the ever-increasing significance of the Internet, and the meaninglessness of transactions in the realm of cyberspace all serve to exacerbate the profound problems confronted by those seeking to establish the provenance of wealth.

Once the money has been agitated to the satisfaction of the launderer, it must be placed in an 'end deposit'. Of course, the nature of this 'end deposit' will depend upon a variety of factors. In many cases, however, it will be desirable to return the money to the jurisdiction in which it was first generated.[24] Those responsible for making such profits will often wish to enjoy at least part of the fruits of their endeavour, and the laundered funds will be crucial where there is an ongoing enterprise to finance.

Therefore, launderers may well be required to ensure that at least a proportion of the money is repatriated to the country of origin. Thus they must create a transaction, or more likely a series of transactions, to bring the 'clean' money back home. This can be achieved in a number of ways, but the repatriation should be achieved in a manner that can be explained and will justify the surfacing of the wealth in the hands, or under the control, of the relevant principal.

One technique that has been employed to some effect is the incorporation of essentially shell companies that can then 'sell' their securities to 'overseas investors'. The 'overseas investors' will be the money laundering puppets. The purchase of such securities, which will be properly documented, will provide a vehicle through which the cleansed money can flow back into the control of issuers.

It is important to recognise the use that such companies may be put to in the context of money laundering operations. There have been cases where the existence of such operations has been mistaken for high-pressure selling frauds or 'boiler room' scams. Although the modus operandi may be somewhat similar, especially at the early stages, the purpose and implications of the operation are very different.

It must be appreciated that money laundering involves a series of stages and that each stage will have its own characteristics. Those charged with the detection and investigation of such matters need to be alerted to the implications of a process that has been carefully designed and structured with the objective of minimising exposure, and thus the risk of interference. Sadly, legislators have often failed to appreciate the complexity of money laundering, in terms of both its character and its objectives. They have taken for granted a somewhat stylised model, which rarely conforms to reality. The deficiencies of essentially western-crafted legislation are perhaps best shown in this regard in the context of underground banking systems.

Beyond the Offshore Dimension. The Underground Banking Systems

Underground banking systems have developed to a level in some societies where they rival the conventional banking system in terms of efficiency and capability.

While many such systems have developed within ethnic societies because of distrust for the host country's institutions, many have a history that is rather more complex and reflects rather more indigenous social and cultural factors. The importance of underground banking systems in money laundering operations has

---

[24] But see in the case of corrupt payments Expert Working Group, *Banking on Corruption: the Legal Responsibilities of Those who Handle the Proceeds of Corruption*, The Society for Advanced Legal Studies, London, 2000.

become more widely appreciated in recent years. And given the dispersal of certain ethnic communities, there is today little doubt that such systems exist on an international basis and play a significant role in the laundering of dirty money. Given the involvement of certain ethnic groups in highly profitable crimes, such as drug trafficking, the significance of these traditional banking systems and more recent adaptations and imitations should not be underestimated.

Furthermore, as governments are increasingly recognising, given the distorting effect that the underground banking system can have on money flows, it cannot be ignored by those who operate wholly within the conventional banking system. Most underground systems will also, at some stage, have to interface with conventional financial or banking institutions.

There are innumerable types of underground banking, ranging from highly sophisticated structures operated by overseas Chinese groups to relatively informal barter- and smuggling-based operations in Africa. Most systems do not involve the movement of cash and depend for their efficacy on tokens. The Chinese 'Chit' or 'Chop' system, the Pakistan 'Hundi System', and the Indian Hawalah operate primarily within defined racial groups, often with some additional bond of a tribal or geographical nature.

They rarely involve the physical movement of cash, or for that matter anything other than tokens, regarded within the special structure of the system as the equivalent in value to the relevant cash sums. The Hawalah system is rather more a system of compensation through related transactions, but given the facility for aggregation, actual payments between those 'funding' the systems are kept to the minimum.

The efficiency of a paperless and practically record-less banking system capable of transferring substantial amounts of wealth is obviously an attraction for those involved in money laundering. Money launderers have emulated the underground systems to some extent, and have shown an increasing willingness to make use of existing systems on a commercial basis.

Laws and enforcement policies fashioned to address money laundering through conventional banking systems are of little practical relevance where such underground systems are involved.

Interest in the underground banking systems, particularly those operational in South Asia and the Middle East, has blossomed after 11 September. While the evidence is somewhat patchy, it is tolerably clear that Al Qaeda and its associated networks utilised various forms of underground banking to move and store its wealth.

What is of particular interest is the way the operations more closely associated with Bin Laden were able to interface these traditional and informal systems into the conventional financial world, largely through the use of nominee and front companies registered in certain 'offshore' jurisdictions.

It is also clear that religious foundations, and even registered charities, were utilised not only to collect funds from supporters but also to facilitate integration. Perhaps one of the most disturbing aspects of these revelations was the apparent and pervasive ignorance of law enforcement and intelligence agencies as to the nature, extent and operation of these underground networks.

Major intelligence agencies were forced to admit that this was largely an uncharted sea, and there was a scrabble to 'recruit' almost any expertise thought to be available and relevant. Perhaps even more disturbingly, recognition is dawning that perhaps these networks cannot be penetrated to the extent necessary to provide the level of intelligence required, at least for predictive intelligence and proactive measures.

If the picture that many have of money laundering is a little misconceived, the general conception of the type of individuals engaged in money laundering is probably erroneous as well. Since the days of Meyer Lansky, there have been individuals who are prepared, for a fee or part of the action, to provide their services to whomever may wish to have their money hidden or laundered.

Many of these individuals are experts in financial and corporate matters and have created a network of corporate and other entities in jurisdictions not known for their willingness or ability to promote financial integrity. In a number of investigations, such individuals have shown a willingness not only to become involved in laundering hot and dirty money but also to facilitate other dubious financial and commercial transactions. In particular, they have been prepared to utilise their corporate identities and offshore banking facilities to front or give credibility to those engaged in advance fee frauds and the like.

Thus, modern money launderers are unlikely to be members of a criminal organisation. They are much more likely to be on the periphery of the financial services or banking industry or professional advisers, such as lawyers or accountants, prepared to make their services available to anyone willing to pay.

'New' Weapons, 'Old' Problems: Pursuing the Proceeds of Crime

Hiding money is one thing but, as we have already indicated, attempting to disassociate wealth from its actual source smacks of something rather more sinister.

While those who obtain their wealth through rather disreputable methods doubtlessly prefer their neighbours and admirers to remain in ignorance, and while unexplained wealth may draw suspicion and unwanted interest from both sides of the law, until very recently there was little risk to those assets as a consequence of legal procedures, other than those associated with taxation.

Although provisions can be found in many ancient systems of law which allow the state or ruler to forfeit the instruments of crime, and even the proceeds of crime, and in extreme cases all the criminal's property, there are few contemporary examples of such laws enduring. Much more recently, governments have realised that where criminal conduct is motivated by economic gain, it makes a great deal of sense to attack the profits of crime, to hit the criminal in his pocket!

Furthermore, where the criminal conduct involves a continuing criminal enterprise, seizing or otherwise interdicting the proceeds of crime might well prevent the investment of this wealth back into the criminal operation, thus causing serious liquidity problems.

US agencies have been particularly attracted by the logic of this approach, the more so because, in the main, those assets that are seized remain within the possession and use of law enforcement agencies. Furthermore, the law as it has developed in the USA, particularly in regard to civil enforcement actions in rem,[25] has proved to be relatively effective.

Indeed, given the manifest failure, viewed from the USA, of various programmes based on drug supply and demand reduction, attacking the assets of the drug barons has appeared increasingly attractive.

The significance of this strategy has been elevated by obtaining the support of other jurisdictions and, in particular, inter-governmental organisations, to almost that of a 'crusade'. A series of international conventions and agreements[26] have directly or indirectly obliged countries to enact legislation that enables their authorities to seize and then, upon conviction for a drug-related offence, confiscate property that represents the proceeds of that crime. Most states have extended these laws to cover property that can be shown to be directly, or even indirectly, the proceeds of such a crime, even though it took place in another jurisdiction.

More recently, this approach has been sensibly extended to encompass the proceeds of all serious crime, whether drug-related or not. These provisions are also reinforced by laws that facilitate financial investigations and mutual legal co-operation. Indeed, discussion of such laws has dominated international meetings for the last decade, and there is every sign this will continue well into the next millennium.

In the case of crime motivated by economic gain, it makes no sense for the legal system to focus attention on the 'profit' that criminals hope to derive from their illicit conduct. We recognise today that far more crimes are motivated by greed and the prospect of financial gain than those that might be described as 'economic crimes'.

The motivation driving most drug trafficking operations, for example, will be the prospect of financial rewards disproportionate to the risks involved. Organised crime, given its character and often its structures, will be particularly focused on the ability to generate income. Its purpose is to 'wring exorbitant profits from … society, by whatever means, legal or illegal, fair or foul…'[27] It also needs money, as well as the prospect of disproportionate rewards, to retain and foster its operational efficacy and the loyalty of its members.

Because economic and commercial crimes are relatively high-reward and low-risk activities, organised crime groups have become increasingly attracted to them.

---

[25] See for example Fletcher Baldwin, 'All funds and International Seizure Cooperation of the USA and UK', *Journal of Financial Crime*, 5, 1997, p. 111.

[26] See B. Rider and C. Nakajima, *Money Laundering*, Sweet & Maxwell, London, 1999, pp. 80-850; W.C. Gilmore, *Dirty Money*, Council of Europe, Paris, 1995, Chapter III and Commonwealth Secretariat, *Basic Documents on International Efforts to Combat Money Laundering*, London, 1991 and generally P. Bernasconi (ed.), *Money Laundering and Banking Secrecy*, Kluwer, Dordrecht, 1996.

[27] *Statement of Conference of State Attorneys-General on Organised Crime*, USA, 1966, and see B. Rider, 'The Financial World at Risk; the Dangers of Organised Crime, Money Laundering and Corruption', *Managerial Auditing Journal*, 8, 1993, p. 3.

Interdicting the proceeds of crime can also provide a useful mechanism for undermining the ability of criminals to invest in other criminal activities or their own enterprises. Although there is little evidence that such strategies are effective, except on an anecdotal basis, it stands to reason that inhibiting the flow of funds into such activities must have a disrupting effect on the enterprise. This is particularly so when liquidity is at a premium, as it is in drug-related crime, where a high proportion of transactions are spot and in cash and yet the retention of large amounts of cash is both impractical and highly risk for the criminal.

Given the justifiable concern in the USA and other western states about the implications of the illicit narcotics trade, and the elevation of the fight against organised crime to a matter of national security, it is not surprising that there is no shortage of legislation seeking to inhibit the laundering of criminal proceeds. Of course, much of this is related to laws seeking to confiscate and forfeit wealth that can be shown to be derived, directly or indirectly, from serious criminal activity. Indeed, as we have already pointed out, the existence of such provisions affords criminals with an incentive to resort to what is often a relatively expensive and risky laundering process.

There are other devices within the legal system to deprive criminals of the benefits of their illicit enterprise, ranging from taxation to the imposition of fines. It is the fear of confiscation, however, rarely the reality, under these relatively new laws that is thought to have increased the quantity of money laundering activity. Whether this perception is true or not is questionable. It might well be as simplistic and naïve as so many other perceptions in this area of law enforcement.

This is not the place to discuss in detail the many national, regional, and international initiatives against the profits of crime.[28] Suffice it to say that few countries today have not enacted laws, or are not in the course of enacting laws, which provide for the tracing, seizure and confiscature of at least the proceeds of drug-related crime, if not other forms of serious crime, and do not at least to some extent criminalise attempts to launder the proceeds of such criminal activity.

We have already pointed out that, until recently, relatively few countries had laws specifically addressing the funding of terror and terrorist property. Indeed, the United Kingdom, given the problems that it has faced in Northern Ireland, was at the time of the outrages in New York and Washington one of the few countries to have comprehensive legislation and dedicated law enforcement and intelligence resources. Since 11 September 2001, many countries have taken steps to bring into their laws the provisions of the International Convention for the Suppression of the Financing of Terrorism, and give effect to the various initiatives from a host of inter-governmental and non-governmental organisations.[29]

---

[28] See generally B. Rider and C. Nakajima, *supra* at note 22 and T.M. Ashe and B. Rider, *International Tracing of Assets*, Vol. 1, Sweet & Maxwell, London, 1998.

[29] UN, *Security Council Resolution 1373*, September 2001, FATF, *Special Recommendations on Terrorist Financing*, 31 October 2001, G-7, *Finance Ministers' Statement of Terrorist Financing*, 25 September 2001, EU, *The Paris Declaration of the European Union*, 8 February 2002, and Wolfsburg Group, *Additional Recommendations on Terrorist Funds*, January 2002.

A profound weakness of the strategy to attack criminal enterprises through the confiscature and forfeiture of ill-gotten wealth is that the law has proved to be exceedingly difficult to apply.

Outside the USA, the value of property and money actually confiscated is very small when compared with even conservative estimates of the amount of wealth likely to be flowing through the criminal pipeline. Regarding the financing of terrorism, Chapter 3 provides results about the financial flows of international terrorist groups.

In general, estimates (or rather guesstimates) of this figure might vary greatly depending upon the perspective of those concerned. There are no truly reliable figures, and although various attempts have been made to quantify the amount of dirty money that may at any one point in time be flowing through the pipeline, at the end of the day it comes down to speculation and informed guesswork. Of course, the situation is complicated by the presence of money and wealth in the system that, although it is not directly the product of crime, is for some reason or another susceptible to the same processes of laundering.

In 1995, a former senior official in the Legal Directorate of the British intelligence and security service was reported in a newspaper as expressing the view that £200 billion a year of narcotics-related money passes through the City of London.[30] Whether such an astronomical amount is anywhere near the truth remains to be seen. While some have 'confirmed' the accuracy of this guesstimate, others have been somewhat more conservative. The truth is that so little work has been done on this question in Britain, or for that matter anywhere outside the USA, no one really knows the extent of the problem.

Ms Elisabeth Bresee, then Assistant Secretary (Enforcement) in the US Department of the Treasury, in giving evidence to the Financial Institutions and General Oversight and Investigations subcommittees of the House of Representatives' Committee on Banking and Financial Services, was asked to quantify the amount of money being laundered through the USA.[31] She stated:

> partial figures can give one some idea of the problem. The Office of National Drug Control Policy estimates that approximately $60 billion is now expended in the purchase of illegal narcotics each year. If 80 per cent of that represents profit, the sales generate $48 billion to be laundered each year, simply on account of narcotics sales, without taking into account all of the other crimes whose proceeds require laundering. And even a fraction of that number, reinvested year after year, generates a sizeable and frightening war chest of criminal capital.

---

[30] J. Adams, '200bn in Drugs Cash Heads for London Markets', *Sunday Times,* 19 November 1995 and see generally B. Rider, 'Organised Crime in the United Kingdom: A Personal Perspective', 1994, mimeo; Home Affairs Committee, *Organised Crime, Minutes of Evidence and Memoranda,* Memorandum 15, House of Commons, HMSO, 16 November 1994.

[31] 15 April 1999, and see B. Rider, 'What do We Mean By "Dirty" Money?', *Money Laundering Monitor*, 3, June, 1999.

Ms Bresee then pointed out that if one sought to obtain a picture of the total amount of wealth being laundered in the USA, then one had to add the profits from crimes committed outside the USA that were laundered through the USA, or by utilising US currency or US institutions, and also the repatriation, either permanently or as part of the laundering cycle, of wealth generated by US criminals at sometime in the past, that had been held outside the USA. When one takes all this into account, perhaps the comment reported in the British press in 1995 was not as preposterous as some have made out.

What is manifest and indisputable is that the amount of money that would, in theory, be susceptible to the application of legal forfeiture laws is vast. In Britain, however, the Third Report of the Home Office Working Group on Confiscation[32] stated that between 1987 and 1997 the authorities in England and Wales had been able to confiscate only £37,261,600 of drug-related wealth. Under legislation designed to take the profit out of all serious crime, whether drug-related or not, the amount, since the law came into force in 1989 is just £4,484,659.

If even a conservative estimate of the amount of wealth liable to confiscation during this period were compared with these figures, the results obtained would be laughable, if the matter were not so serious. The Performance and Innovation Unit of the UK Cabinet Office in its Report *Recovering the Proceeds of Crime*, published in June 2000, indicated that the results since 1997 have been no less disappointing.

Indeed, the Report states that the law is simply not working. Perhaps even more surprisingly, the results under the various measures passed to deal with terrorism in Northern Ireland have been equally uninspiring. The Special Branch of Scotland Yard, which has national responsibility for policing this legislation, has failed to confiscate even one pound from Irish terrorists!

It remains to be seen whether the new legislation that is currently before Parliament, completely overhauling the British law on the proceeds of crime, and in particular providing for civil recovery by a new Assets Recovery Agency, will produce more acceptable results.[33]

Of course, there are mitigating factors: the law is relatively new; financial investigations are always difficult, time-consuming and often complex; it is only recently that law enforcement agencies have been able and willing to commit the necessary resources to this strategy; and the courts and prosecutors have yet to become entirely comfortable with this body of law.

On the other hand, the world community is heralding this strategy as the way ahead, and Britain is not the least bit coy about 'advising' if not 'encouraging' other states to follow it down this path. In evaluating the efficacy of this strategy, however, it is most important to remember that the criminal law is only one

---

[32] Home Office Working Group on Confiscation, *Third Report*, London, 1998, pp. 12-13. See also B. Rider, 'Taking the Gloves Off', *Journal of Money Laundering Control*, 2, 1999, p. 196.

[33] See Home Office, *The Proceeds of Crime Bill 2001* and *The Proceeds of Crime, Consultation on Draft Legislation*, London, 2001, p. 5066.

weapon and that much can be achieved, as it has in Britain, under tax law and the civil law.[34]

It might be argued that the very presence of confiscature and anti-money laundering laws discourage criminal organisations from placing their wealth in the relevant jurisdiction, either as part of the laundering process or by way of investment. The presence of such laws is an unnecessary risk, and the regulatory obligations that the laws impose on those who handle other peoples' wealth imposes an additional cost on criminals doing business in the jurisdiction.

While it is true that money laundering, like any economic activity, is susceptible to being influenced by cost considerations, it is not necessarily the case that even a high level of control, and effective control at that, will render the jurisdiction unattractive to criminal enterprises. The organisations will require a place to hold their wealth which is secure and well respected. The 'end-deposit' country must be reputable so that the organisations can deploy their laundered and now 'clean' money as they see fit with the minimum of suspicion.

Specifically in regard to money laundering, the laws that have been advocated around the world operate at three levels. Firstly, most impose obligations on those who manage other peoples' money to record and report transactions over a certain value to the authorities. Such laws are aimed at photographing the 'splash' to which we referred earlier, when the money in question enters or moves within the conventional financial system.

Secondly, there are laws making it a criminal offence to do anything in furtherance of the laundering process, knowing or suspecting that the property in question is the proceeds of crime.

Thirdly, there are various compliance obligations concerning knowledge of customers, recording transactions, and to a greater or lesser degree satisfying oneself that the transactions in question are proper. Of course, as has already been pointed out, these laws are invariably supported by other provisions, both legal and regulatory. Indeed, it is important to view the specific laws designed to address money laundering in the wider context of general criminal law, and in particular the regulatory system pertaining to financial and banking institutions.[35]

Together with determined and relatively enthusiastic domestic initiatives against money laundering, there has been a host of programmes designed to promote and facilitate investigation of financial transactions and, in particular, international mutual assistance. In many cases, these have manifested themselves in new laws allowing the use of exceptional powers of investigation domestically and other forms of legal coercion to be exercised on behalf of other states.

In fact, it is the international crusade against illicit drug trafficking, and thus the laundering of the proceeds of such crimes, that has been the catalyst, if not the raison d'être, for the many significant developments that have taken place in recent

---

[34] See in a different, although related, context, B. Rider, 'Civilising the Law – the Use of Civil and Administrative Proceedings to Explore Financial Services Law', *Journal of Financial Crime*, 3, 1995, p. 2.

[35] See S. Savla, *Money Laundering and Financial Intermediaries*, Kluwer, Dordrecht, 2001.

years, politically, institutionally and legally, in regard to international mutual assistance in criminal matters.

As has already been pointed out, it is somewhat naïve to evaluate the efficacy of the various laws allowing the state to confiscate the proceeds of crime simply by adding up the amounts of money that have in fact been successfully seized. The same is equally true, if not more so, in contemplating the efficacy of the anti-money laundering laws.

Convictions for the specific offence of money laundering, outside North America, have been few indeed! In Britain, convictions for this offence can be counted on the fingers of one hand, and there has never been a conviction under the money laundering regulations that impose regulatory and compliance obligations on intermediaries. The experience of other countries is not dissimilar. Under these circumstances, and given the high profile of this area of the criminal justice system, it is not surprising that thought is being given in many countries to ways in which the law may be better enforced.

Finally, a serious issue in the minds of many is the price the financial and banking system is required to pay for the strategy of taking the profit out of crime.

It is not an exaggeration to claim that the impact of an anti-money laundering law on the way in which business is carried out in the British financial sector, is greater than that of legislation, such as the Financial Services Act 1986, which is directly aimed at the conduct of financial business.[36]

The costs involved in establishing, maintaining and demonstrating compliance are considerable by any standard. It is also clear that in many jurisdictions even dedicated attention to compliance will only serve as mitigation should an offence actually occur.

The total cost of compliance, training and supervision in regard to the control of money laundering in Britain can only be very roughly guesstimated, like so much in this discussion. It has been put at £600 million a year.

Of course, there are those who would wish to add the cost of 'loss of opportunity'. Whether they have in mind the business that they cannot undertake because their resources are otherwise employed in compliance, or the loss of 'good' money laundering business, remains to be seen.

What is clear is that policing the anti-money laundering laws and their regulations represents a considerable in-house cost within the financial services and banking industry. There is also the important issue, which has yet to be fully grasped in many countries, of the impact of anti-money laundering laws on other areas of legal responsibility.

---

[36] See N. Clark, 'The impact of Recent Money Laundering Legislation on Financial Intermediaries', in B. Rider and T.M. Ashe (eds.), *Money Laundering Control*, Sweet and Maxwell, London, 1996 and also B. Rider, C. Abrams, T.M. Ashe, *Guide to Financial Regulation*, (3rd Edition), CCH, London, 1994, p. 268, and R. Bosworth-Davies and G. Saltmarsh, *Money Laundering*, Chapman & Hall, London, 1994, Chapter 3.

Little thought has been given, for example, to the relationship, if any, of the obligation cast upon financial intermediaries to know more about their customers and the responsibility on certain intermediaries to ensure that their advice and management is suited to the circumstances of their customers.[37] In other words, does the 'know your customer rule' impact on the duty of care and suitability of advice?

Furthermore, while most legal systems protect intermediaries from direct legal liability to their customers when they report their suspicions to the authorities, few protect against defamation suits or collateral and transactional liability to third parties.

The possibility also exists, at least in some common law jurisdictions, of a conflict between the law pertaining to the protection of fiduciary interests and the offence of disclosing that an anti-money laundering investigation is imminent.[38] All these and many other issues represent a real risk to those who handle other peoples' wealth and need to be placed in the balance when evaluating the 'cost-benefit' of the strategy we have all so enthusiastically adopted – and imposed on those who want to join the West's global economy.[39]

Conclusion

This chapter, devoted to the legal view on the OFCs issues, analysed the offshore dimension in a general discussion of the international legal and regulatory framework in which the anti-money laundering policies are defined.

In particular, the author would not wish to create the impression that he considers that focusing upon the assets of criminal organisations has not played, and will not continue to play, a significant role in the control of organised crime and terrorism.

Indeed, he was one of the first to advocate such a strategy and has been a staunch supporter of it over the years.[40] However, he is convinced that it is no panacea.

---

[37] See B. Rider, 'The Limits of the Law: An Analysis of the interrelationship of the Criminal and Civil Law in the Control of Money Laundering', *Journal of Money Laundering Control*, 2, 1999, p. 209.

[38] See *Governor & Co of the Bank of Scotland v. A Ltd* (2001) 3 All. ER. 58 and C. Nakajima, *Conflicts of Interest and Duty*, Kluwer, Dordrecht, 1999, Chapter 8.

[39] It is not without significance that in the United Kingdom the Financial Services Authority must ensure that the regulatory obligations that it imposes on the financial sector are 'proportionate to the benefits, considered in general terms which are expected to result from the imposition of that burden or restriction'; see FSA, *Financial Services and Markets*, section 2 (3), 2001. Under section 119, the Authority must prepare and publish 'a cost benefit analysis'; see section 121 (2) (a).

[40] See B. Rider, *Combating Organised Crime*, Memorandum, Meeting of Commonwealth Law Ministers, Zimbabwe, 26 July – 1 August 1986, and UNCTAD Secretariat, *Maritime Fraud – the Feasibility of Improving the Administration and Legal Procedures of Prosecuting Authorities in Cases of Maritime Fraud*, Geneva, 12 August 1985.

There is a real danger that the understandable desire on the part of leaders and politicians to come up with a 'solution' to the problem of organised crime and terrorism has rendered them too willing to seize upon what is no doubt a good weapon, when used with others, but in no way a solution.

To some extent, those responsible for the management of law enforcement have also found it convenient to espouse this strategy when confronted by the problems of serious financially-orientated crime.[41]

The attention of the media and the political implications of the nature of the problem have underlined the need for prompt action that can be at least represented as directly attacking the primary threat. Furthermore, newspapers tend to report the value of seizures but often do not follow the story through from confiscature of the proceeds of the crime to subsequent conviction.

Thus, in the mind of the public, the law does appear to be far more effective than it actually is – judged purely in terms of the amount of money that has been taken out of the criminal pipeline.[42]

Mention has already been made of the various international and regional initiatives that require, or at least encourage, states to adopt more or less uniform laws providing for the confiscature of the proceeds of serious crime, or at least those associated with the illicit trade in drugs, the investigation and interdiction of the proceeds of such offences, the criminilization of money laundering, the reporting of suspicious transactions, the imposition of reporting and due diligence requirements on those most likely to confront money laundering and the facilitation of international mutual legal assistance. All this is highly commendable.

As in other areas, however, the laws and legal procedures of one jurisdiction are not always easily transported, without significant adaptation, to the legal system of another, with quite different traditions and structures.[43]

If more than cosmetic surgery is to be achieved, considerable attention needs to be given to a host of issues – legal, procedural, evidentiary, institutional and cultural. There are innumerable examples in financial law where devices that have proved effective in, for example, the US Federal Courts, have looked very much out of place in a wholly alien environment.

The present writer is not advocating a parochial attitude to the reception of experience, legal and otherwise, from foreign jurisdictions. Indeed, there is much to be gained. What he is concerned about is the imposition of alien concepts and mechanisms without due regard to the particular sensitivities and needs of the

---

[41] See for example B. Rider, 'Policing the City – Combating Fraud and Other Abuses in the Corporate Securities Industry', *Current Legal Problems,* 47, 1998, and B. Rider and M. Ashe, *Insider Crime,* Jordans, Bristol, 1993, p. 86.

[42] For a similar discussion in regard to insider dealing and securities fraud see B. Rider, 'The Control of Insider Trading – Smoke and Mirrors', in E. Ledeman and R. Shapira (eds), *Law Information and Technology,* Kluwer, Dordrecht, 2001.

[43] See B. Rider, 'Blindman's Bluff - a Model for Securities Regulation?', in J.J. Norton and M Andenas (eds), *Emerging Financial Markets and the Role of International Financial Organisations,* Kluwer, Dordrecht, 1997.

jurisdiction concerned. In fashioning the laws and procedures, we need to be able effectively to discourage the international criminal, we need to look rather more at substance and place rather less emphasis on form.[44]

If we are going to make a significant attack on those who corrupt, exploit and subvert our systems, rather more radical strategies will be required than those we have adopted, or perhaps dared to contemplate, in the past.

It appears increasingly obvious that any strategy based on the ability of a prosecutor to prove, to the satisfaction of the court, that wealth represents the proceeds of a crime or even a pattern of criminal activity, can be expected to have only minimal impact on the totality of criminal and subversive assets.

Although it may be possible to facilitate law enforcement by providing more resources, fostering meaningful international co-operation, improving training, and even lowering thresholds of proof, the needs to establish a nexus between wealth and specific crime will result in the vast majority of criminal assets remaining well beyond the reach of the law.

While the costs to criminals of using their ill-gotten gains may also be increased through taxation, regulatory laws and requirements, and even by law enforcement adopting a strategy of disruption, the impact is likely still to fall far short of that required.

Consequently, the present author is convinced that governments will need to devise a much more radical approach to this problem.

The notion of taxing unaccountable wealth is not novel. Furthermore, there are many examples around the world of laws that attach certain presumptions to the holding of wealth that cannot be satisfactorily explained.

Thus, in Hong Kong,[45] if a public servant is in possession of wealth beyond his salary, he is legally obliged to explain its source. The possession of unaccountable wealth is presumptive of corruption.

In Britain, the prosecution may request, on a second conviction for a serious offence within a period of six years, that the court regard any property in the possession of the defendant acquired during the last six years, from a source that he cannot properly explain, to be presumed to be the proceeds of a criminal lifestyle.[46] The provisions in the Proceeds Crime Bill 2001 will take this further.

However, the author remains convinced that over the next decade more and more legal systems will move over to imposing obligations on those in possession of significant amounts of wealth whose source cannot be publicly justified. These obligations may range across the spectrum, from mere transparency to effective

---

[44] See, in another but related context, B. Rider, 'Policing Insider Dealing in Britain', in K. Hopt and E. Wymeersch (eds), *European Insider Dealing,* Butterworths, London, 1991; B. Rider, 'Fraud in the Financial Markets', in C. Lye and R. Lazar (eds), *The Regulation of Financial and Capital Markets*, Singapore Academy of Law, Singapore, 1990, and B. Rider, 'Insider Trading – A Crime of Our Times', in D. Kingsford Smith (ed.), *Current Developments in Banking and Finance*, Stevens, London, 1989.
[45] See for example Sect 10 of the Prevention of Bribery Ordinance CAP 201.
[46] Proceeds of Crime Act 1995.

confiscature. It will be for the society in question to determine the appropriate balance.

What this new strategy will require, however, is a very different approach by law enforcement, where the skills of tax investigators and financial intelligence officers will be paced at a premium. The challenge for the future is to ensure that the steps we take to promote probity and stability do not stifle the very enterprise that drives our economies or trespass too much on the very ideals that remain so precious to civilisation.[47]

A related issue is the extent to which we recognise that our objective in dealing with serious crime and even terrorism is not to place behind bars the 'minnows' that we manage to catch but to disrupt the enterprise.

While it is becoming far more common for senior police officers, although still not many politicians, to admit that the primary strategy today is one of disruption, the implications of this are rarely considered. Policing is essentially reactive, and even when we contemplate pro-active measures we require the commission of a crime, or at least the reasonable suspicion of one, and one that might be proved in the courts according to our exacting standards of justice.

Consequently, disruption of enterprises, whether organised crime or subversion, requires skills and perhaps resources, not always easily identified within traditional policing agencies. In particular, the kind of intelligence that is required for effective disruption is rarely available in police agencies.

Hence the tendency to develop dedicated and special resources, often outside the traditional law enforcement environment. We have already seen this in regard to other areas of activity, which present practical and resource problems for ordinary police structures. Even if such activity remains properly within the law, both civil as well as criminal, there are profound issues of accountability.

It is in the areas that we have been discussing that the real war on serious enterprise crime and terrorism will likely be fought over the next few years. Sadly, I am not convinced that we have even started to frame the right questions yet, let alone devise answers. Success, however it is judged, will be achieved not merely by passing more or even better laws, or by pouring more resources in to the battle – let alone by worthy efforts by bodies such as the Wolfsberg Group – but by a thoughtful and measured balancing of our response to the real threats.

The consequences of our general conclusion for the OFC issues are evident. The need to establish a convincing and workable balance is all the more important in the context of small, developing and transitional economies.

These highly vulnerable states may well find themselves effectively deprived of the advantages and services of those more developed and stable countries that are able to espouse the sort of measures found in legislation such as the PATRIOT Act.

The costs for those operating under these new laws in satisfying the extended and expanded due diligence requirements, in relation to business from many

---

[47] The private sector is well aware of the need to at least be seen to be properly concerned; about these issues see for example, Wolfsberg Group, *The Global Anti Money Laundering Guidelines for Private Banking – the Wolfsberg AML Principles*, October 2000.

smaller, developing and less stable economies, are likely to be extremely expensive.

Together with the legal and regulatory risks, these may persuade the providers of banking and financial services in the 'West' simply to deny access to the 'Western' banking and financial system to those in these other countries. Indeed, even if access is available, it may well be at a cost beyond the reach of many individuals and institutions within these more vulnerable economies.

The implications in terms of stability, both financial and political, are profound. The effective isolation of a significant proportion of the world's commercial and financial activity and the creation of parallel systems cannot be in the interests of any society.

Indeed, once this occurs, and there are many indications that it is becoming a reality, the war may be over and those of us who cherish the values that were so viciously attacked on 11 September 2001, will have lost.

References

Adams, J. (1995), 200bn in Drugs Cash Heads for London Markets, 19 November, *Sunday Times*.

Alberga, M.L. (1998), Cayman Islands: Privacy – A Balancing Act in Changing Times, *Journal of Financial Crime*, 6.

Alexander, K. (1998), Trafficking in Confiscated Cuban Property: Lender Liability Under the Helms-Burton Act, *Journal of Financial Crime*, 5.

Ashe, T.M. and Rider, B.A.K. (1998), *International Tracing of Assets*, Vol. 1, Sweet & Maxwell, London.

Baldwin, F. (1997), All funds and International Seizure Cooperation of the USA and UK, *Journal of Financial Crime*, 5.

Bernasconi, P. (ed.) (1996), *Money Laundering and Banking Secrecy*, Kluwer, Dordrecht.

Birks, P., *Laundering and Tracing*, Clarendon Press, Oxford, 1995.

Birks, P. (1992), Trusts in the Recovery of Misapplied Assets; Tracing, Trusts and Restitution, in E. McKendrick (ed.), *Commercial Aspects of Trusts and Fiduciary Obligations*, Clarendon Press, Oxford.

Blum, R. (1984), *Offshore Haven Banks, Trusts and Companies: The Business of Crime in the Euromarket*, Praeger, New York.

Bosworth-Davies, R. and Saltmarsh, G. (1994), *Money Laundering*, Chapman & Hall, London.

Bower, T. (1997), *Blood Money: The Swiss, the Nazis and the Looted Billions*, Pan Macmillan, London.

Campbell, D. (1992), *International Bank Secrecy,* Sweet & Maxwell, London.

Clark, N. (1996), The impact of Recent Money Laundering Legislation on Financial Intermediaries, in B. Rider and T.M. Ashe (eds), *Money Laundering Control*, Roundhall, Sweet and Maxwell, London.

Commonwealth Secretariat, *Basic Documents on International Efforts to Combat Money Laundering*, London, 1991.

Council of Europe (1999), *International Co-operation in the Fight Against Corruption and Offshore Financial Centres: Obstacles and Solutions*, 4th European Conference of Services Specialized in the Fight Against Corruption, Limassol (Cyprus).

Edwards, A. (1998), *Review of Financial Regulation in the Crown Dependencies*, UK Home Office, London, 1998.

Expert Working Group (2000), *Banking on Corruption: the Legal Responsibilities of Those who Handle the Proceeds of Corruption*, The Society for Advanced Legal Studies, London.

FAFT (2002a), *Report on Money Laundering Typologies 2001-2002*, Paris.

FAFT (2002b), *The Paris Declaration of the European Union*, 8 February, Paris.

FAFT (2001a), *Special Recommendations on Terrorist Financing*, 31 October, Paris.

FAFT (2001b), *G-7 Finance Ministers' Statement of Terrorist Financing*, 25 September, Paris.

FAFT (2001c), *Review to Identify Non-Cooperative Countries and Territories: Increasing the Worldwide Effectiveness of Anti-Money Laundering Measures*, 22 June, Paris.

Findlay, M. (1998), Crime as a Force in Globalisation, *Journal of Financial Crime*, 6.

Friedrich H.P. (1962), The Anonymous Bank Account in Switzerland, *Journal of Business Law*, 15.

Froomkin, S. (1988), *The White House Conference for a Drug Free America*, 3 March, Washington DC.

Gilmore, W.C. (1995), *Dirty Money*, Council of Europe, Paris.

Grundy's Tax Havens (1993), *Offshore Business Centres: A World Survey*, Sweet & Maxwell, London.

Harris, D. and Hellman, S. (1997), Cayman Islands; Anti-Money Laundering Legislation – the Proceeds of Criminal Conduct Law 1996, *Journal of Money Laundering Control*, 1.

Home Office, *The Proceeds of Crime Bill 2001* and *The Proceeds of Crime, Consultation on Draft Legislation*, London, 2001, p. 5066.

Kenny, M.S. (1998), The Penetration of Asset Protection Trusts, *Journal of Financial Crime*, 6.

Nakajima, C. (1999), *Conflicts of Interest and Duty*, Kluwer, Dordrecht.

Nayler, R.T. (1987), *Hot Money and the Politics of Debt*, Unwin, London.

Oakley, A.J. (1997), *Constructive Trusts* (3rd Edition), Sweet & Maxwell, London.

OECD (2001), *Report on the Misuse of Corporate Vehicles for Illicit Purposes*, OECD Steering Group on Corporate Governance, Paris.

Rickett, C.E. (1996), Where are we going with Equitable Compensation? in A.J. Oakley (ed.), *Trends in Contemporary Trust Law*, Clarendon Press, London.

Rider, B.A.K. (2001), The Control of Insider Trading - Smoke and Mirrors, in E. Ledeman and R. Shapira, (eds), *Law Information and* Technology, Kluwer, Dordrecht.

Rider, B.K.A. (2000), The Limits of the Law: An analysis of the inter-relationship of the criminal and civil law in the control of money laundering, *Journal for Juridical Science*, 25.

Rider, B.K.A. (1999a), The Limits of the Law: An Analysis of the interrelationship of the Criminal and Civil Law in the Control of Money Laundering, *Journal of Money Laundering Control*, 2.

Rider, B.A.K. (1999b), What do We Mean By "Dirty" Money?, *Money Laundering Monitor*, 3.

Rider, B.A.K. (1999c), Taking the Gloves Off, *Journal of Money Laundering Control*, 2.

Rider, B.A.K (1998), Policing the City - Combating Fraud and Other Abuses in the Corporate Securities Industry, 41, *Current Legal Problems*.

Rider, B.A.K (1997), Blindman's Bluff - a Model for Securities Regulation?, in J.J. Norton and M. Andenas (eds), *Emerging Financial Markets and the Role of International Financial Organisations*, Kluwer, Dordrecht.

Rider, B.A.K. (1996), The Practical and Legal Aspects of Interdicting the Flow of Dirty Money, *Journal of Financial Crime*, 3.

Rider, B.A.K. (1995), Civilising the Law – the Use of Civil and Administrative Proceedings to Explore Financial Services Law, 3 *Journal of Financial Crime* II.

Rider, B.A.K. (1994), *Organised Crime in the United Kingdom: A Personal Perspective,* mimeo.

Rider, B.A.K. (1993), The Financial World at Risk; the Dangers of Organised Crime, Money Laundering and Corruption, *Managerial Auditing Journal,* 8.

Rider, B.A.K. (1991), Policing Insider Dealing in Britain, in K. Hopt and E. Wymeersch (eds), *European Insider Dealing,* , Butterworths, London.

Rider, B.A.K. (1990), Fraud in the Financial Markets, in C. Lye and R. Lazar (eds) *The Regulation of Financial and Capital Markets,* Singapore Academy of Law, Singapore.

Rider, B.A.K. (1989), Insider Trading - A Crime of Our Times, in D. Kingsford Smith (ed.), *Current Developments in Banking and Finance,* Stevens, London.

Rider, B.A.K. (1986), *Combating Organised Crime,* Memorandum, Meeting of Commonwealth Law Ministers, Zimbabwe, 26 July.

Rider, B.A.K. (1985), Combating International Commercial Crime – a Commonwealth Perspective, *Lloyds Maritime and Commercial Law Quarterly,* 6.

Rider B.A.K. (1983), *Commercial Crime Co-operation in the Commonwealth,* Proceedings and Papers of the 7th Commonwealth Law Conference, Hong Kong, 18-23 September.

Rider, B.A.K. (1980), *The Promotion and Development of International Co-operation to Combat Commercial and Economic Crime,* Memoranda, Meeting of Commonwealth Law Ministers, Barbados, Commonwealth Secretariat, London.

Rider, B.A.K. and Ashe, T.M. (1993), *Insider Crime,* Jordans, Bristol.

Rider, B.A.K. and French, H.L. (1979), *The Regulation of Insider Trading,* Macmillan, London.

Rider, B.A.K. and Nakajima, C. (1999), *Money Laundering,* Loose Leaf Service, Sweet & Maxwell, London.

Rider, B.A.K., Abrams, C. and Ashe T.M. (1994), *Guide to Financial Regulation* (3rd Edition) CCH, Bicester.

Savla, S. (2001), *Money Laundering and Financial Intermediaries,* Kluwer, Dordrecht.

Shipman, A. and Rider, B. (1987), Organised Crime International, *Security and Defence Reference Book,* Cornhill Publications, London.

Smith, L. (1997), *The Law of Tracing,* Clarendon Press, Oxford.

UNDCP, *Financial Havens, Banking Secrecy and Money Laundering,* Vienna.

Chapter 3

Macroeconomics: The Financial Flows of Islamic Terrorism

Friedrich Schneider

Introduction

Since the disastrous terror activities in the United States on September 11, 2001, international – and especially Islamic – terror organisations have gained great attention all over the world.[1]

These terrorist activities had a great economic and political impact,[2] and such activities could not have been undertaken without an appropriate and well-functioning financing system. Hence, it is the goal of this chapter to provide some empirical results about the financial flows of international (mainly Islamic) terrorist groups. In addition, a rudimentary attempt is made to analyse economically how these organisations 'raise' their financial means. Finally, some countermeasures are developed on how these financial flows can be reduced or even stopped.

As mentioned in Chapters 1 and 2, crime in general and the financial flows of criminal organisations have gained great importance with respect to their size and their development over time in the western world. This will be demonstrated with the following four tables and three figures.

---

[1] There is rather extensive literature on the analysis of terrorism; compare Enders and Sandler (1991, 1993, 1996, 1999, 2000), Stern (1999), Wilkinson (2000), as well as Henderson (2001) and Bloomberg et al. (2002).

[2] Compare Drakos (2002), Chen and Siems (2002) and Sandler and Enders (2002).

Tables 3.1-3.4 and Figures 3.1-3.3 show how large the size and the development of the shadow economies and the classical underground economies were for Germany, Italy, France and the United Kingdom over the period 1996 to 2001.[3]

If one considers Germany as a first case, one realizes that, in the second half of the 1990s, the underground economy grew faster and was larger than the shadow economy, and initial preliminary estimates for 2001 clearly demonstrate that the underground economy, i.e. classical crime activities (such as burglary, drug dealing, etc), will reach € 355 billion or 16.9 per cent of official GDP.

These criminal activities are larger than the classic shadow economy, with a volume of € 336 billion (or 16.0 per cent of official GDP), and this development shows that criminal activities in Germany have been sharply rising; these criminal branches are growing 2-3 times faster then official GDP.

In Germany, the underground economy is not as large as in Italy: Italy has by far the largest underground economy of the four countries studied here, with a size of 18.2 per cent of official GDP in 1996, which rose to 20.6 per cent of official GDP in 2000.

In France, the size of the underground economy was 8.9 per cent of official GDP in 1996 and grew to 10.9 per cent of official GDP in 2000. In the UK, it rose from 9.4 per cent of 'official' GDP in 1996 to 10.6 per cent of 'official' GDP in 2000.

In Italy, UK and France, the traditional shadow economy is larger than the underground economy, and only in Germany is the underground economy growing faster then the shadow economy and was larger in 2001.

What can we conclude from these figures regarding the growth of the shadow and underground economies in Germany, France, UK and Italy?

- Both are important economic sectors with more then 10 per cent of the official GDP.
- The shadow economy has more or less stagnated in recent years (except for Germany), whereas the underground economy (classic criminal activity) is still strongly increasing.
- The German underground economy reached a far bigger size than the shadow economy in 2000 and 2001.

These empirical results clearly demonstrate that not only is the shadow economy growing, but classic criminal activities (captured as the underground

---

[3] The shadow economy (i.e. in principal, legal activities, but withholding tax and social security payments, and violating other labour market regulations) and the underground economy are different activities, which cannot be summed, as the underground economy (typical crime activities, such as burglary, drug dealing, etc.) produces no positive value added for an economy. Hence, they cannot be treated as a complement to the official GDP, whereas to the traditional shadow economy can be seen as a complement to the official GDP. For both economies we have overlapping areas. For further definitions, see Schneider and Enste (2000a).

economy) are also growing rapidly in most western countries. Hence, the requirement to detect and reduce the financial flows of classic and terrorist criminal organisations by public authorities is an absolute necessity.[4]

Furthermore, there is an urgent and growing need for more and continuing empirically informed research on the efficacy of international regulatory initiatives. Some empirical studies in these areas are now appearing. For example, Johnson and Lim seek to measure the effects of the FATF initiatives against money laundering. Their overall results are by no means conclusive, but they imply on a tentative basis that, in the majority of FATF member countries, membership of the FATF and the FATF initiatives seem to have weakened the relationship between banks and money laundering.[5] Exceptions to this seem to be Germany, Italy and Singapore. Johnson and Lim also found that jurisdictions that were not members of the FATF: '...have on average a much stronger bank/illegal economy relationship than FATF countries in the post-FATF period.'[6]

The following section will include some short remarks about the structure of international (mainly Islamic) terrorist organisations and will analyse the ways their activities are financed. The structure of terrorist organisations will be only briefly discussed, while most of the analyses relate to the type of financing and to calculating the amount of financial flows of Islamic terrorist organisations.

The subsequent section discusses initial strategies and countermeasures to detect and reduce the financial flows of international terror organisations from an economic point of view, indicating initial single (i.e. national) countermeasures and strategies. Then three suggestions are developed about: (i) an efficient international task force; (ii) criminal network analyses to detect and reduce the financial flows of international terror organisations; and (iii) an award system. The final section summarises the major results and draws some conclusions.

The Structure and Financial Systems of Islamic International Terror Organisations and their Ways of Financing

Most international terrorist groups have an organisational structure involving many single terrorist cells that work independently of each other and whose members have little or no knowledge about other cells.[7] In this chapter we investigate such an Islamic terrorist organisation.

The hierarchical structure is organised top down, and only a few leaders know the number and structure of the individual cells and are able to guide them. As mentioned, the cells work independently of each other and are quite often occupied

---

[4] Compare Alexander (2001), Fitzgerald (2002), Masciandaro and Portolano, Chapter 4 in this volume.

[5] Johnson and Desmond Lim (2002).

[6] *Ibid* p. 18.

[7] For a microeconomic approach of terrorist behaviour, which is not developed here, compare Frey and Lüchinger (2002), Wintrobe (2002) and Epstein and Gang (2002).

by inactive (sleeping) members, who can be activated using certain code words in order to fulfil specific criminal terrorist activities.

The terrorist cells are financed independently, and the financial flows are transferred to the cells in small amounts (between US$ 10,000 and 15,000) in order to create no suspicion from state authorities.

Quite often these financial flows for terrorists are camouflaged by totally normal import/export businesses, such as selling and buying honey, and if honey-stores or import/export organisations belong to terrorist groups, they can provide legitimate revenue for terrorist networks.

However, not only may the income generated by the honey business be valid for terrorist groups, but the operational assistance of the honey business is also quite important, because the smell and consistency of honey make it easy to hide weapons and drugs in the shipments. Thus, using a normal export/import business might be a quite efficient way to steer financial flows to terrorist cells.

The methods the international terror organisations use to move money from the regions that finance them to their target countries are often identical to those used by criminal gangs. This issue was thoroughly discussed in Chapter 2.

It is sufficient to note here some examples. Money laundering experts,[8] for instance, say that both groups use a technique known as a 'starburst'. A deposit of dirty money is made in a bank with standing instructions to wire it in small, random fragments to hundreds of other bank accounts around the world, in both onshore and offshore financial centres (OFCs). Tracking down the money becomes a war of attrition, since getting legal permission to pursue bank accounts in multiple jurisdictions can take years.

The 'boomerang' method is another technique: money is sent on a long arc around the world before returning to its country of origin. En route it travels through what money launderers refer to as 'black holes', meaning countries that lack the means or inclination to investigate banks.[9] In Chapter 4 these countries with lax financial regulation are thoroughly analysed from the economic point of view.

Another method of financing is when the source of terrorist money might, for a start, be legal. It might come from a wealthy individual or religious charity or as a donation from a country. If so, the money starts off clean, becoming 'dirty' only when the terrorist crime is committed later on. Furthermore, as pointed out in Chapters 2 and 4, these flows may use the underground banking system. This makes it almost impossible for the authorities to trace or spot this money.

Another way of financing terrorist organisations is to use 'tax optimisation experts'. These are people who know how to construct 'shell companies' and other structures to hide wealth or dirty money, and they also introduce their clients to banks as new customers. They know far more than bank officials about any new

---

[8] Compare Lemay (1998) and (2001), Savona (2001), Seymour (2001), Tarrat (2001), Fitzgerald (2002), and Masciandaro and Portolano (2003), Chapter 4 in this volume.
[9] Compare Financial Action Task Force (2000a), US Financial Crimes Enforcement Network (2000) and Fitzgerald (2002).

customer's potential link with terrorism or organised crime. The role of tax haven countries is discussed in Chapter 5.

The various kinds of financial flows that supply terrorist cells with money are shown in Table 3.5.

In this chapter, an initial attempt is made to estimate the amount of financial flows and analyse the ways international terror organisations are financed. Before showing the results, the estimation procedure is briefly described.

The estimation procedure is the latent estimator DYMIMIC approach. As the size of financial flows to Islamic terrorist groups is an unknown (hidden) figure, a latent estimator approach using a DYMIMIC (dynamic multiple indicators, multiple causes estimation) procedure is applied.

The DYMIMIC method has been used quite successfully to estimate the size of the shadow economy and is now briefly described.[10]

This estimation procedure is called the 'model approach', which explicitly considers the multiple causes and multiple indicators of the shadow economy. The method is based on the statistical theory of unobserved variables, which consider multiple causes and multiple indicators of the phenomenon (size of the shadow economy, size of the financial flow of Islamic terrorist organisations).

A factor-analytic approach is used to measure the hidden variable (the size of financial flows to terrorist organisations in this case) as an unobserved variable over time.

The unknown coefficients are estimated in a set of structural equations within which the 'unobserved' variable cannot be measured directly. The DYMIMIC model consists, in general, of two parts. The measurement model links the unobserved variables to observed indicators. The structural equations model specifies causal relationships among the unobserved variables.

There is one unobserved variable, the size of the shadow economy. It is assumed to be influenced by a set of indicators of the shadow economy's size, thus capturing the structural dependence of the shadow economy on variables that may be useful in predicting its movement and size in the future.

The interaction over time between the causes Z_{it} ($i = 1, 2, ..., k$) of the size of the shadow economy X_t, and the indicators Y_{jt} ($j = 1, 2, ..., p$) is shown in Figure 3.4. The estimation results using the model approach for the size of the shadow economy are shown in Figure 3.5, and the estimation results to estimate the size of financial flows of Islamic terrorist groups are shown in Figure 3.5.

As causes for estimating the size of the financial flows to Islamic terrorist groups, we have taken the following variables:

1. number of active members,
2. number of active supporters,
3. tribute payments from Islamic countries,
4. financial flows from wealthy people in Islamic countries,
5. financial flows from Islamic religious organisations,

---

[10] For a detailed discussion compare Schneider and Enste (2000b) and Giles and Tedds (2002).

6. amount of diamond trading,
7. amount of drug trading, and
8. GDP per capita in Islamic countries.

As indicators we use the following variables:

1. the cash flows in Islamic countries,
2. the rate of GDP adjusted for the means of all Islamic countries,
3. the amount of financial means trading in Islamic countries,
4. and the amount of currency trading.

What type of results do we now achieve using this estimation method? This will first be demonstrated in the case of Al Qaeda. The main results are shown in Table 3.6.

We find that the wealth of Al Qaeda as an average over 1999-2001 is US$ 5 billion and the annual financial flows (i.e. the budget) of Al Qaeda varies between US$ 20 to 50 million per year.

What is the origin of these annual financial flows? This is shown in the second part of Table 3.6. The drug business (mainly transporting drugs) contributes 30-35 per cent, donations or tribute payments of governments, wealthy individuals, and religious groups vary between 20-30 per cent, classic criminal activities (i.e. blackmail and, in particular, kidnapping) contribute between 10-15 per cent, and unknown is between 30-35 per cent.

Table 3.7 provides a rudimentary overview of the preliminary results of the financial flows of Arab and Islamic terror organisations. Roughly 25 different organisations have been identified, and Table 3.7 shows that the financial flows of most Islamic terror organisations are quite sizeable. These organisations have enough financial means to train and equip their active terrorist members in order to create a maximum destruction when the terrorists are given orders to operate.

If one compares these financial flows with the overall figure of 'dirty money' given by the IMF, these financial flows of Islamic terrorist organisations are quite sizeable. The IMF calculates that the total sum of 'dirty money' being 'whitewashed' through the financial system is huge: between US$ 500 billion and 1.5 trillion a year, which amounts to 5 per cent of the gross world product. The financial flows of Islamic terrorist organisations range between 0.9 and 5.8 per cent of the total sum of 'dirty money' and are therefore quite sizeable.

Strategies and Countermeasures to Detect the Financial Flows of Terror Organisations and Prevent Attacks

Since the terrorist activities in the United States on September 11, 2001, an intensive discussion has started all over the world about what measures can be undertaken to detect and reduce the financial flows of international terrorist organisations and, of course, to prevent future attacks.

In a lot of countries, measures have been undertaken to detect and reduce the financial flows of terrorist organisations. Chapters 1 and 2 review all the issues from the legal and institutional points of view. Here we introduce an economic point of view that will be further developed in Chapters 4 and 5.

There are two major problems in undertaking countermeasures: the first is that the fiscal and financial offshore centres are also quite attractive to terrorist organisations,[11] for the following reasons:

1. there is almost total business discretion;
2. money-laundering laws are weak;
3. the level of communications (air travel, information and communication technologies) is high;
4. the US dollar is often used as everyday currency;
5. the governments are independent;
6. all large international banks have subsidiaries located on these islands;
7. businesses can be readily formed and implemented;
8. many local intermediaries can set up complex operations to camouflage their real purpose.

The second main problem is that, in many countries not only in the OFCs with lax regulations as just discussed – bank customers are protected by privacy and secrecy laws.

Political pressure on these countries has intensified in recent years, and sanctions have been implemented against countries with particularly unhelpful laws or inept enforcement. But this has had a limited impact. Banking secrecy is lucrative for those who practice it. When money passes through secret centres, it is hard to see where it has come from or where it goes. For foreign banks with clients in such centres, knowing the customer can be all but impossible, particularly given the global network of correspondent banks.

Regarding the single country countermeasures, Table 3.8 shows the reaction and the strategy to detect and reduce financial flows of terrorist groups for the United States, the European Union and Germany.[12]

The US has created the FATAC (Foreign Terrorist Asset Tracking Center), with a budget of US$ 6.4 million. This organisation should detect the wealth and financial flows of criminal and terrorist organisations and undertake direct

---

[11] The role of Lax Financial Regulation (LFR) countries in international money laundering schemes has long attracted the attention of policymakers. Virtually all initiatives aimed at combating money laundering, at both the domestic and international levels, tackle the issue. In the aftermath of September 11, growing attention has been paid to the role of LFR countries in ensuring terrorist financing, adding new perspectives to the debate concerning the initiatives to be taken against such countries. For further details compare Masciandaro and Portolano, Chapter 4.

[12] Compare Financial Action Task Force (2000a), Lemay (2001), Fitzgerald (2002) and Masciandaro and Portolano, Chapter 4, for these and other countermeasures or suggestions against money laundering and the detection of terrorist financial flows.

investigation policies to control foreign money with the help of the internal Revenue Service as well as the Custom Authorities. The FATAC can also use the help of the FBI and CIA in financial operations.

In the European Union, the FATF (Financial Action Task Force) has also been given competence not only to fight money laundering but also to fight the financial flows of terrorist organisations. Also, however, the single European countries provided initiatives in preventing and combating the increasing risk of global financial crime.

In Germany a 'Zentralstelle für verfahrensunabhängige Finanzermittlungen' has been founded which should be a competence centre against money laundering and the financial flows of terrorist organisations. In addition, a central database at the 'Bundesaufsichtsamt für Kreditwesen' will be created with the goal of detecting dirty money and the financial flows of terror organisations. Additional powers have also been given to existing state institutions such as the 'Bundesaufsichtsamt für Wertpapierhandel' and 'Bundesaufsichtsamt für Versicherungswesen'.

All these countermeasures are definitely useful and can help to detect and reduce the financial flows of terrorist organisations. The question is whether this is enough or whether much more should be done.[13]

Having analysed the origin of the financial flows and the amount of international terrorist groups, international cooperation is the key to developing some efficient instruments to detect and reduce the financial flows of terrorist groups. In Arab and Muslim countries there is no traceable trail to follow in the kind of traditional, trust-based underground banking known as 'Hawalah', described in Chapters 1 and 2. Al Qaeda may have used this payment method extensively.

Here, Muslim bankers in different places make payments on the promise that the corresponding payment has taken place in other banks – with no money necessarily passing into accounts that can be linked to the owners. As Al Qaeda has relied most heavily on cash so that no 'financial trace' will be left, this type of banking system might be ideal but only operates within Arab and Muslim countries and not outside. Hence, there is a chance something can be accomplished with more efficient international cooperation.

Table 3.9 shows three additional strategies or countermeasures to detect and reduce the financial flows of criminal and also Islamic terror organisations.

The idea behind the table is that efficiently reducing international organised criminal activities (like those of the terrorist organisations) requires a global vision and global activities and countermeasures.

This means, first, the widest possible cross-checking of financial activities and crosschecking between different financial activities and trade activities. This also

---

[13] In Chapter 4, Masciandaro and Portolano develop an interesting and challenging model of why a country offers money laundering services. These countries are grouped in a list of LFR (Lax Financial Regulation) countries, empirically identified with the Non Co-operative Countries and Territories listed by the Financial Action Task Force; see Financial Action Task Force (2000b and 2001).

means transverse and coherent communication around the world about possible terrorist financial activities, and starting and developing a competitive intelligence culture in order to break down the network and/or tools of these terrorist activities.

In order to do so, one should buy and install the latest technologies and software and put together a task force and develop communications platforms at the team level, so that all necessary information can be communicated and provided around the globe in an extremely short time.

This should be supplemented by guided criminal search and criminal network analyses so that an intelligently guided search that links all possible traces can detect (at least partly) the financial flows of terrorist organisations.

Here, the criminal network analysis, which is a method of graphic representation of criminal networks, comes in. Criminal network analyses allow the reproduction of the structures of criminal networks, the analysis of these structures using classic social network analyses, and the simulation of actions.

In combination with a guided criminal search using all possible information on the financial markets, this type of investigation may lead to a higher success rate. The greatest obstacle to international cooperation against money laundering seems to be the lack of regulation, because it is very difficult to identify the real beneficial owner. Here, new regulations should be put forward such that the real beneficial owner would be tracked down, possibly with the help of an electronic system for earmarking financial transactions.

The main problems with the guided criminal research and criminal network analyses are the authorisation and implementation of the necessary authorities and guidelines in the individual countries and the creation of the respective national and international organisations.

A second suggestion may be a worldwide financial Interpol task force. This should be a task force with specialists working in crime detection, in all financial 'deals' and in other terrorist activities, in order to fight terrorism and its financial flows using guided criminal research and network analyses with the help of the respective national jurisdictional institutions and police forces.

The idea here is that this task force should be able to operate in all countries around the world under the respective laws of the individual countries, but all possible legal help should be given to the task force so that it can efficiently work and move as quickly as terrorist groups. The crucial questions are: who should supervise this task force (e.g. the United Nations, the IMF or the World Bank)? And can this task force be given clear goals as well as the instruments to work efficiently?

A third suggestion may be a reward and/or another incentive system, with the idea that key terrorists might be tempted to leave their units and work with state and public authorities. There is some doubt whether this is possible with Islamic terrorist organisations, but at least these reward and other incentive systems should be installed so that those who would like to leave the terrorist organisations are given the opportunity.

A fourth suggestion is proposed by Fitzgerald (2002, pp. 20-21), where he argues that the nature of the international financial system makes limiting terrorist finances more difficult.

Even within formal institutional structures, however, the nature of bank secrecy makes the tracking of transactions difficult. With the growth of the Internet and the increasing impersonalisation of the banking industry, banks find it more difficult to detect suspicious transactions. For many offshore banking companies, their very comparative advantage lies in total secrecy and minimal records. As a result, cooperation faces obstacles from all sides.

Indeed, governments are often unwilling to share information with banks, expecting instead that banks will act as conduits for government information. There is no strong economic incentive for non-bank financial intermediaries to comply in reporting dubious transactions, as the probability of conviction is low and fines small. There are strong incentives for non-compliance as the sums of money involved are large and the costs of monitoring are substantial, especially since wealthy clients value secrecy highly.

As proposed by Fitzgerald (2002, p. 20), one solution to this problem could be to shift from the present 'blacklist' system administered by the US Office of Foreign Asset Control to an equivalent 'white list' system based on persons or firms registered for tax purposes (and thus monitored) in OECD countries and qualified emerging markets.

Basically, transactions with entities that are not properly registered for tax purposes would be subject to a substantial withholding tax (e.g. 25 per cent of the gross transaction). This would create a strong incentive against dealing with unregulated agents. This would have three strong positive effects.

- First, it would make handling unregistered funds unprofitable – or at worst cost criminals a great deal to transact, reducing their liquidity and eroding their assets.
- Second, the process of levying the tax would provide a steady information flow on the pattern of payments not now available.
- Third, it would mean the virtual closure of tax havens and a large increase in fiscal resources both for developed countries (to balance increased security expenditure) and developing countries to reduce social disparities.

A fifth suggestion is proposed by Frey and Lüchinger (2002, pp. 9-10). They suggest that one of the most effective ways to immunise a country against terrorist attacks is to decentralise actively both with respect to the polity and the economy.

They argue that strengthening political decentralisation via the division of power and federalism contributes strongly to a country being less vulnerable to terrorist attacks. The attraction of such actions for terrorists may be diminished. The marginal benefit of terrorism falls, and the equilibrium level of terrorism is reduced. Such measures may be attractive but they can only be realised under a long-term perspective.

What can we expect, if these five suggestions/countermeasures are implemented? I think we would have much more efficient tools of detection and prevention, because the conditions to fight terrorist organisations efficiently would be fulfilled to a greater extent: linking all transactions, people and situations in order to track down terrorist activities, and to use comprehensive and intelligent means that combine functions for quick registration, detection and workflow management.

In this toolbox, information technology is the key element of the detection process. One should realise, however, that it is essential in this environment, characterised by complexity and an extremely high level of automatic financial and commercial transactions, for all necessary information to be screened and efficiently examined.

Conclusion

This preliminary work first elaborated how Islamic terrorist organisations work, how they finance their activities and what type of financial means they use. Then, with the help of a latent estimator approach, we investigated how large the financial flows of the terrorist organisations are and what their ways of financing are. Finally, some suggestions were advanced on how to fight terrorist activities more efficiently and detect and reduce their financial flows.

Let me clearly summarise and emphasise that this is a very preliminary work with rough initial findings, especially the estimations, which should only be viewed as crude figures. What can we conclude from the findings of this chapter?

- For the western world, it is a major political and economic problem to fight terrorism and to detect and reduce the financial flows of terrorists. This means, on the one hand, that we should not make excessive use of instruments of repression and, on the other, we should have efficient instruments to detect and reduce the financial flows of terrorists so that their actions are impeded or made impossible.
- This difficult trade-off will only be masterminded with a lot of goodwill in the western hemisphere. Only with source interaction and the creation of new international organisations and task forces will it be possible to overcome the threat and challenge of Islamic and other international terror organisations without giving up key elements of our democracy.

References

Alexander, K. (2001), The need for efficient international financial regulation and the role of a global supervisor, *Journal of Money Laundering Control* , 5, pp.52-65.

Bloomberg, S.B., de Hess, G. and Weerapana A. (2002), *Terrorism from Within: An Economic Model of Terrorism*, Paper presented to the DIW Workshop 'The Economic Consequences of Global Terrorism', Berlin, June 14-15.

Chen, A.H. and Siems, T.F. (2002), *An Empirical Analyses of the Capital Markets' response to Cataclysmic Events*, Paper presented to the DIW Workshop 'The Economic Consequences of Global Terrorism', Berlin, June 14-15.

Drakos, K. (2002), *The Financial and Employment Impact of 9/11: The Case of the Aviation Industry*, Paper presented to the DIW Workshop 'The Economic Consequences of Global Terrorism', Berlin, June 14-15.

Enders, W. and Sandler, T. (2001), *Pattern of transnational terrorism, 1970-1999: Alternative time series estimates*, unpublished manuscript.

Enders, W. and Sandler, T. (2000), Is transnational terrorism becoming more threatening?, *Journal of Conflict Resolution*, 44, pp. 307-332.

Enders, W. and Sandler, T. (1999), Transnational Terrorism in the post-cold war-area, *International Studies Quaterly*, 43, pp. 145-167.

Enders, W. and Sandler, T. (1996), Terrorism and Foreign Direct Investment in Spain and Greece, *Kyklos*, 49, pp. 331-502.

Enders, W. and Sandler, T. (1993), The effectiveness of anti-terrorism policies: vector auto-regression intervention analyses, *American Political Science Review*, 87, pp. 829-844.

Enders, W. and Sandler, T. (1991), Causality between transnational terrorism and tourism: The case of Spain, *Journal of Terrorism*, 14, pp. 49-58.

Epstein, G. S. and Gang, I.N. (2002), *Understanding the Development of Fundamentalism*, Paper presented to the DIW Workshop 'The Economic Consequences of Global Terrorism', Berlin, June 14-15.

Financial Action Task Force on Money Laundering (2001), *Developments in Non-Cooperative Countries and Territories*, September, Paris.

Financial Action Task Force on Money Laundering (2000a), *Report on Money Laundering Typologies 1999-2000*, Paris.

Financial Action Task Force on Money Laundering (2000b), *Report on Non-Cooperative Countries and Territories*, Paris.

Fitzgerald, V. (2002), *Global Financial Information, Complaints, Incentives and Conflict Funding*, Paper presented to the DIW Workshop 'The Economic Consequences of Global Terrorism', Berlin, June 14-15.

Frey, B.S. and Lüchinger, S. (2002), *Terrorism: Deterrence may Backfire*, Paper presented to the DIW Workshop 'The Economic Consequences of Global Terrorism', Berlin, June 14-15.

Giles, D.A. and Tedds, L.M. (2002), Taxes and the Canadian Underground Economy, *Canadian Tax Paper*, No. 106, Canadian Tax Foundation, Toronto.

Henderson, H. (2001), *Global Terrorism: The Complete Reference Guide*, Checkmark Books, New York.

Johnson, J. and Desmond Lim, Y.C. (2002), Money Laundering: Has the Financial Action Task Force Made a Difference?, *Journal of Financial Crime*, 10, pp. 7-22.

Lemay, T. (2001), *Money Laundering and the International Community: The United Nations and other Multi-lateral Responses*, in: Geldwäsche und verdeckte Terrorfinanzierung: Bedrohung der Staatengemeinschaft, Bundesnachrichtendienst, Pullach (Deutschland).

Lemay, T. (1998), *Financial Heavens: Banking, Secrecy and Money Laundering*, Research Study of the United Nations, New York.

Sandler, T. and Enders, W. (2002), *An Economic Perspective on Transnational Terrorism*, Paper presented to the DIW Workshop 'The Economic Consequences of Global Terrorism', Berlin, June 14-15.

Savona, E. U. (2001), *Money Laundering Activities and Counter Measures: Off-Shore Centers and the Transparency of Company Law*, in: Geldwäsche und verdeckte Terrorfinanzierung: Bedrohung der Staatengemeinschaft, Bundesnachrichtendienst, Pullach (Deutschland).

Schneider, F. and Enste, D. (2000a), *Schattenwirtschaft und Schwarzarbeit: Umfang, Ursachen, Wirkungen und wirtschaftspolitische Empfehlungen*, R. Oldenbourg-Verlag, München and Wien.

Schneider, F. and Enste, D. (2000b), Shadow Economies: Size, Causes and Consequences, *Journal of Economic Literature*, 38, pp. 77-114.

Seymour, C. H. (2001), *E-Commerce, Cyber Laundering and Securities Trading – New Techniques and Counter Measures*, in: Geldwäsche und verdeckte Terrorfinanzierung: Bedrohung der Staatengemeinschaft, Bundesnachrichtendienst, Pullach (Deutschland).

Stern, J. (1999), *The Ultimate-Terrorist*, Harvard University Press, Cambridge and London.

Tarrat, A. (2001), *Money Laundering: Approaching Methods and Tools*, in: Geldwäsche und verdeckte Terrorfinanzierung: Bedrohung der Staatengemeinschaft, Bundesnachrichtendienst, Pullach (Deutschland).

US Financial Crimes Enforcement Network (2000), *A Survey of Electronic Cash, Electronic Gaming and Internet Banking*, www.ustreas.gov/FINCEN.

Wilkinson, P. (2000), *Terrorism versus Democracy: The Liberal State Response*, Frank Cass, London.

Wintrobe, R. (2002), *Can Suicide Bombers be Rational?*, Paper presented to the DIW Workshop 'The Economic Consequences of Global Terrorism', Berlin, June 14-15002.

Table 3.1 Shadow Economy and Underground Economy in Germany, 1996-2001

Year	Germany			
	Shadow economy [1]		Underground economy [1]	
	% of official GNP	€ (billions)	% of official GNP	€ (billions)
1996	14.50	263	10.4	189
1997	15.00	280	11.6	217
1998	14.80	286	12.8	248
1999	15.51	308	14.1	280
2000	16.03	329	16.3	334
2001[2]	16.00	336	16.9	355

[1] Shadow economy (= in principle legal activities, but withholding tax and social security payments, and violating other labour market regulations) and underground economy are different activities, which *cannot* be summed, as the underground economy (typical criminal activities, like burglary, etc) produces no positive value added for an economy and hence cannot be treated as a complement to the 'official GNP', whereas the 'traditional' shadow economy can be seen as a complement to the 'official' GNP. For both 'economies' we have overlapping areas.
[2] Preliminary estimates.

Source: Own calculations.

Figure 3.1   Shadow economy and Underground economy in Germany, 1996-2001, as % of official GNP

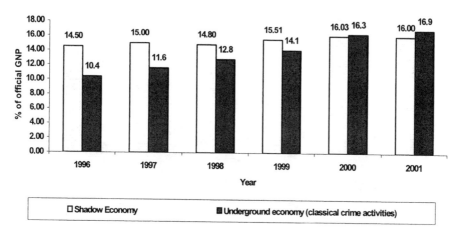

Figure 3.2 Shadow economy and underground economy in Germany, 1996-2001, in € billions

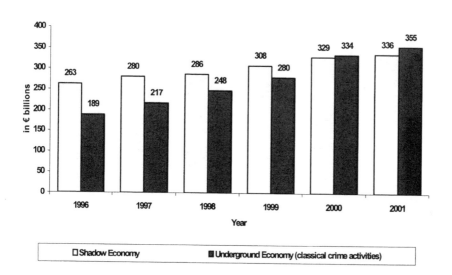

Figure 3.3 Underground Economy for Germany, Italy, France and UK, 1996-2001, as % of official GNP

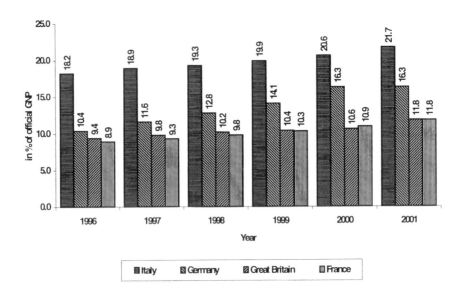

Table 3.2   Shadow economy and underground economy in Italy from 1996-2001

Year	Italy	
	Shadow Economy1) **% of official GNP**	**Underground Economy** [1] **% of official GNP**
1996	27.0	18.2
1997	27.3	18.9
1998	27.8	19.3
1999	27.1	19.9
2000	27.2	20.6
2001 2)	27.0	21.7

[1] Shadow economy (= in principle legal activities, but withholding tax and social security payments, and violating other labour market regulations) and underground economy are different activities, which *cannot* be summed, as the underground economy (typical crime activities, like burglary, etc) produces no positive value added for an economy and hence cannot be treated as a complement to the 'official GNP', whereas the 'traditional' shadow economy can be seen as a complement to the 'official' GNP. For both 'economies' we have overlapping areas.

[2] Preliminary estimations.

Source: Own calculation.

Global Financial Crime

Table 3.3 Shadow Economy and Underground Economy in France from 1996-2001

Year	France	
	Shadow economy [1] % of official GNP	**Underground economy** [1] % of official GNP
1996	14.9	8.9
1997	14.7	9.3
1998	14.9	9.8
1999	15.2	10.3
2000	15.2	10.9
2001 [2]	15.1	11.8

[1] Shadow economy (= in principle legal activities, but withholding tax and social security payments, and violating other labour market regulations) and underground economy are different activities, which *cannot* be summed, as the underground economy (typical crime activities, like burglary, etc) produces no positive value added for an economy and hence cannot be treated as a complement to the 'official GNP', whereas the 'traditional' shadow economy can be seen as a complement to the 'official' GNP. For both 'economies' we have overlapping areas.
[2] Preliminary estimations.

Source: Own calculations.

Table 3.4 Shadow Economy and Underground Economy in the UK, 1996-2001

Year	United Kingdom	
	Shadow Economy [1] **% of official GNP**	**Underground Economy** [1] **% of official GNP**
1996	13.1	9.4
1997	13.0	9.8
1998	13.0	10.2
1999	12.7	10.4
2000	12.7	10.6
2001 [2]	12.6	11.8

[1] Shadow economy (= in principle legal activities, but withholding tax and social security payments, and violating other labour market regulations) and underground economy are different activities, which *cannot* be summed up as the underground economy (typical crime activities, like burglary, etc) produces no positive value added for an economy and hence cannot be treated as a complement to the 'official GNP', whereas the 'traditional' shadow economy can be seen as a complement to the 'official' GNP. For both 'economies' we have overlapping areas.
[2] Preliminary estimations.

Source: Own calculations.

Table 3.5 The Kind of Financial Flows Used to Supply Terrorist Cells

1) Starbust:	A deposit of dirty money is made in a bank with standing instructions to wire it in small, random fragments to hundreds of other bank accounts around the world. *Goal: To hide the original source of the money and increase the financial flows for terrorist groups organised in cells.*
2) Boomerang:	Money is sent on a long arc around the world before returning to the country whence it came. En route it travels through what money launderers refer as "black holes", meaning countries that lack the means and/or inclination to investigate banks. *Goal: same as 1)*
3) Charity money:	The source of terrorist money might initially be legal. It might come from a wealthy individual or from a religious charity.
4) Shell companies:	Via faked firms and with the help of "tax optimisation experts", dirty money will be whitewashed. *Goal: same as 1)*

Figure 3.4   Development of the Shadow Economy (size of Financial flows of Islamic terrorist organisations) Over Time

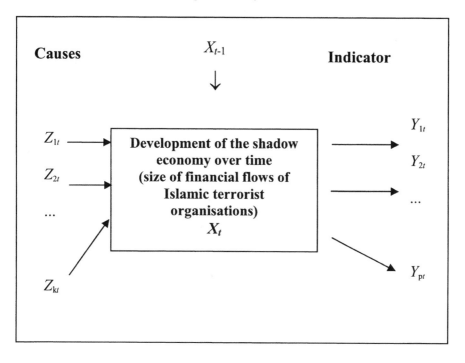

Figure 3.5　Estimatio (latent estimation approach) of the Size of the Shadow Economy using Causes (determinants) and Traces (indicators), DYMIMIC Estimation Procedure, Combined Cross Section and Time Series over 17 OECD Countries and over the Period 1984-1999

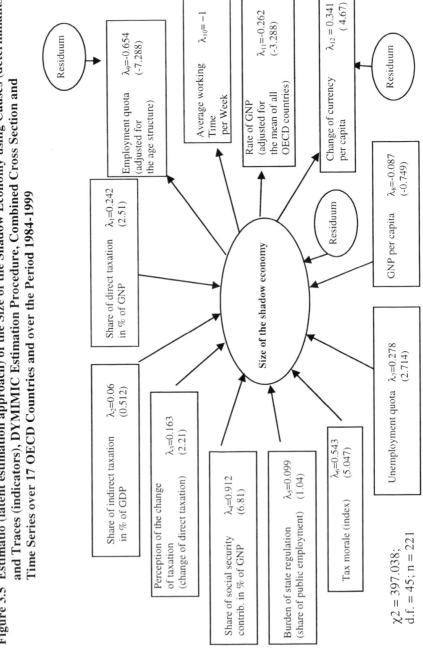

Figura 3.6 Estimation (Latent Estimator Approach) of the Financial Flows (Budget) of Islamic Terrorist Groups using Causes (Determinants) and Traces (Indicators), DYMIMIC Estimation Procedure, Combined Cross Section and Time Series

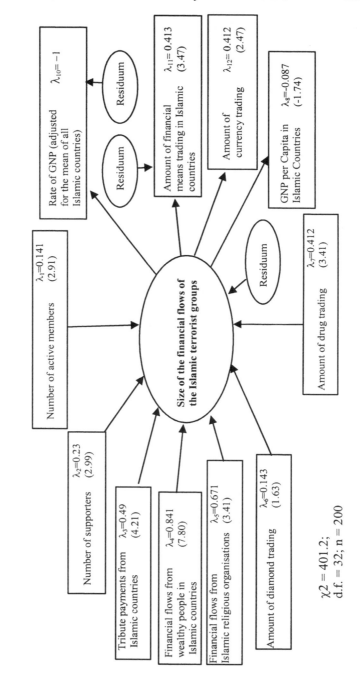

Table 3.6 The Financial Flows and the Kind of Finances of Al Qaeda and other Terror Organisations

Wealth (Stock value) of Al Qaeda (Average 1999-2001)	~ US$ 5 billion
Annual financial flows (budget) of Al Qaeda (Average 1999-2001)	US$ 20-50 million
Ways of financing of terror organisations (using the example of Al Qaeda)	
Drug business (mainly transporting drugs)	30-35%
Donations/tribute payments of governments or wealthy individuals or religious groups	25-30%
Classic criminal activities (blackmail, kidnapping, etc)	10-15%
Illegal diamond trading	10-15%
Additional unknown financial means (legal + illegal)	25-5%

Source: Own calculations.

Table 3.7 Preliminary Overview of Financial Flows of Arab Islamic Terror Organisations

Name	Members (worldwide)[1] Year 2001/02	Current financial flows (annual budget) Year 2001/02
Al Qaeda	1500-3000	20-50 million $
Front Islamique du Salut (Algeria)	~ 400	~ 5 million $
Hammas	~ 1000	~ 10 million $
Hezbollah	~10.000	~ 50 million $
Arab Mujaheddin (terror) organisations:		
- Iraq	~ 800	~ US$ 5 million
- Iran	~ 600	~ US$ 5 million
- Libya	~ 600	~ US$ 10 million
- Egypt (Egyptian Islamic Jihad; most likely united with Al Qaeda; Islamic/Arab)	~ 600	~ US$ 8 million
additional 17 Organisations	~ 27.000	~ USD 150 mill.
PKK (Turkey)	~ 2.000	~ USD 10 mill.

[1]   Active (well-trained) members belonging to the hardcore (stock).

Source: Own calculations.

Table 3.8   Reactions/Strategies to Fight Terror Organisations and their Financing

1) USA:	*FTATC (Foreign Terrorist Asset Tracking Center)* Budget: USD 6.4 million To detect the wealth of criminal/terrorist organisations. Direct investigation policies of the bureau to control foreign money with the help of the Internal Review Service as well as Customs Authorities. Direct use of the staff against the FBI, CIA and NSA. Additional competences for the FBI + local investigation teams.
2) EU	*FATF (Financial Action Task Force)* Fighting of money laundering and fighting the financial flows of terror organisations.
3) Germany (i)	New founding of a *„Zentralstelle für verfahrensunabhängige Finanzermittlungen"* Task: Competence centre against money laundering.
(ii)	*Additional competence to servile of financial transfers*; Creation of a central database at „Bundesaufsichtsamt für Kreditwesen (KAKred)". Goal: to detect "dirty" money and the financial flows of terror organisations and money laundering activities of classical crime groups.
(iii)	*Additional competences and power for the existing state institutions*, for example: „Bundesaufsichtsamt für Wertpapierhandel oder Bundesaufsichtsamt für Versicherungs-wesen".

Table 3.9 Further and Comprehensive Ideas/Countermeasures to Detect and Reduce the Financial Flows of International Terror Organisations

1)Guided criminal search and criminal network analyses	*Goal: guided search and linking all possible traces of the financial flows of terrorist organisations with the link to the traditional criminal search.* Problems/questions: (1) Authorisation and implementation of the necessary competences and guidelines in the single nations (2) national/international institutions to be created
2)The Financial Interpol/Task Force (worldwide)	Goal: International unit to fight terrorism and their financial flows using guided criminal search and network analyses with the help of national jurisdictional and police force. Control: UNO (IMF, World Bank) and/or national parliaments? Problems/questions as 1)
3)High award and other incentive systems	Goal: to create incentives that key terrorist or other active members leave their unit. Promise of new identity and a lot of money.

Chapter 4

Financial Policy: Offshore Centres and Competition in Regulation: The Laxity Problem

Donato Masciandaro and Alessandro Portolano

Introduction

Chapters 1 to 3 highlighted how relevant the potential role of the offshore countries and territories has been in the international debate on money laundering and terrorism financing.

Now, to be precise from an economic point of view, an 'offshore financial centre' is a generic term applied to a variety of financial centres, which offer a wide range of services to their customers in a loose regulatory, supervisory, accounting and tax environment. In the most general sense, this term should also apply to activities such as the trust business, financing vehicles and other corporate entities. It is common for these centres to benefit from bank secrecy laws.

Offshore financial centres (OFCs) have been used for decades by corporate entities to reduce their tax burden through complex tax planning strategies and by individuals for tax avoidance and evasion. Chapter 5 will analyse the relationships between OFCs and taxation policies.

Similarly, many of these same OFCs could be utilised for money laundering. Therefore, in order to analyse the relationship between the financing of terrorism and organised crime, on one hand, and the design of financial regulation, on the other, we would prefer to introduce the term Lax Financial Regulation (LFR) countries.

An LFR country is a jurisdiction in which the features of the financial regulations increase the likelihood that money laundering services, utilised by terrorist and criminal organisations, will be offered.[1]

---

[1] It is important to stress – as Rider (2002) noted – that the laundering process is determined by the need of those agents and organisations seeking to hide or to be disassociated from the wealth, and that there are important differences between terrorists and conventional criminal organisations.

The role of LFR countries in international money laundering schemes has long attracted the attention of policymakers. Virtually all initiatives aimed at combating money laundering, at both the domestic and international levels, tackle this issue.

In the aftermath of 11 September, as the previous chapters stressed, growing attention has been paid to the role of LFR countries in providing terrorist financing, adding new perspectives to the debate over what initiatives should be taken against such countries.

In fact, as has been correctly pointed out,[2] the first official reaction against terrorism after the September 2001 attacks was a financial one: not two weeks had passed since the attack when President Bush signed an executive order freezing the US assets of suspected organisations and individuals.[3]

Policymakers concentrated their attention on the negative qualitative[4] and quantitative[5] effects of money laundering and on the possibility that LFR centres might facilitate the task of terrorist and criminal organisations. Concerns are raised by regulations adopted in LFR centres that may greatly contribute to the laundering of money from illicit sources.

Two intertwined postulates commonly feature in the debate concerning the international market for money laundering services: a) money laundering is facilitated by lax financial regulation; b) countries that do not co-operate in the international effort aimed at combating money laundering adopt lax financial regulation.

The ensuing observation is that non-co-operative countries contribute to the functioning of the international market for money laundering, and therefore to the world social and economic pollution caused by terrorism and organised crime.

The Financial Action Task Force (FATF) for the prevention of money laundering has launched an initiative aimed at identifying countries that do not co-operate in the global fight against money laundering.

As Chapter 1 well introduced, since 2000, the FATF has monitored a total of 45 countries that, following our definition, can be identified as potential LFR countries.

Using a worldwide data set on the main 130 countries – note that the United Nations member countries total 189 – we can note that these 45 countries represent

---

[2] Wasserman (2002).

[3] On the US new legislation on money laundering see Banoun, et al. (2002) and Rider (2002).

[4] Policymakers are mainly concerned with two sources of cost stemming from money laundering. Firstly, the possibility of laundering proceeds of crime affects the incentive of a potential criminal. In a world where money of illicit origin cannot be laundered, the possibility of linking the capital to the crime reduces the ex ante incentive of the criminal to commit the crime in the first place. At the margin, more crimes will be committed if money laundering is possible. From this perspective, combating money laundering is equal, in the aggregate, to combating predicate offences. Secondly, capital that is laundered returns to the legal financial sector generating serious negative effects: competition is distorted, and the allocative efficiency of the market is undermined.

[5] The extent of money laundering flows is unknown by definition. The IMF (1998) estimated laundered funds as 2-5 per cent of global GDP.

8 per cent of total GDP, 15 per cent of total population, and 25 per cent of world foreign bank deposits. In addiction, as the OECD pointed out, other LFR countries may exist or emerge.

The FATF produces periodic reports on non-co-operative countries and territories (NCCTs) in an international effort to combat money laundering. These reports are commonly, although somewhat incorrectly, described as blacklists. Since June 2000, seven NCCT lists have been published (June 2000, June 2001, September 2001, February 2002, July 2002, October 2002, February 2003), indicating the jurisdictions that fail to conform to the criteria.

Therefore, issues related to the link between black finance and lax financial regulation seem to be qualitatively and quantitatively relevant.

Discussions concerning these issues, however, often take as a *given* the existence of some countries that offer financial services to terrorism and organised crime via the adoption of lax financial regulations. In other words, the supply of money laundering services is treated as an *exogenous variable*.

This chapter builds on previous work by the same authors,[6] taking a different perspective. We start from the assumption that financial regulation may be a strategic variable for countries seeking to maximise the revenues produced by money laundering. A country may find it profitable to adopt financial regulations that attract capital of illicit origin or destination.

We argue that LFR countries are structurally different from other countries. More specifically, we shall argue that:

- the utility function of countries that favour money laundering is positively correlated to the existence of terrorism or criminal activities abroad;
- the utility function of such countries is not influenced by the negative effects of such illegal activity, i.e. they do not bear the negative consequences of the terrorist and criminal activity.

Our view is that there may be features of a given country that will naturally support the decision to adopt financial regulations that may, in fact, facilitate money laundering.

In so doing, we take a relational approach, on the assumption that it 'takes two to tango': we treat regulation that can affect the ease by which money of illicit origin is laundered as a product. Within this framework, we focus on the relationship that is established between a given LFR country and its customers, i.e. terrorist and/or criminal organisations.

We are less concerned with the main product offered by LFR countries to potential launderers (for example, a strict banking regime) and more concerned with the features of LFR countries that help to support the exchange between those jurisdictions, on one hand, and terrorist and criminal organisations, on the other.

---

[6] Masciandaro (1996, 1998, 1999 and 2000), Masciandaro and Portolano (2003).

These features may be of various natures. Particular attention will be paid, however, to the economic and institutional environment, as generally defined.[7] We look for features in the legal system, as well as for specific rules that help to sustain the relationships that LFR countries and terrorist or criminal organisations establish, thus determining the ultimate success of some LFR centres over others.

Examining the determinants of success in the competition among LFR countries, it is hoped, will help to identify which countries are likely to be involved in money laundering. Grasping the factors that determine the success of some countries in the race to the bottom might also prove useful for policymakers in devising the most appropriate countermeasures.[8]

In examining the factors that may put a given country in an advantageous position over other countries, we take an evolutionist perspective.[9] These factors need not necessarily be the result of a 'conscious' choice by the country. Rather, they need to prove useful in the competition with other countries. The competitive advantage of a country might also be ascribed to the accidents of history, to geographical factors, or even to sheer chance.

For example, the language spoken in the country might obviously play a role in the choice made by criminal or terrorist organisations. An evolutionist approach implies that while we expect a great degree of functional convergence, different countries may choose different strategies to achieve the same end.

In discussing the possibility that some countries may act in order to maximise profits stemming from money laundering, we make a simplifying assumption, in that we treat a single LFR country as a unitary decision agent. This assumption, albeit naïve, is consistent with the goal of the chapter, i.e. an evaluation of the dynamics of competition among jurisdictions by identifying the 'typical' features of LFR countries.[10]

Finally, some remarks on our interdisciplinary methodology. From the standpoint of economic literature, we clearly follow the classic intuitions of the new political economy, basing our work on the three hypotheses: that the definition of regulatory policy is not exogenous, as in conventional economics, but endogenous; that policy is not determined by maximising its social welfare

---

[7] For example, as defined in North (1990), institutions include both formal and explicit rules and less formal rules such as norms.

[8] Our attention focuses on countries that try to attract proceeds of crime by offering financial services to criminal organisations abroad. We leave aside the broader question of the possible role of offshore centres in generating and facilitating international financial crises. The latter issue has obviously attracted the attention of policy makers. This interest has also been spurred by the ever-increasing integration of financial markets, which has increased the threat to financial stability posed by offshore centres. See Errico and Musalem (1999), Financial Stability Forum (2000).

[9] As defined in Alchian (1950) and Becker (1962).

[10] However, we will sometimes try to shed some light on the black box, in order to look at the possible role of interest groups within the offshore center. Further research may try to write a thorough "public choice" history of the confrontation that we expect to take place in the political arena within each offshore country.

function but by taking the political cost-benefit analysis into account;[11] and policymaker optimisation is constrained and influenced by institutional design.[12]

We are also indebted to a strand of literature – usually associated with the 'law and economics' movement – which we deem to be strictly, although indirectly, related to the subject matter of our research, i.e. the literature on the competition for corporate charters among the American states that constitute the Union. More specifically, we take the approach developed by authors that have tackled the issue in the 'transaction cost economics' tradition[13] and apply it in a novel area.

The importance of institutions is the common element of both our economic and law references. Therefore it is quite natural to acknowledge the suggestions of recent Law, Endowments and Finance literature.[14]

In fact the importance of the institutional determinants of different national financial structures has originated two different bodies of work: law and finance theory,[15] more focused on the legal traditions, and endowment theory,[16] more concentrated on geography/disease endowments. In our work we try to consider both the traditional and natural endowments in determining the degree of laxity.

---

[11] For the new political economy see Drazen (2000) and Persson and Tabellini (2000).

[12] See, for example, Grilli et al. (1991).

[13] See Romano (1985, 1993 and 1999). To be sure, the situation we are examining is not directly comparable to the one examined by American corporate law scholars. The most obvious difference is that competition among the 50 American states takes place under the eye of Federal authorities, namely the Federal Government and the Supreme Court. In particular, the latter has shown remarkable attention to the need to reduce the externalities produced by the states. On the other hand, the results of a lively debate – dating almost 30 years – provide us with fundamental insights even in the context we are dealing with. The results of such a strand of literature help to develop a theoretical framework of analysis that may be applied with promise to our subject. The fact that competition among states takes place in completely different environments – be it the United States, the European Union, or the international market for money laundering services – does not invalidate the idea that competition is likely to respond to the same logic. Indeed, what started out in the mid-1970s as a purely theoretical debate, has evolved over the years into a feast of empirical studies. Measuring the impact of competition on the value of listed companies tests the validity of the theoretical conclusions. Despite occasional evidence to the contrary, that literature has gained a solid hold on the dynamics of competition among jurisdictions. More specifically, there appears to be a certain degree of consensus on when and why competition will evolve into a race to the bottom or to the top. We expect empirical research on competition among offshore countries to be extremely difficult. Obvious factors suggest an almost complete lack of information: parties to money laundering schemes do not publish reports on the success of their operations. In contrast, listed companies supply a goldmine of data for financial economists to measure the impact of the various actions taken by the actors involved. The precision reached by event or accounting data studies does not appear duplicable in the context of the competition among offshore centres. We therefore have at our disposal an analytical framework whose reliability has been thoroughly tested in the field.

[14] See Beck et al. (2002).

[15] La Porta et al. (1998).

[16] Acemoglu, Johnson and Robinson (2001).

The chapter proceeds as follows. In the first part we explore, from a more general point of view, the possible determinants of success of a given LFR country in the market for money laundering.

In other words, we try to examine the conditions under which becoming an LFR jurisdiction can be 'convenient' for a given country: what are the geographical, institutional, and economic features that increase the probability that a given country becomes an LFR country?

The second part of the paper provides a formal theoretical analysis and description of the possible dynamics governing the decision of policymakers to design financial regulations in such a way as to enter the market for money laundering.

In the third part we empirically verify whether the theoretical features of LFR countries are consistent with those of the countries in the FATF's analysis of effective and potential NCCTs. The empirical evidence, as we shall see, is consistent with the hypothesis.

However, we must also consider the possibility of facing both Type I and Type II errors. On the one hand, there may be de facto LFR countries that are not included in the FATF analyses; on the other hand, the evidence shows that the NCCTs included in the lists are not entirely homogeneous.

Both observations appear to be important for an overall assessment of the adequacy of the international response, in the fourth and concluding part.

Money Laundering and Money Dirtying: Key Concepts

Since 11 September 2001, the financial systems, overt and covert, have come increasingly into the sights of the state agencies appointed to combat terrorism. In that context, the need to increase the fight against the laundering of illicit capital was included in the agenda.

We should immediately stress that in terms of economic analysis the financing of terrorism (money dirtying) is a phenomenon conceptually different from the recycling of capital (money laundering).

To understand the similarities and differences, therefore, we must briefly review the economic peculiarities of the money-laundering phenomenon. In recent years, particular emphasis has been placed on the study of that phenomenon because of its central theoretical and practical role in the development of any crime that generates revenues.

In fact, the conduct of any illegal activity may be subject to a special category of transaction costs, linked to the fact that the use of the relative revenues increases the probability of discovery of the crime and therefore incrimination.

Those transaction costs can be minimised through an effective laundering action, a means of concealment that separates financial flows from their origin, an activity whose specific economic function is to transform potential wealth into effective purchasing power.

In this sense, money-laundering performs an illegal monetary function, responding to the demand for 'black finance' services expressed by individuals or groups that have committed income-producing crimes.

The financing of terrorism resembles money-laundering in some respects and differs from it in others. The objective of the activity is to channel funds of any origin to individuals or groups to enable acts of terrorism, and therefore crimes. Again in this case, a party with such an objective must contend with potential transaction costs, since the financial flows may increase the probability that the crime of terrorism will be discovered, thus leading to incrimination. Therefore, an effective money dirtying action, an activity of concealment designed to separate financial flows from their destination, can minimise the transaction costs. Thus, money dirtying can also perform an illegal monetary function, responding to the demand for 'covertness' expressed by individuals or groups proposing to commit crimes of terrorism.

The phenomena of money laundering and money dirtying may coexist, of course, when terrorism is financed through the use of funds originating from criminal activities. A typical example is the financing of terrorism with the proceeds from the production and marketing of narcotics. In those specific situations, at least on the logical level, the importance of the transaction costs is at least doubled, since the need to lower the probability of incrimination concerns both the crimes that generated the financial flows and the crimes for which they are intended. As a result, the value of a concealment operation is even more significant.

But who satisfies the demand for concealment, whether its purpose is money-laundering or financing terrorism?

Drawing upon the literature on information asymmetries, it is easy to demonstrate that banking and financial intermediaries can perform an important function in the concealment activity, whether the underlying motive is money-laundering or financing terrorism.

By reducing the overall transaction costs for the other economic agents, financial intermediaries improve the consumers' capacity to decide how to allocate their purchasing power in terms of consumption, savings and investment. Thus, intermediaries ultimately animate an industry in which the services offered and sold are intrinsically intangible, with an information content that is high but not uniformly distributed among all the market participants. The diverse characteristics of the operators are thus known to, and coordinated by, the financial firms through the supply and sale of their services, and the individual intermediaries seek to maximise their profit precisely through the management and enhancement of their information assets, in a sector where information is not uniformly distributed. Therefore, financial firms are ultimately characterised as having information assets greater than, different from and more specialised than, all the others. As a result, the financial industry acquires a reputation for two crucial attributes with regard to the purpose of concealment:

- a greater-than-normal degree of 'opacity' (information asymmetry), since the exchanges and flows of purchasing power are filtered, coordinated and administered by specialised operators;
- the privileged position of those intermediaries.

It should be stressed, however, that the connotation of incomplete, asymmetrical distribution of information between the parties stipulating the various forms of contract or agreement is accentuated in the provision of financial services but is not the exclusive prerogative of those markets. It manifests itself, for example, when the characteristics of the provision of professional services are examined. In any case, the quantitative and qualitative centrality of the financial industry within the overall economic system clearly evidences information asymmetry and centrality of the specialised operators.

Within the financial sector, a particular role is played by banks, intermediaries distinguished by the simultaneous offering of a) deposit contracts, fungible for payment and monetary requirements, and b) credit contracts, generally not transformable prima facie into market-negotiable assets. Banks thus emerge as a 'special' intermediary, since both their deposit and loan contracts provide them with significant economies of scale and diversification in the management of information. In markets 'opaque' by definition, they therefore become a depositary of confidential information on both the beneficiaries of loans and on the users of payment services, or whatever services they provide.

Management of the payments system also puts banks in a crucial position regarding the purpose of concealment. The more a payments system minimises the costs that operators pay to transform their potential options for allocating purchasing power into actual options, the more efficient it becomes. But, if this is true, that system can be a potentially optimal, efficient vehicle for transforming the potential purchasing power of illicit revenues into actual purchasing power and therefore for performing money laundering functions effectively. At the same time, through the payments system, the provision of funds to terrorist organisations can be concealed.

In other words, management of the payments system has a positive value for legal economic agents, since it facilitates their resource allocation decisions. At the same time, it may be crucial for illegal parties, which are seeking not only to reduce transaction costs but especially to minimise the risks of discovery – and therefore the costs of sanctions and punishment – associated with both money-laundering and terrorism financing activities.

Banking and financial intermediaries are therefore at the centre of attention of both criminal and terrorist organisations and the law enforcement authorities. For criminal parties, the presence of intermediaries that are cooperative (contaminating intermediaries) or inefficient in protecting their integrity (unknowing intermediaries) increases the possibility of using the payments or lending systems, or financial services system in general, for their concealment objectives. At the same time, for the inquiring and investigative authorities, the information assets in the possession of those companies can serve an essential reporting function in the identification and verification of the presence of criminal or terrorist organisations or individuals.

To cast light on the similarities and differences between money laundering and money dirtying, we should dwell on the role of the unknowing intermediaries, to which the authorities assign the task of reporting suspicious financial movements.

Starting with money-laundering phenomena, we reconsider the definition of money laundering with respect to any financial transaction: that transaction not only performs an economic function of its own but, if its purpose is to launder funds, it also performs an additional irregular function.

The hypothesis is that precisely because the transaction in question is responding to an uncommon (and illegal) purpose, it will possess irregular features that distinguish it from normal, physiological characteristics. What will the sources of the irregularity be? The irregularity could arise from at least one of the base-elements of the definition of money laundering, in which an economic agent institutes procedures to transform a given amount of potential purchasing power into actual purchasing power. The irregularity could therefore refer to at least one of the three elements: the party, the procedures and the amount of a given banking or financial contract.

Thanks to past evolution, money-laundering techniques now pose greater difficulties of identification and monitoring, precisely because they have made concealment and the separation of the three components of a laundering operation increasingly effective. A first important point is therefore the growing difficulty of recognising money-laundering irregularities. A second important point is the fact that a banking or financial transaction may embody irregular elements without this signifying that it derives from a laundering attempt: irregularity can therefore be considered a necessary but insufficient condition for identifying money-laundering activity.

These reflections on the logical and operational difficulties related to the hypothesis of irregularity are strengthened when this postulate becomes the cornerstone on which the obligations of intermediaries to collaborate in the war on the financing of terrorism are based. It is wholly evident, in fact, that the existence or detectability of irregular elements can become even more problematic when the sources of the financial flows to be concealed are totally licit activities conducted by individuals or organisations equally overt and legal.

In summing up our analysis regarding the relationship between the laundering of capital and financing terrorism, one is prompted to think that the operational techniques, and therefore the channels of dissemination, of the two phenomena are at least in part coincident. It is important, however, for the partial or total coincidence of money dirtying and money laundering to remain a working hypothesis rather than a theorem, so that it is possible to attempt the construction of a system of rules that can combine the effective enforcement of laws with the efficiency of the banking and financial markets.

And it is precisely from the standpoint of possible channels for financing terrorism that the theme of informal finance emerges, although it is not a new concept.

The focus on the relationship between informal banking and financial systems, on the one hand, and the potential risks of money laundering and terrorism financing, on the other, is quite recent, and the few studies on the subject are exclusively descriptive in nature. There are several systems of informal finance, but considerable attention has been reserved for the Hawalah system (described in Chapters 1 and 2), for reasons that will be illustrated as we proceed.

From the standpoint of economic analysis, the description of those systems leads us to conclude that those informal networks, beyond the obvious historical, geographical and technical-operational differences, seem to be distinguished by the following: informality and trust on an ethical basis.

Informal finance systems, in fact, develop without the stable or long-lasting support of a system of formal laws, administrative rules, and relative documentary, paper-based records, as is characteristic of overt finance systems, bank-based and otherwise. The fuel and catalyst of these systems is ethics-based trust: in individual communities, strongly identified on the ethnic level, financial transactions are carried out that create de facto debtor–creditor relations of variable duration on the basis of a common fiduciary heritage. In informal systems, the reliability of these relations cannot be based, by definition, on the threat of legal sanctions but rests instead on the advisability of avoiding the social and moral sanctions that strike members of the reference community who fail to fulfil their obligations, with highly concrete effects associated with exclusion and isolation.

The systems of informal finance thus seem to be heavily used by migrants belonging to the ethnic communities from which these systems originated. This observation is obviously not based on robust statistical series, given the covert nature of the phenomenon, but on a growing volume of specific case studies and on specific sample surveys.

The combination of high fiduciary content and ethnic affinity makes those informal, naïve channels – consisting of networks among friends and relatives of the same ethnic group as the immigrant or by more complex structures of informal finance – particularly attractive. The use of ethnic-national networks is strictly tied to the strength of relationships of trust among immigrant compatriots.

Informal finance is characterised by great simplicity and rapidity of procedures, operational flexibility, and a capacity to adjust to the needs of the migrants. Informal finance also displays maximum capacity in integrating the economic element into the social context and in linking organisational decisions to cultural influences and traditions. The operations of informal financial institutions are based on trust and on gradually established schemes and procedures and customary rules. The functioning of informal finance mechanisms is normally ensured by 'social control', i.e. the censure of improper conduct exercised by the community through the marginalisation of migrants who fail to adhere to the rules (typically ethical or religious rules linked to the cultural background). It is not rash to maintain, in fact, that the mechanism for enforcing the relations created within informal networks is repeated within the local immigrant communities, which are particularly sensitive to cultural identity and relative 'marginalisation risk'.

The assurance of confidentiality and the minimal request of information are known to be crucial aspects of the banking and financial industry, and become even more so where some specific customer characteristics are present: illegal immigrants; legal immigrants but with little clarity/legality regarding their social-security, employment and residential positions; legal immigrants with a preference for informal channels for regulatory reasons (fiscal aspects, rules on currency flows, etc) in the country of origin; legal immigrants who, for psychological motives, dictated by the social context of the host country, desire minimal visibility and do not appreciate any type of control or disclosure of personal information.[17]

In the relationship between informal finance and migrants, in essence, we find yet another example of the now-classic lesson of recent economic analysis: exchanges occur only where there is information and sufficient trust. In effect, the capacity of the informal systems to succeed where the formal systems tend to fail has been explored by economic analysis, particularly regarding credit mechanisms.

Under certain conditions, therefore, the informal systems are more efficient than the formal systems. Unexplored, on the other hand, is the relationship between covertness and integrity, in terms of the risk that these channels may satisfy the demand for illegal financial services, and particularly serve for purposes of money-laundering and financing terrorism.

Based on the considerations advanced earlier regarding the characteristics that make a system attractive to those individuals or organisations wishing to conceal the origin or destination of given monetary flows, it seems evident that covert finance may appear particularly effective with respect to these purposes.

Both money laundering and money dirtying are based on a need for concealment. Informality, other conditions being equal, reduces the traceability of both the origin and destination of the financial flows. While the sharing of common fiduciary assets also imposes confidentiality, or better secrecy, the impermeability of informal systems to the acquisition of information by outsiders is greatly reduced, especially if the outsiders are authorities, and all the more if they are representatives of foreign countries. Therefore, at least at the level of deductive reasoning, the riskiness of informal finance systems, in terms of their use by criminal or terrorist organisations, seems greater than that attributable to overt finance, banking and non-banking.

Lax Financial Regulation: Key Concepts

As noted earlier, we treat the regulation of money laundering as a product, with a demand and supply schedule. But whose demand schedule is driving the system?

We assume that the policymaker in a given country has not yet decided the direction that it will impose on its financial regulation, with specific regard to money laundering. The policymaker may thus decide to implement regulations that create serious obstacles to money laundering, and thus to terrorism and organised crime, or it may decide – at the other extreme – to make the opposite choice, devising lax regulations that facilitate money laundering.

---

[17] See Ferri and Masciandaro (2003).

Global Financial Crime

Money laundering generates costs as well as benefits for the parties involved. The costs for society depend on the fact that more predicate offences will be committed by terrorist or criminal organisation if money laundering is possible, and on the possible negative impact that money laundering will have on the economic system.[18]

The benefits of money laundering accrue, first of all, to terrorist and criminal organisations, which can employ the proceeds of crime and avoid the threat of prosecution for predicate offences (money laundering in the strict sense), or which can use legal capital to finance illegal activities (money dirtying). The similarities and differences between money laundering and money dirtying were discussed above and in Chapters 1 and 2.

On the other side of the transaction, money laundering offers the host country the possibility to earn a 'commission' in exchange for its services – what we can call *the expected national benefits* due to lax financial regulation.

Therefore, we can identify four different categories of actors potentially interested in regulation: a) the policymakers; b) terrorist and criminal organisations, deriving utility from the possibility of laundering money; c) those who bear the costs of money laundering; d) the financial community and, in general, the citizens that receive benefits from the inflow of foreign black and grey capital.

Starting with this last category, it seems difficult to predict which side the financial community will take. In general, we tend to think that the utility function of financial intermediaries does not appear to be affected by whether profits stem from legal or illegal financial activities (*pecunia non olet*). We think that they simply maximise the expected revenues, and that, given the asymmetric information issues, they are not able to distinguish clearly the customers' nature, legal or illegal.[19]

The interests of b) and c) are obviously incompatible, as the gains of the former depend on the losses of the latter; a) appears to be caught in the middle, having to decide which demand schedule to follow.

Note that we are not assuming that b) and c) are necessarily based *outside* the country where the policymaker we are concerned with is based. This is not an assumption, but rather the consequence of our line of argument. As with all policy issues, as long as the costs and benefits of a decision fall within the boundaries of the area of influence of the policymaker, we expect to have an efficient decision. Policymakers in countries where crime or terrorism is pervasive will tend to bear at least some of the costs associated with a decision to favour money laundering.

Countries where organised crime or terrorism is pervasive might appear to play a minor role in the offer of black or grey financial services at the international level, because they are sensitive to terrorism – and crime – related national costs. This might be so because the widespread presence of organised crime or terrorism

---

[18] For an economic analysis of money laundering as a multiplier of the economic and financial impact of criminal organisations, see Masciandaro (1998 and 1999).

[19] For an economic analysis of the role of banking and financial intermediaries in the money laundering process, see Masciandaro (1996) and Johnson and Lim (2002).

in the country increases, for the policymaker, the costs of regulations that favour money laundering.[20]

The public will bear the costs of the decision and will hold the policymaker responsible. Entering the international market for money laundering services has a greater potential for countries that are immune from terrorist or criminal activities. By definition, such countries will almost be able to externalise the costs associated with the increase of predicate offences.[21] A negative correlation between crime rate or terrorist episodes in the country and the role played in the offering of money laundering services appears likely.

As a result of this process, some countries which do not bear the costs associated with money laundering become predisposed to adopting lax regulations that facilitate money laundering. The other side of the coin is that both criminal and terrorist organisations and those who bear the costs stemming from money laundering will 'naturally' tend to be situated in countries other than the one where the regulations are adopted.

We have thus limited our attention to policymakers that are based in countries different from those which the other actors potentially interested in the regulations are based in. From this starting point, the confrontation between those who benefit from money laundering and those who suffer from it is almost a 'win-win' game for criminal and terrorist organisations.

Organised crime and terrorism enjoy huge asymmetrical organisational advantages over those who bear the costs of money laundering. A small, powerful group opposes a large, dispersed group, thus making the outcome predictable.[22]

---

[20] We are here leaving aside the possibility of corruption or even mere lobbying by groups interested in having regulations favourable to money laundering. Through corruption, organised crime might be able to urge the adoption of legislation that facilitates money laundering. We believe this possibility to be less important than it may appear at first glance. For reasons that are developed below, a corrupted state will find it difficult to make a credible commitment not to expropriate the assets of illicit origin.

[21] These countries will still be exposed to the other source of costs identified above, i.e. distortion in the functioning of the financial market. This source of costs, however, can be controlled through 'ring fencing' practices. Thus, offshore centres might try to build a Chinese wall to insulate their financial system from the effects of involvement in money laundering schemes. A regime favourable to money laundering, for example, might explicitly or implicitly exclude residents from taking advantage of its benefits. Conversely, 'firms' that benefit from a given regime may be explicitly or implicitly prohibited from operating in the domestic market. Both of these provisions would ensure the offshore centre that criminal organisations seeking to benefit from the regime do not 'reside' in the OFC. A similar goal is served by multi-tiered licensing systems. Under such a system, an OFC offers two rather different licences to financial intermediaries, one 'restricted' and the other 'unrestricted'. A typical multi-tiered regime states that restricted licensees may not engage in transactions with residents inside the OFC. They may not collect deposits or even make certain investments. Similar restrictions may also apply to the ability of restricted licensees to solicit funds from the general public. The raison d'être of rules of this type is easily perceived: they aim at generating externalities, or more precisely, at avoiding the internalisation of costs associated with money laundering.

[22] See Olson (1965) for a classical exposition of the dynamics of collective action.

To be sure, money-laundering regulation could be opposed, and indeed is opposed, by political authorities that represent the public interest. The dispersion of the costs, however, makes money laundering a low salience issue for the public, and consequently quite low on the political agenda. The man on the street simply does not feel the bite of money laundering, and political actors will act as a consequence.

These hypotheses – i.e. the role of *expected national benefits* and of *terrorism and crime expected national costs* – will be formalised in the analytical part of the paper and tested in the empirical part.

The foregoing line of argument will help us in the following paragraphs to shed light on the explanations of the simple observation that LFR countries tend to be small. Most often they also tend to be islands. In explaining the determinants of the size of 'political units', economic historians have focused on the pressure generated by the need to internalise the costs associated with economic activities. For example, the growth of nation states in the Middle Ages can be explained by the need for 'political units' that could internalise the costs required to support the expansion of trade.

In the competition among 'political units', only those that were able to grow were able to exploit the opportunities offered by the expansion of trade. A converse effect appears to be at work when we come to LFR countries. The need to externalise costs associated with money laundering generates pressures that tend to select countries that are better equipped for the job, countries that may keep organised crime or terrorism – and the costs associated with it – outside the country.

Opportunism, Commitment and Reputation: Lax Financial Regulations as a Contractual Device

The paragraph above shows that some countries will be able to externalise the costs associated with lax financial regulations, thus being in an advantageous position vis-à-vis their competitors in the supply of money laundering services. This advantage, however, does not resolve all the problems faced by a potential LFR country.

A closer look at the exchange reveals the problems that need to be solved by both parties. For sake of simplicity, we will juxtapose two parties, the Criminal (or Terrorist) and the LFR country.

Consider a single money-laundering operation: it is not a simultaneous game. Parties do not exchange at arm's length a service for a price or a good for a price. It is rather a game in which one party moves first and the other moves second. That is to say, Criminal or Terrorist has to move first, deciding whether to put his assets into the hands of the LFR country or not. Criminal (Terrorist) is therefore a particularly vulnerable consumer of the LFR country's products.

Assume that the Criminal (Terrorist) decides to move. Once the capital is in the domain of the LFR country, the latter moves. The agreement is that the LFR country will launder the assets, keep a commission for this service, and then return the laundered assets to the Criminal (Terrorist). So the LFR country will earn the commission, a fraction of the overall value of the assets.

The LFR country, however, may choose another strategy. It may decide not to co-operate and appropriate the assets. By definition, this strategy implies that the payoff to the LFR country will be larger than the co-operation pay off.[23] In game theory jargon, the strategy of non-co-operation is a strictly dominant strategy: the LFR country will always decide to appropriate.[24]

There is, in short, the threat of ex post opportunistic switches by LFR countries. In the context of relations between LFR countries and illegal organisations, appropriation might take several forms, running the full gamut from outright taking to merely not responding to the need to keep financial regulations up to date.

The threat of opportunistic behaviour feeds back into the incentive structure of the Criminal (Terrorist). Ex ante the exchange, the Criminal (Terrorist) perceives the possibility that the LFR country will appropriate the assets. This result unravels, thus implying that the Criminal (Terrorist) will not put the assets in the hands of the LFR country in the first place, in order to avoid a sure loss. The threat of ex post opportunistic behaviour by the LFR country translates into the absence of any exchange.

Note that this is a negative result for both parties to the (potential) exchange. Had they been able to co-operate and to realise the exchange, they would have both gained: the Criminal (Terrorist) from the laundering of the proceeds, and the LFR country from the price charged for the service.

Despite the potential for a mutually beneficial exchange, the non-simultaneous nature of the game will result in a Pareto move not being made. Unless the Criminal (Terrorist) is assured that the LFR country will not behave opportunistically, the exchange will not take place. In other words, the problem is to transform a non-co-operative game into a co-operative one.

The problem is exacerbated by the environment in which the relation between Criminal (Terrorist) and LFR country takes place. As is well known, the existence of a state providing an efficient contract law and an efficient enforcement system might manage to help the party to co-operate. The LFR country and the Criminal (Terrorist), however, bargain in the absence of a superior authority that might perform such a function. The threat of opportunistic behaviour is further exacerbated by the circumstance that one of the parties, i.e. the LFR country, also plays the role of the enforcer.

But this is not the end of the story. To be sure, the Criminal (Terrorist) perceives the threat of ex post opportunistic behaviour by the LFR country and will act consequently, but also the LFR country perceives that the Criminal (Terrorist) will not accept the exchange. Solving the problem is in the interest of both parties: in the absence of a superior authority, this becomes the province of endogenous mechanisms of governance.[25] More specifically, the parties will have two different

---

[23] That is to say that the pay-off to the OFC will be represented by the *whole* amount of the assets and not by a mere commission.

[24] For a classical account of an ex post opportunistic breach by a state, see Grandy (1989).

[25] Williamson (1985) and (1996).

but interrelated lines of action that are capable of transforming a non-co-operative game into a co-operative one.

On the one hand, a non-co-operative game may become a co-operative game if repeated over time.[26] We expect the LFR country and the Criminal (Terrorist) to develop a relational contract, a relation between parties that lasts over a long period of time.[27] Rather than playing single money laundering games with different counterparts, parties will have an incentive to play repeatedly with the same opponent. From this point of view, the regulation adopted by the LFR country can be regarded as the *contractual device* that will govern the relationship as events unfold.[28]

This is the main reason why, in our view, in order to analyse the optimal policy against terrorism finance and organised crime finance, we have to concentrate our attention on the regulation architecture.

The second and interrelated line of action aims at reinforcing the relationship. If the main difficulty for the LFR country is gaining the Criminal's (Terrorist's) confidence that it will not renege on the agreement, then the issue becomes one of devising a credible commitment not to behave opportunistically. The competition for attracting the black capital will be won by countries that are able to resolve the commitment problem credibly.

On the face of it, this observation explains why we do not expect to find 'corrupted' or 'criminal' countries on the supply side of the market for illegal financial services. A Banana Republic, for example, would face immense difficulties in making a credible commitment not to switch course in the middle of the contract. The mere threat that a coup d'état might at any moment overthrow the current regime makes the commitment non-credible. Successful states will tend to show a stable political situation.

Extreme cases of political instability aside, however, the way the LFR country can commit not to behave opportunistically ex post the exchange depends on its ability to invest in what Williamson terms 'transaction specific assets'.[29]

Transaction specific assets cannot be profitably redeployed outside the original relationship. Once a party has invested in such assets, therefore, it has an incentive to continue the relationship, lest it lose the value of the investment. In other words, the LFR country will need to post a hostage,[30] i.e. an asset whose value will be lost if the relationship breaks down due to an opportunistic switch by the LFR country itself.

---

[26] This is only true, however, apart from end game problems, i.e. problems that arise when the last period comes and the parties know that they will not play together anymore.

[27] The literature on relational contracting is immense; leading contributions are Williamson (1979, 1985 and 1996); MacNeil (1978).

[28] Of course, bounded rationality implies that this contract cannot be complete, i.e. cannot foresee all contingencies. As we shall see in the next paragraph, this limitation has fundamental consequences for the governance of the relationship, mandating the adoption of some form of *ex post* governance structure.

[29] Williamson (1985 and 1996).

[30] Williamson (1983).

The most obvious hostage, commonly used in such settings, is reputation. Reputation is often of one and only one use, thus making investments in this asset sunk. While asset specificity is a common feature of reputation, reputation for offering efficient money laundering services, free from the risk of ex post opportunistic behaviour, appears to show an extreme degree of asset specificity.

Such reputation requires an intricate set of rules and mechanisms. More specifically, regulation of the financial sector will need to be tuned to reach this goal. The rules concerning banking secrecy, incorporation of business entities, co-operation with supervisory authorities abroad, the duties to report suspicious transactions, to identify and register customers: all these rules will need to be shaped so as to provide an efficient money laundering service.[31] Investments need to be made in order to gain a reputation for providing such an efficient service.

Paradoxically, the value of these investments in the closest use is probably negative, rather than being merely zero or slightly more. A country that has chosen to invest – in a broader term – in the technology necessary to build a solid reputation as a supplier of first class money laundering services will experience serious difficulties in converting such investments into the next best use. Potential partners of the financial sector situated abroad may be rather sceptical about the credibility of the change in strategy by the LFR country.

Should these LFR countries decide to switch course and convert their financial systems to lawful uses, they may well start from a negative point rather than merely from zero. Investments will be needed to nullify the reputation as a supplier of criminal financial services. Once this goal is reached, further investments will be required to build from scratch a new reputation as a supplier of lawful financial services. On this point of view, in the theoretical section, we have to investigate the role of such *international reputation expected costs*.

So far we have examined reputation as a pre-commitment device. The LFR country may, however, use other means to obtain the same results. LFR countries tend to rely on the income generated by their financial activity, so a change in policy would be extremely costly for them. This because they would experience severe damage to their level of income.

This observation helps to explain why we can imagine finding among LFR countries some territories that experience a low level of income and a high dependence on the revenues of their financial industry: they need continuously to offer financial services to criminal and terrorist organisations, because they want to preserve their level of income or perhaps increase it.

Furthermore, dependence on income generated by money laundering is yet another committing device.[32] A country whose level of income is dependent on the supply of illegal financial services will be committed to offering those services. Such a country might need to fight vigorously in order to preserve its level of

---

[31] Of course, for some of the subjects mentioned in the text, the efficient rule, from the reputational point of view, will be simply no rule, as is the case with duties to report suspicious transaction reports.

[32] Romano (1993) interprets Delaware's dependence on income generated by franchise taxes as a pre-commitment device.

income. Countermeasures taken by the international community may drive it to aggressively defend its position.

Compare this case with that of a country whose level of income stems from several sources. The loss generated by the repeal of a policy that attracts capital of illicit origins will represent a fraction of the overall income generated by the state. The incidence of the loss is thus, by definition, less severe.

Dependence on revenues – i.e. the level of *expected national benefits* – produced by money laundering makes an LFR country a hostage to its own success. In turn, this hostage-like dependence reinforces the bilateral relationship between criminal/terrorist organisations and LFR countries. The former are exposed to the threat of opportunistic behaviour, but the latter are exposed to the risk of losing reputation and revenues should they behave opportunistically. Both parties gain from preserving their relationship.

Lax Financial Regulations and Institutions

Some natural features of certain countries appear to put them in an advantageous position in comparison to other countries. The reference to the 'natural' character of such features is intended to imply that such features are not only the result of a specific choice by the LFR country.

The opposite is true, in fact. These features are sometimes the result of accidents of history; and in some cases they have even been imposed on the LFR country – as in the case of the colonisation of the country by another country that adopted that system. The 'natural' features of a winning LFR country will show a sort of 'macro' aspect – a low crime rate, the lack of natural resources, the adoption of a common law regime – just to anticipate some macro variables that we will use in the empirical part of this chapter.[33]

Once these features have put the specific LFR country down the path of competition with other LFR centres, however, a demand will arise for institutions to help the LFR country compete more vigorously. Competitive pressure will urge the adoption of tools useful in the struggle for survival. Starting from the initial positions, a process of refinement through the adoption of newer institutions seems likely.

As this process proceeds, 'micro' institutional devices will be put in place. Interest groups inside the FLR centre will lobby for complementary institutions that increase the value of the existing ones. The institutional environment inside the LFR country will thus be driven, domino-like, by a chain of linked

---

[33] Of course, the distinction between 'macro' and 'micro' institutional devices should not be regarded as one of 'quality' but rather of 'quantity', and we use it for mere sake of presentation. With the former we refer to more general and profound institutional features that tend to characterise a given country with respect to another. By 'micro' institutional devices, we mean rules of a more detailed nature.

complementary institutions,[34] that will add to the survival value of the overall package.

The task of newer institutions appears to be twofold. First, the institutions need to contribute to the overall efficiency of the regulation offered to customers of the OFC; a strict banking secrecy regime, for example, or rules that protect the anonymity of beneficial owners of accounts.

Far more interesting for the subject of this chapter, however, is the second function of these 'micro' institutional devices: over time, institutional devices that buttress the commitment by the LFR centre are likely to materialise.

What will these pre-commitment devices look like? Anything that limits the ability of the LFR country to renege on its agreement with the criminal and terrorist organisations will do the job. The process of differential survival will select the solutions that serve the pre-commitment function. While we expect to observe functional convergence, we also expect to observe a diversity within these devices, whose spectrum is likely to range from a formal and explicit set of rules, such as constitutional rules, to mere norms.

The most obvious case is a supermajority requirement for the repeal of certain pieces of legislation. For example, a rule that states that banking secrecy regulation can be repealed only by the vote of two-thirds of the legislative body makes it more difficult for the LFR country to switch course after Criminal or Terrorism has made its move.[35] A second device could be a provision to the effect that repeal or modification of a given regulation requires prior approval by organisations representing interests that benefit from regulations sympathetic to money laundering.

For example, the need to obtain the consensus of the bankers' association or the bar will make it more difficult for the LFR country to renege on the agreement. Financial institutions, lawyers, and any other group that makes a business of supplying financial services within an international money-laundering scheme will fiercely lobby against any initiative that undermines the credibility of the commitment. Even a mere customary norm that requires consultations with the interest groups involved will do, as long as it increases for the LFR country the costs of changing its course of action and behaving opportunistically.

To be sure, none of these devices is, in itself, a showstopper. Any rule that aims at making the procedure more cumbersome might be repealed, thus allowing for the subsequent repeal of the pro-money laundering rule. Consider a procedural rule that requires consultations to be held before any modification of rules concerning the financial system may be approved. In anticipation that the financial sector will oppose a change in the regulations that implies an opportunistic switch, the legislative body might first vote to repeal the procedural requirement and then move on to approve the modification to the regulations. Yet, such a procedure would appear cumbersome on the face of it. The rule still achieves the goal of increasing the costs of an ex post opportunistic switch, thus helping to fortify the credibility of the commitment.

---

[34] The observations in the text are based on Gilson (2000).

[35] See Romano (1993) for the description of a similar provision in Delaware.

A final remark: the contractual relationship between the LFC country and the Criminal or Terrorist is governed, in the first place, by the regulations put in place by the LFR country. In a world of bounded rationality, however, contracts are hopelessly incomplete. The implicit contract stipulated by the LFC country and the Criminal or Terrorist is no exception. The regulation cannot specify ex ante all future contingencies.

Contractual gaps are always inescapable but, in the setting we are concerned with, the problem appears to be exacerbated by the possibility that one party to the exchange might not reveal all relevant information to the other. The illicit nature of the capital involved appears to create an incentive for the Criminal (Terrorist) to hide some information from the LFR country. In fact, there may well be instances in which the Terrorist or Criminal will have a clear incentive to disclose false information to the LFR country. Beyond the ordinary incompleteness deriving from the costs necessary to write contract clauses,[36] there is an increased risk that the contract will suffer from 'strategic incompleteness'.[37]

Whether it is the result of transaction costs or of strategic behaviour, less information translates into more gaps in the contract. The need arises for gap-filling devices that allow the parties to work out contingencies that were not provided for at the outset.

A country that is able to offer better gap-filling devices will be in an advantageous position. This shifts the focus of attention towards those features of the legal system that come under severe pressure when it comes to the ex post governance of unspecified contingencies.

We focus on one specific feature that supports the exchange, i.e. the judicial system. The regulations adopted by the LFR country fill gaps ex ante, up to the point where the marginal cost and benefit of an added rule are equalised. Remaining gaps can be filled ex post by the courts.

To be sure, the likelihood that a given dispute between illegal organisations and their counterparts inside the LFR country will go to court might appear low, and indeed it seems reasonable to assume this is so.

At the same time, however, remembering the IMF money-laundering estimations and Schneider's terrorism finance estimations in Chapter 3, the huge amounts of capital at stake implies that even with a low probability that a dispute will actually go to court, an efficient judiciary might still represent a high present value for the parties. An efficient judiciary works as a last resort mechanism, capable of generating positive externalities on ongoing relations, regardless of whether the question actually goes to court.

Keeping the quality of regulation constant, therefore, the package that includes the most efficient judicial system will tend to prevail in the competition.

The importance of the judicial power in ensuring the success of an LFR country also appears underscored from a different perspective. The need to fill gaps ex post does not necessarily imply that the gap-filling function *must* be entrusted to judges.

---

[36] On which see Williamson (1985).
[37] Strategic incompleteness is explored for example in Ayres and Gertner (1989).

At a purely theoretical level, LFR countries could choose to allocate the gap-filling function to the same decisional centre responsible for the adoption of the regulation. This solution would probably be infeasible for very practical reasons. When the decision-making agent that drafted the regulations in the first place is a collective body – a parliament – entrusting the gap-filling function to it would be highly impractical.[38]

But let us assume, for add the sake of argument, that the ex ante and ex post gap-filling functions are joined. Problems of opportunism aside, this might imply greater familiarity with the issues involved and therefore a higher probability that gaps will be filled in a way consistent with the interest of both parties. By contrast, this advantage is partially lost if the function to decide ex post what the parties involved would have wanted is shifted to a third party.

However, putting the threat of opportunistic behaviour back in the picture reveals another potential advantage of an efficient judiciary. An increased role of judges in filling gaps can also be thought of as one more tool in the 'pre-commitment' package that a country offers to potential customers. Assigning the task to fill the gaps in the incomplete contract to a judge might also serve another function: À *la* Madison,[39] fragmenting the powers among many decision-making agents helps to ensure that none of them will be able to abuse those powers. An opportunistic switch by the legislative body is likely to require validation by the judiciary. The country that strictly separates the ex ante and ex post gap-filling functions will make its commitment more credible.[40]

Lax Financial Regulations as an Endogenous Variable: the Model

Now we can try to design analytically the key elements of our approach. In defining the optimal characteristics of financial regulations aimed at promoting an influx of hidden funds into a given country, we focus on the actions of a national policymaker in what we shall call a Lax Financial Regulation (LFR) country.

Let us assume that this policymaker is aware that a potential demand for money laundering exists on the part of one or more criminal or terrorist organisations for a total amount equal to W. We analyse a situation in which the international market of money laundering is demand-driven, as it is likely to be in the real world: every potential LFR jurisdiction is a relatively 'small country'.

---

[38] Every dispute should be examined by a structure whose decision making costs are high, especially if compared with those borne by a single decision making agent, say a judge. The latter can ensure a much higher speed of response, thus being able to handle more issues than the former. Quite obviously, the mere circumstance that in the real world the task to resolve disputes ex post the exchange is indeed entrusted in third parties shows that different solutions would be impracticable.

[39] See the 'famous' Madison (1787).

[40] This observation obviously paves the way for questions concerning the procedures by which judges are appointed and the possible effects of the procedures on the incentive structure of the judge. For example, life tenure is likely to produce different results from a short term tenure with the possibility of reappointment.

Each LFR country can define the optimal degree of financial laxity and then determine its own optimal level of money laundering services. The design of financial regulations represents the contractual device that determines the relationships between the country and the illegal organisations.[41]

The policymaker may decide to launder an amount of cash equal to Y, where of course $0<Y<W$. In our simple model, the decision on the optimal level of money laundering services is equivalent to the choice of the optimal degree of financial laxity.

Calling U the utility function of the policymaker, it is obvious that the expected utility from unlaundered profits is zero, whatever their amount:

$$U(W - Y) = 0 \qquad\qquad\qquad (4.1)$$

On the other hand, every dollar (or euro?)[42] laundered can have a positive expected value for the policymaker, since the LFR country can derive benefits from offering financial services that facilitate money laundering. In the preceding paragraphs we showed how a country could derive economic advantages from favouring money laundering.

For example, one might hypothesise that the *lower* the national income and the *higher* the proportion of that income dependent on the financial industry, the greater the propensity to offer money laundering services, all other things being equal. In general, let us define those expected national benefits as *laxity benefits*.

Then the fact that the laundered cash, which we shall indicate with Y, has a positive expected profitability for the policymaker may be grasped by imagining that the monetary value B of this benefit is equal to:

$$B = mY \qquad\qquad\qquad (4.2)$$

where $m>0$ is the expected net rate of return on the money laundering services offered (i.e. on the degree of laxity) by the LFR country. The inflow of black and grey foreign capital produces national revenues, increasing activity in the financial industry and then through the traditional macroeconomic multiplier effects.[43]

---

[41] In the model, the policymaker's choice of the optimal degree of financial laxity is assumed to be equivalent to the decision on the optimal supply level of money laundering financial services. An alternative view should be to consider the degree of regulation laxity as one of the possible instrumental variables in order to define the optimal supply of money laundering services. It is a fact, however, that the link between money-laundering supply and other kinds of public policy is logically and empirically weaker. Furthermore, it should be easy to model the relationship between laxity and money laundering, considering both random effects and lag effects.

[42] For the use of the dollar or euro in the black economy, see Boeschoten and Fase (1992), Rogoff (1997), Sinn and Westermann (2001).

[43] For a macroeconomic analysis of the relationships between money laundering, legal and illegal economic sectors see Masciandaro (2000).

If the decision to launder were cost-free, indicating with Y the amount of illegal funds for which the policymaker institutes the money-laundering service, it would be a simple matter to see that $Y = W$. But things are not that simple.

In the first place, an LFR country may be subject to *international reputation expected costs*. In the preceding paragraphs we stressed that to be more attractive to criminal or terrorist organisations a country must make legislative and regulatory choices that increase its credibility as an LFR country. These choices may carry a reputation cost, however, since being an LFR country may result in negative backlashes, whether in relation to capital, intermediaries and companies sensitive to integrity or to international relations in general. In fact, we have stressed the possibility that under-regulation may be as unattractive for some legal investors as over-regulation.[44]

Secondly, an LFR country must consider that laundering money means strengthening internal organised crime or terrorism, i.e. there may be *crime and terrorism expected national costs*. The policymaker must first consider the possibility that domestic social damage may derive from the fact that the country is a possible growth engine for criminal organisations. It is obvious, on the other hand, that the less the LFR country registers the actual or potential presence of criminal or terrorist organisations internally, the lower the perceived costs of crime will be.

In our framework we do not separate the crime expected costs from the terrorist expected costs. From the theoretical point of view, we prefer to stress the difference in policymaker sensitivity between international expected costs and national expected costs, based on a clearly different political cost-benefit analysis, that characterised every LFR country. Furthermore, for each LFR country, it should not be difficult to introduce in expression (4.3) a specific parameter for each national expected cost factor.

The cost C of offering money laundering for an LFR country will therefore consist of two parts.

First, let us assume that the reputation cost is proportional – according to a parameter $c>0$ – to the amount of cash it is asked to launder. Secondly, there will be a crime or terrorist cost whose expected value rises as the laundered money increases, for a multiple of the parameter $\gamma>0$.

Let us assume, in other words, that for political-electoral reasons the policymaker in the LFR country, all other things being equal, is more sensitive to the crime and/or terrorist cost, which can weigh directly on the country's citizens, than to the reputation cost, whose effect on the citizens-voters is probably less perceptible and direct. We therefore have:

---

[44] The inflow of legal capital can be assumed as negatively correlated with financial laxity, because of two main effects: a) a competitive effect: in the overt financial sector, competition is distorted and the allocative efficiency of the market is undermined because of extreme financial laxity; and b) a reputation effect: legitimate customers may fear suffering a loss of reputation from locating their businesses in a country highly suspected of money laundering.

$$C = cY + \gamma^2 Y \tag{4.3}$$

Lastly, we must consider, as pointed out earlier, that the existence of an LFR country is an increasing source of economic, political and social risk for the international community. Therefore, when a country decides whether and to what extent to institute a regulatory design that will, in essence, offer money laundering services, it must consider that this activity bears risks: we assume that the international community might consider it a censurable policy, perhaps even prohibited, and as such subject to sanctions and punitive countermeasures.

Let us assume, therefore, that offering money-laundering services may bring with it an international sanction, whose equivalent monetary value is S, and a probability p that this conduct will be discovered by the international community and thus sanctioned.

The probability p can be defined as the *degree of technical enforcement* of the international sanction. Let us call these risks the *international sanction expected costs*. In this way we are able to reflect in our model the possibility that the international community may issue explicit sanctions against the LFR country.

The monetary value of the damage from sanctions S against the money laundering must be at least equal to the value Y of the laundered money. In reality, the damage from a sanction is certainly a multiple, because of the value of the intangible damage related to such international sanctions. So we can assume that the amount of the international sanctions is a multiple of the 'laundry' volume, equal, for simplicity of computation, to the square of that sum.

And we should also consider that once the crime is discovered, the international community would apply the sanctions with varying degrees of severity, based on a political cost-benefit analysis. The rapidity and procedure for applying the punishment may be variable, affected by national or international structural variables; this *severity* (or, if you wish, *the degree of political enforcement*)[45] by which the sanctions are applied can be expressed by variations in the parameter t:

$$S = tY^2 \tag{4.4}$$

Thus, the dilemma of choice facing the policymaker is the following: if I design lax regulations that favour the offering of money laundering, and the international community does not impose sanctions, the benefit for the LFR country is positive, net of the expected cost associated with reputation costs and crime and terrorism risks. If, on the other hand, the LFR country is hit by explicit international sanctions, it will not only sustain the expected costs but will also be damaged by the international sanctions. The game is between the policymaker and Nature, since we will assume the 'small country' hypothesis.

Having defined the terms of the problem, the policymaker is thus faced with the problem of deciding whether and how much to launder, i.e. defining the optimal

---

[45] Rider (2002) noted that international monetary policy is susceptible to political considerations.

level of laxity. The optimal policy is not derived by any social utility function but is the result of the policymaker's maximising process, based on his own political cost-benefits analysis. The policymaker's expected utility E can now be better specified as:

$$E(U) = u[(1-p)(B-C) - p(C+T)] \tag{4.5}$$

But since we have defined $B = m\,Y$ and $C = c\,Y + \gamma^2\,Y$, then (4.5) becomes:

$$E(U) = u(1-p)\{mY - cY - \gamma^2 Y\} - up(cY + \gamma^2 Y + tY^2) \tag{4.6}$$

The linear specification of the function of policymaker utility tells us that it is a neutral risk subject. This utility function is consistent with the better economic characteristics in this situation. In fact:

$$\frac{\partial E}{\partial p} = u\left[-mY + cY + \gamma^2 Y - (cY + tY^2 + \gamma^2 Y)\right]$$
$$= uY(-tY - m) = -uY(tY + m) < 0$$
$$\frac{\partial E}{\partial t} = -upY^2 < 0$$
$$\frac{\partial E}{\partial m} = u(1-p)Y > 0$$

In other words, we find that the utility for the policymaker, and therefore for the FLR country, declines as the probability of international sanctions and their severity increase, while it increases as the expected return on the money laundering activity increases.

The policymaker must now determine the optimal level Y^* of money to launder, bearing in mind that the maximum resources available to him, given the potential demand expressed by the criminal or terrorist organisations, amounts to W. Differentiating (4.6) for that variable subject to the policymaker's decision – to observe the conditions necessary and sufficient for a maximum – we find that:

$$\frac{\partial E}{\partial Y} = u\left[(1-p)(m-c-\gamma^2) - pc - 2tpY - p\gamma^2\right]$$
$$= u\left[(1-p)m - c - \gamma^2 + cp - cp - 2ptY\right]$$
$$= -u(2ptY + c + \gamma^2 - m(1-p))$$
$$\frac{\partial^2 E}{\partial Y} = -2upt < 0$$

Proposition One*: it is possible to define the optimal level of laxity.*

The function reaches its maximum at the point

$$\frac{\partial E}{\partial Y} = 0$$

i.e.:

$$\left(2ptY + c + \gamma^2 - m(1-p)\right) = 0$$

which gives us:

$$Y^* = \frac{m(1-p) - c - \gamma^2}{2pt}$$

where Y^* represents the optimal level of money laundering supply services that is equivalent to the optimal degree of financial laxity. Let us observe that for $Y^* > 0$ it must be $m(1-p) - c - \gamma^2 > 0$, i.e. the factor of expected benefit from the money-laundering activity, considering the probability of international sanctions, is greater than the sum of the reputation and crime and terrorism cost factors. Let us define this condition as the *laxity condition*.

It is also possible to define the critical value Y' that marks the limit beyond which it is definitely optimal for the policymaker to abstain from offering money-laundering services. Over a certain amount, the damage associated with the risk of being punished by the international community is so high that the expected utility is negative, so being an FLR country would not be beneficial.

All other conditions being equal, this result depends on the fact that the amount of the sanction is a multiple of the cash to be laundered, so as this value rises the damage from detection of the crime rises more than proportionately. In general, this result stresses the importance of having an effective design for the international sanctioning mechanisms.

The critical value Y' must, of course, be compared with the level of potential demand for resources to launder W. If $Y' < W$, the amount of resources $(W - Y')$ will be excluded a priori by any laundering decision. If $Y' > W$, on the other hand, laundering is potentially advantageous for all the available illegal resources. We must then determine the actual level Y'.

Let us see to what value Y' corresponds:

$$E(U) = u\left[(1-p)\{(1+r)Y - cY - \gamma^2 Y\} - p\left(cY + \gamma^2 Y + tY^2\right)\right]$$

$$E(U) = uY\left[(1-p)\left(m - c - \gamma^2\right) - cp - p\gamma^2 - tpY\right]$$

therefore $E(U) = 0$ when

$$
\begin{cases}
Y = 0 \\[2ex]
Y' = \dfrac{\left[(1-p)\left(m - c - \gamma^2\right)\right] - cp - p\gamma^2}{tp} \\[2ex]
 = \dfrac{(1-p)m - c - \gamma^2 + \gamma^2 p - \gamma^2 p + cp - cp}{tp} = \dfrac{(1-p)m - c - \gamma^2}{tp}
\end{cases}
$$

We can show the relationships with the structural variables of the model for the optimal level of laxity Y^*. Firstly, the optimal offering of money laundering will be inversely proportional to the probability of international sanctions:

$$Y^* = \frac{m(1-p) - c - \gamma^2}{2pt} = \frac{1}{2}Y'$$

$$\frac{\partial Y^*}{\partial p} = \frac{-2mpt - 2t\left[(1-p)m - c - \gamma^2\right]}{(2pt)^2}$$

$$= \frac{-2mpt - 2tm + 2ptm + 2ct + 2t\gamma^2}{(2pt)^2}$$

$$= \frac{-2tm + 2ct + 2t\gamma^2}{(2pt)^2}$$

$$= \frac{\left(c + \gamma^2 - m\right)}{2p^2 t} < 0$$

$$\frac{\partial^2 Y^*}{\partial p} = \frac{-4pt\left(c + \gamma^2 - m\right)}{4p^4 t^2} = \frac{m - c - \gamma^2}{p^3 t} > 0$$

Therefore, since we have assumed $m > c + \gamma^2$, we find that the first derivative is negative, so the function decreases as the probability of detection increases and the concavity faces upward, i.e. the second derivative is greater than zero. This implies proposition two.

Proposition Two: *the optimal degree of laxity increases as the degree of technical enforcement decreases.*

$Y^*(p) = 0$, i.e. it intersects the x-axis at point:

$$Y* = \frac{m(1-p)-c-\gamma^2}{2pt} = 0 \text{ which means:}$$

$$(1-p)m-c-\gamma^2 = 0$$

$$\Rightarrow m-pm-c-\gamma^2 = 0 \Rightarrow p = \frac{m-c-\gamma^2}{m}$$

and we can also say that for

$$p \rightarrow 0 \qquad\qquad\qquad Y* \rightarrow +\infty$$

$$p \rightarrow 1 \qquad\qquad\qquad Y* \rightarrow \frac{-c-\gamma^2}{2t}$$

As expected, when there are no costs to the LFR country related to its laxity (i.e. $c+\gamma^2 = 0$), that country will abstain from offering money-laundering services ($Y*=0$) only when the international sanctions are absolutely certain ($p=1$).

As p tends toward zero, the optimal level of laxity for the Policymaker tends to $Y* \rightarrow +\infty$, but the Policymaker has available a maximum demand of W, so it must stop with the curve on the probability level at the point where $Y* = W$.

Let us then find the minimum possible value p can take (p_m), i.e. at the point where $Y* = W$:

$$Y* = \frac{m(1-p_m)-c-\gamma^2}{2p_m t} = W$$

$$m-p_m m-c-\gamma^2 = 2Wp_m t$$

$$\Rightarrow 2Wp_m t + p_m m = m-c-\gamma^2$$

$$\Rightarrow p_m(2Wt+m) = m-c-\gamma^2$$

$$\Rightarrow p_m = \frac{m-c-\gamma^2}{2Wt+m}$$

Secondly, the laxity of the LFR country is affected by the severity of the international community in applying the sanction.

Proposition Three: *the optimal degree of laxity increases as the level of political enforcement decreases.*

$$Y* = \frac{m(1-p)-c-\gamma^2}{2pt} =$$

$$\frac{\partial Y*}{\partial t} = \frac{-2p[m(1-p)-c-\gamma^2]}{4p^2 t^2} < 0$$

Therefore, Y^* decreases as t increases. When t tends to $+\infty$ the first derivative is nullified.

What we said about the case where $p = p_m$ also applies here. If, in fact, t tends to zero, we see that Y^* tends to $+\infty$. But this is not possible, because the maximum level of illegal funds available is W. Therefore we must also find the minimum value of t (t_m) at which $Y^* = W$;

$$Y^* = \frac{m(1-p)-c-\gamma^2}{2pt} = W$$

$$= \frac{m(1-p)-c-\gamma^2}{2pt_m} = W$$

$$\Rightarrow m(1-p)-c-\gamma^2 = 2Wpt_m$$

$$\Rightarrow t_m = \frac{m(1-p)-c-\gamma^2}{2Wp}$$

The laxity of the LFR country will depend also on the profitability of the money-laundering services.

Proposition Four: *the optimal degree of laxity increases as the level of national benefits increases.*

$$Y^* = \frac{m(1-p)-c-\gamma^2}{2pt}$$

It is a function of the type $Y = a\,x + b$ where

$$a = \frac{1-p}{2pt} \quad \text{and} \quad b = \frac{-c-\gamma^2}{2pt}$$

$$\frac{\partial Y^*}{\partial m} = \frac{(1-p)}{2pt} > 0$$

$$Y^* = \frac{m(1-p)-c-\gamma^2}{2pt} = 0$$

$$\Rightarrow m(1-p)-c-\gamma^2 = 0$$

$$\Rightarrow m = \frac{c+\gamma^2}{(1-p)}$$

$$Y^* = \frac{m_{max}(1-p)-c-\gamma^2}{2pt} = W$$

$$m_{max} = \frac{2Wpt + c + \gamma^2}{(1-p)}$$

The money-laundering will therefore be non-zero if the profitability lies in the range $[m_m, m_{max}]$.

Finally, we can then analyse the relationship between the reputation cost of money-laundering operations and the amount of money to be laundered.

Proposition Five: *the optimal degree of laxity increases as the level of international reputation costs decreases.*

As one might expect, the relationship is inverse and equal to:

$$Y* = \frac{m(1-p) - c - \gamma^2}{2pt}$$

$Y*(c)$ is a straight line of the type $Y = -ax+b$

If the reputation cost is extremely high, then $Y* = 0$. Let us see for what value of c

$$Y* = \frac{m(1-p) - c_{max} - \gamma^2}{2pt} = 0$$

$$\Rightarrow \frac{m(1-p) - c_{max} - \gamma^2}{2pt} = 0$$

$$\Rightarrow m(1-p) - c_{max} - \gamma^2 = 0$$

$$\Rightarrow c_{max} = m(1-p) - \gamma^2$$

$$\frac{\partial Y*}{\partial c} = \frac{-1}{2pt} < 0$$

$$Y* = \frac{m(1-p) - c - \gamma^2}{2pt} = W$$

$$\frac{m(1-p) - c_m - \gamma^2}{2pt} = W$$

$$\Rightarrow m(1-p) - c_m - \gamma^2 = 2Wpt$$

$$\Rightarrow c_m = m(1-p) - \gamma^2 - 2Wpt$$

Lastly, the money-laundering activity of the LFR country will also depend on the expected crime and terrorism costs, summarised by the parameter γ.

Proposition Six: *the optimal degree of laxity increases as the level of national crime and terrorism costs decreases.*

$$Y* = \frac{m(1-p)-c-\gamma^2}{2pt}$$

$$Y* = \frac{m(1-p)-c-\gamma^2}{2pt} = 0 \Rightarrow \gamma_{max} = \sqrt{[m(1-p)-c]}$$

$$\frac{\partial Y*}{\partial \gamma} = \frac{-\gamma}{pt} < 0$$

$$\frac{\partial^2 Y*}{\partial \gamma} = \frac{-1}{pt} < 0$$

if

$$\gamma = 0 \Rightarrow Y* = \frac{m(1-p)-c}{2pt}$$

As the criminal and terrorism risks for its citizens increase, the propensity of the LFR country to offer money-laundering services decreases. As usual, we can also determine the maximum and minimum values of the parameter γ to which the minimum and maximum values of the optimal laundering activity instituted by the policymaker correspond:

$$Y* = \frac{m(1-p)-c-\gamma^2}{2pt} = W$$

$$\Rightarrow m(1-p)-c-\gamma^2 = 2Wpt$$

$$\Rightarrow \gamma^2 = m(1-p)-c-2Wpt$$

$$\Rightarrow \gamma_{min} = \sqrt{[m(1-p)-c-2Wpt]}$$

Lax Financial Regulations and Non Co-Operative Countries: An Empirical Analysis

In the previous pages, we analysed theoretically the following hypothesis: a given country may find it advantageous to design its financial regulations so as to attract capital of illegal origin, essentially by offering money-laundering services. We have designated these states as LFR countries. The activities of LFR countries produce benefits for terrorism and organised crime.

A country finds it advantageous to become an LFR country because, in defining its objective function, the economic benefits expected from offering money-laundering services are greater than the relative expected costs associated with the internal risk of the development of terrorism and of organised crime, the international risk of loss of reputation, and the possibility of sanctions by the international community. Therefore, the greater the sensitivity of a country to the benefits of money laundering, and the lower its sensitivity to the related costs, the greater is the probability that it will become an LFR country (*Proposition One*).

The utility function assumed here must therefore meet these two fundamental requirements: insensitivity to the production of pollution (terrorism and/or organised crime) and a strong sensitivity to the benefits of providing money laundering services. But what are the economic and institutional characteristics that help define an LFR country? Based on our earlier reflections, taking the international context (i.e. the technical and the political enforcement) to be constant, we can state that:

- An LFR country will be one that, in terms of economic characteristics, has relatively scant physical resources to spend in international trade, and this is an initial channel of *national benefit* expected from lax regulations (*Proposition Four*).
- At the same time, an LFR country has the potential for developing financial services, also useful for money-laundering purposes, and this is a second channel of *national benefit* expected from lax regulations (*Proposition Four*).
- An LFR country also has geographical and social characteristics that shield it, to some extent, from the risks of terrorism and/or organised crime and thus reduce the *expected cost* of lax regulations (*Proposition Six*).
- An LFR country is relatively indifferent to the *expected costs* due to international reputation risks (*Proposition Five*).

However, in reality, what category of countries is actually closest to the LFR country model? The answer is immediate, thinking of the activities of the FATF. As described in Chapter 1, the Financial Action Task Force (FATF) is an intergovernmental body whose objective is to develop and promote policies to combat money laundering, a dangerous process aimed at concealing the illegal income generated by criminal activities.

The FATF currently has 29 member countries[46] and two international organisations.[47] Its membership therefore includes the principal financial centres of Europe, North and South America and Asia.

The organisation is multidisciplinary, a fundamental condition for effectively combating money laundering, and possesses the knowledge of experts in legal, financial and economic questions. The need to cover all the aspects of the war

---

[46] Argentina, Australia, Austria, Belgium, Brazil, Canada, Denmark, Finland, France, Germany, Greece, Hong Kong, Ireland, Iceland, Italy, Japan, Luxembourg, Mexico, Norway, New Zealand, Netherlands, Portugal, United Kingdom, Singapore, Spain, United States, Sweden, Switzerland and Turkey.

[47] The two international organisations are the European Commission and the Gulf Cooperation Council.

against money laundering is reflected in the Forty Recommendations of the FATF, an instrument that the Task Force decided to adopt and that all countries are asked to follow.[48]

These Recommendations were drafted for the first time in 1990 and later revised (1996 and 2003) to incorporate the experience gained in those years and to reflect the evolution in money laundering. They form the working base for the Task Force and an essential framework of effectiveness in combating money laundering.

In particular, since 22 June 2000 the FATF has been publishing a periodic report on non-co-operative countries and territories (NCCTs) in an international effort to combat money laundering: the blacklist. This report lays down 25 criteria, plus eight recent special recommendations, on terrorist financing (Appendix 1) for each country that, if violated, identify the national rules in each country detrimental to international co-operation in the fight against money laundering. These criteria are consistent with the Forty Recommendations.

From June 2000 to February 2003, 45 countries have been monitored (Table 4.1) and seven blacklists have been published, indicating the jurisdictions that fail to conform to the criteria. A total of 23 countries have been identified as effective NCCTs at least once (Figure 4.1).[49]

Analysing the nature of the violations in the NCCTs, country by country, (Table 4.2), we discover an interesting fact: over 50 per cent of the violations concern deficiencies in financial regulation: a lack of, or inadequate, regulations and supervision of financial institutions, inadequate rules for the licensing and creation of financial institutions, inadequate customer identification requirements, excessive secrecy provisions regarding financial institutions, and lack of an efficient system for reporting suspicious transactions.

The principal violations concern the criteria that require co-operative countries to have an efficient mandatory system for reporting suspicious or unusual transactions to a competent authority, provided that such a system aims to detect and prosecute money laundering (criterion 10), the presence of internal regulations on monitoring, and criminal or administrative sanctions in respect of the obligation to report suspicious or unusual transactions (criterion 11), and the presence of a centralised financial intelligence unit for the collection, analysis and dissemination of information on suspicious transactions to competent authorities (criterion 25).

The NCCTs thus tend primarily to violate the criteria related to financial regulation. It is therefore natural to think that the FATF list of the potential NCCTs is, in reality, a list of countries that come closest to our theoretical definition of LFR countries. Furthermore, each potential LFR country tends to differ from the others in the number of times it has appeared on the blacklist and the number of criteria it has violated. So it may be useful to construct a laxity index, based on this

---

[48] See FATF (1990).

[49] Editor note: on 20 June 2003 the FATF published the following updated list of non – cooperative countries and territories: Cook Islands, Egypt, Guatemala, Indonesia, Myanmar, Nauru, Nigeria, Philippines, Ukraine.

information, to measure the extent to which a given country is lax in its regulations.

Based on the available information, we have created a Laxity Index, using a two stage process (Table 4.1). First stage: for each country, in every year from 2000 to 2003, each criterion can be satisfied, or can be fully or partially violated. Therefore, for each country, a weight can be assigned to each criterion: 0 for compliance, 0.5 for partial violation, and 1 for total violation (Appendix 2). Averaging the annual criteria violations, we obtain a preliminary laxity index. Second stage: given the number and extent of the violations, we must consider that each country can be more or less permanently on the blacklist. The presence of each country can potentially range from a maximum of six times to a minimum of one. So by weighting the respective simple laxity index for each country, we can obtain a final *Laxity Index*, in which the degree of laxity is found by considering both the number and gravity of the violations of the criteria and the more or less transitory presence of the country on the blacklist. We can therefore construct a Laxity Index for the list of 45 potential LFR countries.

Having identified a sample of potential LFR countries, it is possible to perform some econometric exercises. Using a worldwide data set on the main 130 countries[50] (see Table 4.3 for the list), we perform a Probit analysis. The dependent variable is a Binary Probit Variable that is equal to 1 for the 45 potential LFR countries and 0 otherwise.

The estimated equation is as follows:

$$(BinaryLI)_t = \beta_1 + \beta_2(A1)_t + \beta_3(B1) + \beta_4(C1)_t + \beta_5(E1)\varepsilon_t$$

with $t = 1 \ldots N$

where:

A1 = Land use;[51]
B1 = GDP per Capita;[52]

---

[50] Given the 267 world countries (the UN members total 180), our 130 countries represent 98 per cent of the world GDP and 90 per cent of the world population.

[51] Land use: This entry contains the percentage shares of total land area for five different types of land use: *arable land* – land cultivated for crops that are replanted after each harvest, such as wheat, maize, and rice; *permanent crops* – land cultivated for crops that are not replanted after each harvest, such as citrus, coffee, and rubber; *permanent pastures* - land permanently used for herbaceous forage crops; *forests and woodland* – land under dense or open stands of trees; *other* – any land type not specifically mentioned above, such as urban areas. Source: Central Intelligence Agency (CIA).

[52] Gdp-capita: This entry shows GDP on a purchasing power parity basis divided by population (year 2001). Source: Central Intelligence Agency.

C1 = Foreign Deposits per capita;[53]
E1 = Terrorism and Organised Crime[54] Index.[55]

Table 4.1 Binary Laxity Index determinants

Dependent variable	Binary Laxity Index		
Land use	0.007***	0.007****	
	(0.003)	(0.000)	
GDP-capita	-7.07E-05****	-8.15E-06**	
	(1.92E-05)	(4.36E-06)	
Fordepositcapita	3.18E-06****	3.52E-08 ***	
	(1.36E-06)	(1.60E-08)	
Terrorismorgcrime	- 0.508***		
	(0.224)		
Orgcrime	- 0.190 ****		
	(0.079)		
Terrorism	- 0.061		
	(0.241)		

Standard Errors in parentheses. Asterisks indicate statistical significance at 0.01 (****), 0.02 (***), 0.05 (**), 0.10 (*).

---

[53] Fordepositscapita: The data on foreign deposits are derived from reporting as such or calculated by subtracting separately reported data on positions other than deposits from total external assets and liabilities. The only exception is the Netherlands Antilles, which does not provide this information separately (year 2001). Source: BRI. The deposit data are then divided by the population (year 2001).

[54] Regarding the Organised Crime Dummy, it is evident that the size of the drug market is an indirect and imperfect indicator of the organised crime problem. It is also true that it is the drug market that has given organised crime its massive resources. It has been correctly noted that, during the 1970s, drugs became a far too profitable and easy trade for even traditional and 'conservative' organised crime organisations to ignore. See Rider (2002, p. 17). Furthermore, it has also been noted that even terrorist groups entered into the market and by so doing became virtually indistinguishable from 'ordinary' organised crime.

[55] Terrorism and Organised Crime Index: we built this variable by summing two separate variables for each country: Organised Crime Dummy = 1 if in the country there are drug production and/or drug markets, 0 otherwise (Source: CIA); Normalised Terrorism Indicator = average number of terrorist episodes in the country (1968-91)/max average number of terrorist episodes in a country 1968-91); the Terrorism indicator therefore ranges from 0 to 1 (Source: Blomberg). Consequently, our Index ranges from 0 to 2. Data Sources; Central Intelligence Agency – www.cia.gov/cia/publications/factbook; Democracy Index – www.geocities.com/CapitolHill/Lobby/3535/country/list-di.htm; Foreign Bank Deposits: Bank for International Settlements – www.bri.org/publ/qtrpdf/r_qa0206.pdf#page=44; Terrorism Indicators, see Blomberg B.S., Hess D.G., Weerapana A., *Terrorism From Within: An Economic Model of Terrorism*, May 2002 and ITERATE Data Set.

The above regression results show that the probability of being an LFR country will depend on economic variables (*Proposition One*).

Firstly, we have stated that an LFR country will be one that, because of its geographical and economic characteristics, has relatively scant physical resources to spend in international trade, and this is the first channel of *national benefit* expected from lax financial regulation (*Proposition Four*). We note that the probability of a country becoming an LFR country tends to be higher:

- the more the country experiences economic growth problems, measuring those problems in terms of per capita GDP and the level of land exploitation.

Secondly, we have affirmed that an LFR country has the possibility to develop its offering of financial services, also useful for purposes of money laundering, and this is a second channel of *national benefit* expected from lax financial regulation (*Proposition Four*). In this regard, we note that the probability of a country becoming an LFR country tends to be higher:

- the more they have developed the flow of foreign deposits.

Thirdly, we have stated that an LFR country will be one that has no terrorism and/or organised crime problems (*Proposition Six*). In the regression we use a joint Index of the terrorism risks and the organised crime risks. In our approach, every national policymaker cares about both risks, and lax financial regulations can, in principle, benefit either terrorism or organised crime. We note that the probability of a country becoming an LFR country tends to be higher

- as the degree of terrorism and organised crime risks decreases.

We must point out that we find no data to test the role of international reputation sensitivity (Proposition Five).[56]

Conclusion

The problem of lax financial regulations that favour money laundering may increase the worldwide risks of terrorism and organised crime. In this chapter we have explored the issue theoretically and empirically.

Theoretically, the degree of financial laxity can be considered an endogenous variable, determined by the policymaker's cost-benefits analysis, depending then on such economic and institutional country variables as the growth level, the role

---

[56] Obviously we cannot use cross-country analysis to test the role of international economic and political enforcement, since from the standpoint of traditional economic policy these variables are not country-specific, while, from the standpoint of new political economy, they should be more testable prima facie using country case studies.

of the financial industry, reputation sensitivity, the absence of terrorism and/or organised crime.

It is also important to stress that the gains and losses of any degree of financial laxity are expected variables, calculated by the agents (i.e. the policymakers) that maintain or reform a given regime. The expectations of policymakers are likely to be influenced by structural economic and institutional variables, which may vary from country to country. Therefore, the policymakers' expectations become the key variable in the relationship between the financial regulation architecture and the specific country variables.

The empirical analysis does not repudiate the theoretical assumption that countries, because of scant resources, foreign dependence in the offering of financial services, and the absence of terrorism and/or organised crime risks – and perhaps insensitivity to the opinion of the international community – can derive net expected national benefits from offering laundering services for illicit foreign capital. Therefore these countries can be, or become, LFR countries.

The empirical relationships developed are probably interesting but not definitive or conclusive. This prompts at least three reflections.

In terms of results, we must stress that potential LFR countries display uniform economic and institutional elements, bolstering the significance of the FATF action, but also marked dissimilarities.

This suggests two indications for designing international policies of prevention and contrast. On the one hand, by modifying their formal rules they do not automatically cease to be LFR countries, since the incentives for laxity in combating the laundering of illicit capital may be very deep-rooted.

On the other hand, the international community can have an impact on those roots through stick-and-carrot policies tailored to each country, precisely because the degree of laxity and its motivations may not be perfectly identical in each case.

On a battlefield where reputation is one of the main weapons, policymakers engaged in the fight against international money laundering schemes should be very cautious in taking initiatives that may affect the reputation of the actors involved. A pure 'name and shame' approach may even prove counterproductive.

At the same time, tampering with reputational mechanisms might not only miss the target but also reach the wrong goal.

First, there is a high risk of false negatives, i.e. of including countries in a hypothetical list of those that supply money laundering services but which merely offer financial services of superior quality. The costs of such an error appear great. As the Financial Stability Forum put it: 'not all [OFCs] are the same. Some are well supervised and prepared to share information with other centres, and co-operate with international initiatives to improve supervisory practices. But the Survey carried out by the [Financial Stability Forum] indicated that there are serious concerns by onshore supervisors about the quality of supervision in, and degree of co-operation provided by, some [OFCs].'[57]

Reputation is also the basic tool of the trade for countries that are not involved in money laundering schemes but are merely aiming at attracting capital from

---

[57] Financial Stability Forum (2000).

abroad through the offer of superior quality financial services. From this perspective, a mistake by the international community to include the wrong country in the list might cause serious distortions in the competition among jurisdictions.

As Chapter 2 pointed out, these countries, like victims of friendly fire, will find their reputation in the financial community seriously hampered, to the detriment of their role in the market. In the long run, mistakes of this type also appear capable of curbing innovation in the financial sector. Regulatory arbitrage is a powerful force in driving innovation, and the international community should recognise that tinkering with the reputation of the actors involved is a dangerous game.

But even assuming that the international community is capable of effectively singling out LFR countries that are indeed involved in money laundering schemes, a cautious approach is still deemed necessary. When the international community points the finger at a given country as a leading supplier of money laundering financial services, it may also be certifying, to the benefit of the country itself, that that country is indeed specialised in that business.

The signalling effect embedded in the 'name and shame approach' should not be underestimated. The main difficulty for an LFR country is to resolve credibly the commitment problem. Then, what is better for the LFR country than having the international community, not exactly its closest friends, resolving that problem with a public statement? Listing should also be regarded as a sort of third party bonding, which is likely to generate two intertwined effects.

First, it may cement the commitment by the LFR country. Secondly, naming increases the transaction specific character of investments in reputation. Inclusion in a list increases the value of the (sunk) investments in reputation.

A state that is engaged in money laundering and finds itself blacklisted will find it even more difficult to switch course and exit the market, thus being encouraged to compete aggressively in the market. The final result does not change much. They still need to move forward.

This is not to say that the international community should not endeavour to list countries that are involved in the market for money laundering services. Quite to the contrary; what this chapter argues is that a 'name and shame' approach per se, without other initiatives, is equivalent to a third-party seal on the reputation of LFR countries. Names should be named, but only if blacklisting goes hand in hand with other measures capable of offsetting the positive effects experienced by the OFC as a result of inclusion in the list.

Appropriate countermeasures should be based on the premise that, in a global world, even the most efficient LFR country will still need to be integrated into the world financial markets.

This implies that no matter how many layers of transactions cover the predicate offence, terrorism or criminal organisations will still need to place that money within the lawful financial sector. This step is necessary, at a minimum, in order to utilise the capital lawfully once it has been laundered. Money laundering is, by definition, instrumental to a later use.

With this regard, it should be noted that there is a fundamental feature of the initiative taken by the FATF that appears to be pivotal for its success. The FATF has not limited its initiative to mere recognition of 'non-co-operative countries and territories.' FATF member states have also applied 'Recommendation 21'[58] to the countries included in the list. 'Recommendation 21' requires a higher scrutiny by financial intermediaries in evaluating the possible suspect nature of transactions with counterparts, including legal persons, based in a country listed as non-co-operative. As a result of the FATF initiative, many countries included in the list have already taken initiatives aimed at overcoming the serious deficiencies observed by the FATF.[59]

These initiatives need to be evaluated in the medium-to-long run because, for example, some of the enacted laws will need secondary regulations to be put in place to become effective or, more generally, the initiatives taken at the legislative level will need to be followed by concrete actions. It can be argued, however, that the threat of being crowded out by the international community has played a major role in spurring the adoption of the above-mentioned initiatives.

The second conclusion that can be reached on the basis of the empirical evidence we have examined is that we must not exclude the possibility that some LFR countries are not presently included in the FATF monitoring action, perhaps because they are highly effective in bringing their formal rules in line with international precepts, while in their deeds they remain lax in the fight against money laundering.

This implies a constant effort on the part of international organisations, particularly the FATF, to update the criteria and monitor the countries.

---

[58] See FATF (1990, 2000).
[59] See FATF press communiqué of 5 October 2000.

Figures and Tables

Figure 4.1 Non-cooperative countries and territories (NCCTs)

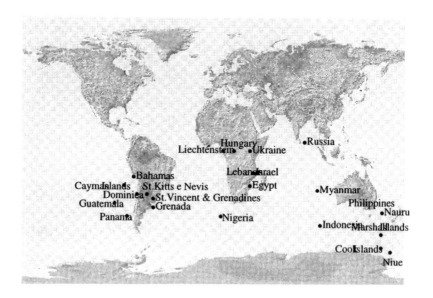

Table 4.2 Laxity Index

N.	Countries	Criteria2000	Criteria2001	Criteria2002	Criteria 2003	Average Criteria	Black List	Laxity Index
1	Antigua	3.0	3.0	3.0	3.0	3.0	1.0	3.0
2	Barbuda	3.0	3.0	3.0	3.0	3.0	1.0	3.0
3	Bahamas	12.0	6.0	4.0	4.0	6.5	2.0	13.0
4	Belize	3.0	3.0	3.0	3.0	3.0	1.0	3.0
5	Bermuda	3.0	3.0	3.0	3.0	3.0	1.0	3.0
6	British Virgin Islands	1.0	1.0	1.0	1.0	1.0	1.0	1.0
7	Cayman Islands	15.0	5.5	0.5	0.5	5.4	2.0	10.8
8	Cook Islands	14.0	12.0	8.0	6.0	10.0	8.0	80.0
9	Cyprus	2.0	2.0	2.0	2.0	2.0	1.0	2.0
10	Czech Republic	-	5.5	3.0	3.0	3.8	1.0	3.8
11	Dominica	15.0	9.0	1.5	1.5	6.8	6.0	40.5
12	Egypt	-	7.5	7.5	6.5	7.2	7.0	50.2
13	Gibraltar	3.0	3.0	3.0	3.0	3.0	1.0	3.0
14	Grenada	-	6.0	3.0	2.0	3.7	5.0	18.3
15	Guatemala	-	7.5	7.5	6.5	7.2	7.0	50.2
16	Guerney	3.0	3.0	3.0	3.0	3.0	1.0	3.0
17	Hungary	-	4.5	3.0	3.0	3.5	4.0	14.0
18	Indonesia	-	11.0	4.0	4.0	6.3	7.0	44.3
19	Isle of Man	3.0	3.0	3.0	3.0	3.0	1.0	3.0
20	Jersey	3.0	3.0	3.0	3.0	3.0	1.0	3.0
21	Israel	5.5	3.0	1.5	1.5	2.9	5.0	14.4
22	Lebanon	15.0	12.0	1.5	1.5	7.5	5.0	37.5
23	Liechtestein	10.0	5.0	0.5	0.5	4.0	2.0	8.0
24	Malta	3.0	3.0	3.0	3.0	3.0	1.0	3.0
25	Marshall Islands	18.0	12.5	2.5	2.5	8.9	6.0	53.3
26	Mauritius	3.0	3.0	3.0	3.0	3.0	1.0	3.0
27	Myanamar	-	15.0	15.0	15.0	15.0	7.0	105.0
28	Monaco	1.0	1.0	1.0	1.0	1.0	1.0	1.0
29	Nauru	16.0	16.0	16.0	16.0	16.0	8.0	128.0
30	Nigeria	-	4.0	4.0	4.0	4.0	7.0	28.0
31	Niue	12.0	4.5	2.5	2.5	5.4	6.0	32.3
32	Panama	8.5	3.0	0.5	0.5	3.1	2.0	6.3
33	Philippines	11.0	11.0	7.0	7.0	9.0	8.0	72.0
34	Poland	-	3.0	3.0	3.0	3.0	1.0	3.0
35	Russia	10.5	10.5	2.5	2.5	6.5	6.0	39.0
36	Samoa	3.0	3.0	3.0	3.0	3.0	1.0	3.0
37	Seychelles	-	4.0	4.0	4.0	4.0	1.0	4.0
38	Slovak Republic	-	6.0	6.0	6.0	6.0	1.0	6.0
39	St. Kitt and Nevis	20.0	8.5	2.0	2.0	8.1	5.0	40.6
40	St. Lucia	1.5	1.5	1.5	1.5	1.5	1.0	1.5
41	St. Vincent & Gren.	16.5	15.5	3.5	3.5	9.8	8.0	78.0
42	Turks and Caicos	-	3.0	3.0	3.0	3.0	1.0	3.0
43	Ukraine	-	12.5	12.5	12.5	12.5	6.0	75.0
44	Uruguay	-	3.0	3.0	3.0	3.0	1.0	3.0
45	Vanuatu	-	3.0	3.0	3.0	3.0	1.0	3.0

Figure 4.2 Signalling in FAFT monitoring countries 2003

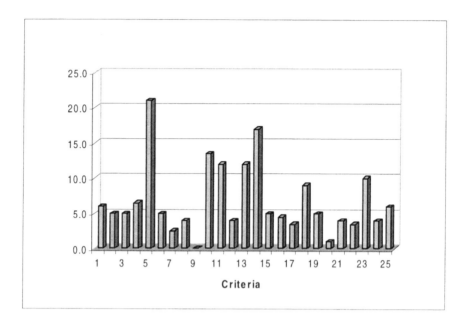

Appendix 4.A List of Criteria for defining Non-co-operative Countries or Territories

Loopholes in financial regulations

(i) Absence of, or inadequate regulations and supervision of, financial institutions

1. Absence of, or ineffective regulations and supervision for, all financial institutions in a given country or territory, onshore or offshore, on an equivalent basis with respect to international standards applicable to money laundering.

(ii) Inadequate rules for the licensing and creation of financial institutions, including assessing the backgrounds of their managers and beneficial owners

2. Possibility for individuals or legal entities to operate a financial institution without authorisation or registration or with very rudimentary requirements for authorisation or registration.

3. Absence of measures to guard against the holding of management functions, and control or acquisition of a significant investment in financial institutions, by criminals or their confederates.

(iii) Inadequate customer identification requirements for financial institutions

4. Existence of anonymous accounts or accounts in obviously fictitious names.

5. Lack of effective laws, regulations, and agreements between supervisory authorities and financial institutions or self-regulatory agreements among financial institutions on identification by the financial institution of the client and beneficial owner of an account:

- no obligation to verify the identity of the client;
- no requirement to identify the beneficial owners where there are doubts as to whether the client is acting on his own behalf;
- no obligation to renew identification of the client or the beneficial owner when doubts appear as to their identity in the course of business relationships;
- no requirement for financial institutions to develop ongoing anti-money laundering training programmes.

6. Lack of a legal or regulatory obligation for financial institutions or agreements between supervisory authorities and financial institutions or self-agreements among financial institutions, to record and keep documents connected with the identity of their clients, as well as records on national and international transactions, for a reasonable and sufficient period of time (five years).

7. Legal or practical obstacles to access by administrative and judicial authorities to information regarding the identity of the holders or beneficial owners and information connected with the transactions recorded.

(iv) Excessive secrecy provisions regarding financial institutions

8. Secrecy provisions which can be invoked against, but not lifted by, competent administrative authorities in the context of enquiries concerning money laundering.

9. Secrecy provisions that can be invoked against, but not lifted by, judicial authorities in criminal investigations related to money laundering.

(v) Lack of an efficient system for reporting suspicious transactions

10. Absence of an efficient mandatory system for reporting suspicious or unusual transactions to a competent authority, provided that such a system aims to detect and prosecute money laundering.

11. Lack of monitoring and criminal or administrative sanctions in respect of the obligation to report suspicious or unusual transactions.

Obstacles raised by other regulatory requirements

(i) Inadequate commercial laws requiring the registration of business and legal entities

12. Inadequate means for identifying, recording and making available relevant information related to legal and business entities (name, legal form, address, identity of directors, provisions regulating the power to bind the entity).

(ii) Lack of identification of the beneficial owner(s) of legal and business entities

13. Obstacles to identification by financial institutions of the beneficial owner(s) and directors/officers of a company or beneficiaries of legal or business entities.

14. Regulatory or other systems that allow financial institutions to conduct financial business where the beneficial owner(s) of transactions is unknown, or is represented by an intermediary who refuses to divulge that information, without informing the competent authorities.

Obstacles to international co-operation

(i) Obstacles to international co-operation by administrative auth

15. Laws or regulations prohibiting international exchange of information between administrative anti-money laundering authorities or not granting clear gateways or subjecting exchange of information to unduly restrictive conditions.

16. Prohibiting relevant administrative authorities from conducting investigations or enquiries on behalf of, or for account of, their foreign counterparts.

17. Obvious unwillingness to respond constructively to requests (e.g. failure to take the appropriate measures in due course, long delays in responding).

18. Restrictive practices in international co-operation against money laundering, between supervisory authorities or between FIUs, for the analysis and investigation of suspicious transactions, especially on the grounds that such transactions may relate to tax matters.

(ii) Obstacles to international co-operation by judicial authorities

19. Failure to criminalise laundering of the proceeds from serious crimes.

20. Laws or regulations prohibiting international exchanges of information between judicial authorities (notably specific reservations to the anti-money laundering provisions of international agreements) or placing highly restrictive conditions on the exchange of information.

21. Obvious unwillingness to respond constructively to requests for mutual legal assistance (e.g. failure to take the appropriate measures in due course, long delays in responding).

22. Refusal to provide judicial co-operation in cases involving offences recognised as such by the requested jurisdiction especially on the grounds that tax matters are involved.

Inadequate resources for preventing and detecting money laundering activities

(i) Lack of resources in public and private sectors

23. Failure to provide the administrative and judicial authorities with the necessary financial, human or technical resources to exercise their functions or to conduct their investigations.

24. Inadequate or corrupt professional staff in either governmental, judicial or supervisory authorities or among those responsible for anti-money laundering compliance in the financial services industry.

(ii) Absence of a financial intelligence unit or of an equivalent mechanism

25. Lack of a centralised unit (i.e. a financial intelligence unit) or of an equivalent mechanism for the collection, analysis and dissemination of suspicious transactions information to competent authorities.

SPECIAL RECOMMENDATIONS ON TERRORIST FINANCING

I. Ratification and implementation of UN instruments

Each country should take immediate steps to ratify and to implement fully the 1999 United Nations International Convention for the Suppression of the Financing of Terrorism. Countries should also immediately implement the United Nations resolutions relating to the prevention and suppression of the financing of terrorist acts, particularly United Nations Security Council Resolution 1373.

II. Criminalising the financing of terrorism and associated money laundering

Each country should criminalise the financing of terrorism, terrorist acts and terrorist organisations. Countries should ensure that such offences are designated as money laundering predicate offences.

III. Freezing and confiscating terrorist assets

Each country should implement measures to freeze without delay funds or other assets of terrorists, those who finance terrorism and terrorist organisations in accordance with the United Nations resolutions relating to the prevention and suppression of the financing of terrorist acts. Each country should also adopt and implement measures, including legislative ones, which would enable the competent authorities to seize and confiscate property that is the proceeds of, or used in, or intended or allocated for use in, the financing of terrorism, terrorist acts or terrorist organisations.

IV. Reporting suspicious transactions related to terrorism

If financial institutions, or other businesses or entities subject to anti-money laundering obligations, suspect or have reasonable grounds to suspect that funds are linked or related to, or are to be used for terrorism, terrorist acts or by terrorist organisations, they should be required to report promptly their suspicions to the competent authorities.

V. International co-operation

Each country should afford another country, on the basis of a treaty, arrangement or other mechanism for mutual legal assistance or information exchange, the greatest possible measure of assistance in connection with criminal, civil enforcement, and administrative investigations, inquiries and proceedings relating to the financing of terrorism, terrorist acts and terrorist organisations. Countries should also take all possible measures to ensure that they do not provide safe havens for individuals charged with the financing of terrorism, terrorist acts or terrorist organisations, and should have procedures in place to extradite, where possible, such individuals.

VI. Alternative remittance

Each country should take measures to ensure that persons or legal entities, including agents, that provide a service for the transmission of money or value, including transmission through an informal money or value transfer system or network, should be licensed or registered and subject to all the FATF Recommendations that apply to banks and non-bank financial institutions. Each country should ensure that persons or legal entities that carry out this service illegally are subject to administrative, civil or criminal sanctions.

VII. Wire transfers

Countries should take measures to require financial institutions, including money remitters, to include accurate and meaningful originator information (name, address and account number) on funds transfers and related messages that are sent, and the information should remain with the transfer or related message through the payment chain. Countries should take measures to ensure that financial institutions, including money remitters, conduct enhanced scrutiny of and monitor for suspicious activity funds transfers that do not contain complete originator information (name, address and account number).

VIII. Non-profit organisations

Countries should review the adequacy of laws and regulations that relate to entities that can be abused for the financing of terrorism. Non-profit organisations are particularly vulnerable, and countries should ensure that they cannot be misused:

- by terrorist organisations posing as legitimate entities;
- to exploit legitimate entities as conduits for terrorist financing, including for the purpose of escaping asset freezing measures;
- to conceal or obscure the clandestine diversion of funds intended for legitimate purposes to terrorist organisations.

Appendix 4.B

Table 4.3 Criteria violations 2000

Countries / Criteria	1	2	3	4	5	6	7	8	9	10	11	12	13	14	15	16	17	18	19	20	21	22	23	24	25	Total Criteria
Antigua					1.0								1.0	1.0												3.0
Barbuda					1.0								1.0	1.0												3.0
Bahamas*					0.5					0.5	0.5	1.0	1.0	1.0	1.0	1.0		1.0		0.5	1.0	1.0	1.0		1.0	12.0
Belize					1.0								1.0	1.0												3.0
Bermuda					1.0								1.0	1.0												3.0
British Virgin Islands														1.0												1.0
Cayman Islands*	1.0	0.5	0.5		1.0	1.0	0.5	1.0		1.0	1.0	0.5	1.0	1.0	1.0	1.0	1.0	1.0					1.0			15.0
Cook Islands*	1.0		1.0	1.0	1.0					1.0	1.0	1.0		1.0				1.0	1.0		1.0	1.0	1.0		1.0	14.0
Cyprus													1.0	1.0												2.0
Czech Republic																										0.0
Dominica*			1.0	1.0		1.0				1.0	1.0	1.0	1.0	1.0	1.0	1.0	1.0		1.0			1.0	1.0		1.0	15.0
Egypt																										0.0
Gibraltar			1.0							1.0	1.0															3.0
Grenada																										0.0
Guatemala																										0.0
Guernsey			1.0							1.0	1.0															3.0
Hungary																										0.0
Indonesia																										0.0
Isle of Man			1.0							1.0	1.0															3.0
Jersey			1.0							1.0	1.0															3.0
Israel*				0.5						1.0	1.0							1.0			1.0				1.0	5.5
Lebanon*	1.0	1.0				1.0	1.0	1.0	1.0	1.0				1.0	1.0	1.0		1.0	1.0	1.0				1.0	1.0	15.0
Liechtenstein*	1.0			0.5						1.0			0.5		1.0	1.0	1.0	1.0		1.0	1.0		1.0			10.0
Malta			1.0										1.0	1.0												3.0
Marshall Islands*	1.0	1.0	1.0	1.0	1.0	1.0	1.0	1.0		1.0	1.0	1.0		1.0	1.0	1.0	1.0	1.0					1.0		1.0	18.0
Mauritius			1.0										1.0	1.0												3.0
Myanmar																										0.0
Monaco																		1.0								1.0
Nauru*	1.0	1.0	1.0	1.0	1.0	1.0	1.0			1.0	1.0	1.0		1.0				1.0					1.0	1.0	1.0	16.0
Nigeria																										0.0
Niue*	1.0	1.0	1.0	1.0	1.0					1.0	1.0	1.0		1.0	1.0			1.0							1.0	12.0
Panama*						1.0	1.0			0.5			1.0		1.0	1.0	1.0	1.0								8.5
Philippines*	1.0		1.0	1.0	1.0		1.0			1.0				1.0				1.0					1.0		1.0	11.0
Poland																										0.0
Russia*	1.0		1.0	1.0	0.5					1.0	1.0						1.0				1.0		1.0	1.0	1.0	10.5
Samoa*	1.0	1.0	1.0																							3.0
Seychelles																										0.0
Slovak Republic																										0.0
St. Kitt and Nevis*	1.0	1.0	1.0	1.0	1.0	1.0	1.0	1.0	1.0	1.0	1.0	1.0	1.0		1.0	1.0	1.0	1.0	1.0				1.0		1.0	20.0
St. Lucia	0.5	0.5	0.5																							1.5
St. Vincent & Gren.*	1.0	1.0	1.0	1.0	1.0	1.0				1.0	1.0	1.0	1.0		1.0	0.5		1.0				1.0	1.0	1.0	1.0	16.5
Turks and Caicos																										0.0
Ukraine																										0.0
Uruguay																										0.0
Vanuatu																										0.0

Data: FATF, www.oecd.org/fatf

Table 4.4 Criteria violations in 2001

Countries / Criteria	1	2	3	4	5	6	7	8	9	10	11	12	13	14	15	16	17	18	19	20	21	22	23	24	25	Total Criteria
Antigua					1.0								1.0	1.0												3.0
Barbuda					1.0								1.0	1.0												3.0
Bahamas					0.5							0.5	0.5	0.5				1.0				1.0	1.0	1.0		6.0
Belize					1.0								1.0	1.0												3.0
Bermuda					1.0								1.0	1.0												3.0
British Virgin Islands														1.0												1.0
Cayman Islands				0.5		0.5							0.5	0.5	0.5	0.5	0.5	1.0					1.0			5.5
Cook Islands*			1.0	1.0	1.0					1.0	1.0	1.0		1.0				1.0				1.0	1.0	1.0	1.0	12.0
Cyprus													1.0	1.0												2.0
Czech Republic	0.5			1.0	1.0	1.0							1.0	1.0												5.5
Dominica*					1.0					1.0	1.0	1.0	1.0	1.0									1.0	1.0	1.0	9.0
Egypt*	0.5			1.0	0.5		0.5			1.0	1.0			1.0					1.0						1.0	7.5
Gibraltar					1.0								1.0	1.0												3.0
Grenada*	0.5	0.5	0.5				0.5	1.0						1.0	0.5	0.5						1.0				6.0
Guatemala*	0.5					1.0	0.5	1.0			0.5				1.0	1.0			1.0						1.0	7.5
Guernsey					1.0								1.0	1.0												3.0
Hungary*				1.0	0.5		0.5				0.5	0.5	0.5	1.0												4.5
Indonesia*	1.0		0.5	0.5	0.5			1.0	1.0	1.0	1.0	1.0				0.5			1.0				1.0		1.0	11.0
Isle of Man					1.0								1.0	1.0												3.0
Jersey					1.0								1.0	1.0												3.0
Israel*													1.0	1.0								0.5			0.5	3.0
Lebanon*								1.0	1.0	1.0	1.0			1.0	1.0	1.0		1.0	1.0	1.0				1.0	1.0	12.0
Liechtenstein											1.0				0.5	0.5	0.5	0.5		0.5	0.5	1.0				5.0
Malta					1.0								1.0	1.0												3.0
Marshall Islands*	0.5	0.5	0.5	0.5	0.5	0.5	0.5				1.0	1.0	1.0	1.0	1.0	1.0	1.0					1.0			1.0	12.5
Mauritius					1.0								1.0	1.0												3.0
Myanmar*	1.0	1.0	1.0	1.0	1.0	1.0					1.0	1.0						1.0	1.0	1.0	1.0		1.0	1.0	1.0	15.0
Monaco																		1.0								1.0
Nauru*	1.0	1.0	1.0	1.0	1.0	1.0	1.0	1.0			1.0	1.0	1.0		1.0				1.0				1.0	1.0	1.0	16.0
Nigeria*					1.0					0.5							1.0		0.5					1.0		4.0
Niue*					1.0	1.0						1.0		1.0					0.5							4.5
Panama							0.5						0.5		0.5	0.5	0.5	0.5								3.0
Philippines*	1.0			1.0	1.0	1.0				1.0	1.0			1.0					1.0						1.0	11.0
Poland					1.0								1.0	1.0												3.0
Russia*	1.0			1.0	1.0	0.5				1.0	1.0							1.0				1.0		1.0	1.0	10.5
Samoa	1.0	1.0	1.0																							3.0
Seychelles															1.0	1.0	1.0	1.0								4.0
Slovak Republic				0.5	0.5										1.0	1.0	1.0	1.0					1.0			6.0
St. Kitt and Nevis*				1.0	1.0	1.0		1.0	1.0	0.5	0.5				0.5	0.5	0.5	0.5					0.5			8.5
St. Lucia	0.5	0.5	0.5																							1.5
St. Vincent & Gren.*	1.0	1.0	1.0	1.0	1.0	1.0				0.5	0.5	1.0	1.0		1.0	0.5			1.0			1.0	1.0	1.0	1.0	15.5
Turks and Caicos					1.0								1.0	1.0												3.0
Ukraine*	0.5	0.5	0.5	0.5	0.5	0.5	0.5	1.0			1.0	1.0		1.0	1.0	1.0							1.0	1.0	1.0	12.5
Uruguay		1.0	1.0																				1.0			3.0
Vanuatu												1.0	1.0	1.0												3.0

Data: FATF, www.oecd.org/fatf

Table 4.5 Criteria violations in 2002

Countries / Criteria	1	2	3	4	5	6	7	8	9	10	11	12	13	14	15	16	17	18	19	20	21	22	23	24	25	Total Criteria
Antigua				1.0									1.0	1.0												3.0
Barbuda				1.0									1.0	1.0												3.0
Bahamas					0.5							0.5	0.5	0.5				1.0		1.0						4.0
Belize				1.0									1.0	1.0												3.0
Bermuda				1.0									1.0	1.0												3.0
British Virgin Islands														1.0												1.0
Cayman Islands																		0.5								0.5
Cook Islands*				1.0	1.0	1.0												1.0			1.0	1.0	1.0		1.0	8.0
Cyprus													1.0	1.0												2.0
Czech Republic	0.5			0.5	0.5	0.5							0.5	0.5												3.0
Dominica																		0.5				0.5	0.5			1.5
Egypt*	0.5				1.0	0.5		0.5		1.0	1.0			1.0					1.0						1.0	7.5
Gibraltar				1.0						1.0	1.0															3.0
Grenada*													0.5	0.5					1.0		1.0					3.0
Guatemala*	0.5				1.0	0.5	1.0			0.5			1.0	1.0				1.0							1.0	7.5
Guerney				1.0						1.0	1.0															3.0
Hungary		0.5				0.5				0.5	0.5	0.5	0.5													3.0
Indonesia*	0.5												1.0	1.0					0.5			1.0				4.0
Isle of Man				1.0						1.0	1.0															3.0
Jersey				1.0						1.0	1.0															3.0
Israel				0.5						0.5	0.5															1.5
Lebanon										0.5	0.5							0.5								1.5
Liechtestein																		0.5								0.5
Malta				1.0									1.0	1.0												3.0
Marshall Islands											0.5	0.5	0.5			0.5							0.5			2.5
Mauritius				1.0									1.0	1.0												3.0
Myanmar*	1.0	1.0	1.0	1.0	1.0	1.0					1.0	1.0						1.0	1.0		1.0	1.0	1.0	1.0	1.0	15.0
Monaco																	1.0									1.0
Nauru*	1.0	1.0	1.0	1.0	1.0	1.0	1.0	1.0		1.0	1.0	1.0		1.0					1.0				1.0	1.0	1.0	16.0
Nigeria*				1.0						0.5						1.0		0.5						1.0		4.0
Niue			0.5	0.5								0.5		0.5				0.5								2.5
Panama																		0.5								0.5
Philippines*				1.0	1.0		1.0			1.0	1.0			1.0								1.0				7.0
Poland				1.0									1.0	1.0												3.0
Russia				0.5						0.5	0.5						0.5			0.5						2.5
Samoa	1.0	1.0	1.0																							3.0
Seychelles													1.0	1.0	1.0	1.0										4.0
Slovak Republic			0.5	0.5									1.0	1.0	1.0	1.0						1.0				6.0
St. Kitt and Nevis																		0.5			0.5	0.5	0.5			2.0
St. Lucia	0.5	0.5	0.5																							1.5
St. Vincent & Gren.*					0.5								0.5	0.5				1.0			1.0					3.5
Turks and Caicos				1.0									1.0	1.0												3.0
Ukraine*	0.5	0.5	0.5	0.5	0.5	0.5	0.5	1.0		1.0	1.0			1.0	1.0	1.0							1.0	1.0	1.0	12.5
Uruguay		1.0	1.0																				1.0			3.0
Vanuatu												1.0	1.0	1.0												3.0

Data: FATF, www.oecd.org/fatf

Table 4.6 Criteria violations in 2003

Countries / Criteria	1	2	3	4	5	6	7	8	9	10	11	12	13	14	15	16	17	18	19	20	21	22	23	24	25	Total Criteria
Antigua					1.0								1.0	1.0												3.0
Barbuda					1.0								1.0	1.0												3.0
Bahamas					0.5							0.5	0.5	0.5				1.0		1.0						4.0
Belize					1.0								1.0	1.0												3.0
Bermuda					1.0								1.0	1.0												3.0
British Virgin Islands														1.0												1.0
Cayman Islands																		0.5								0.5
Cook Islands*			1.0	1.0	1.0													1.0			1.0	1.0	1.0		1.0	8.0
Cyprus													1.0	1.0												2.0
Czech Republic	0.5			0.5	0.5	0.5							0.5	0.5												3.0
Dominica																		0.5			0.5	0.5				1.5
Egypt*	0.5			1.0	0.5		0.5			1.0	1.0			1.0				1.0							1.0	7.5
Gibraltar				1.0						1.0	1.0															3.0
Grenada*																0.5	0.5				1.0		1.0			3.0
Guatemala*	0.5					1.0	0.5	1.0		0.5			1.0	1.0				1.0							1.0	7.5
Guernsey				1.0						1.0	1.0															3.0
Hungary		0.5			0.5					0.5	0.5	0.5	0.5													3.0
Indonesia*	0.5									1.0	1.0								0.5			1.0				4.0
Isle of Man				1.0						1.0	1.0															3.0
Jersey				1.0						1.0	1.0															3.0
Israel				0.5						0.5	0.5															1.5
Lebanon										0.5	0.5							0.5								1.5
Liechtestein																		0.5								0.5
Malta				1.0									1.0	1.0												3.0
Marshall Islands										0.5	0.5	0.5			0.5								0.5			2.5
Mauritius				1.0									1.0	1.0												3.0
Myanmar*	1.0	1.0	1.0	1.0	1.0	1.0				1.0	1.0							1.0	1.0		1.0	1.0	1.0	1.0	1.0	15.0
Monaco																		1.0								1.0
Nauru*	1.0	1.0	1.0	1.0	1.0	1.0	1.0	1.0		1.0	1.0	1.0		1.0					1.0				1.0	1.0	1.0	16.0
Nigeria*				1.0						0.5							1.0		0.5					1.0		4.0
Niue			0.5	0.5					0.5								0.5	0.5								2.5
Panama																		0.5								0.5
Philippines*				1.0	1.0			1.0		1.0	1.0			1.0									1.0			7.0
Poland				1.0									1.0	1.0												3.0
Russia				0.5						0.5	0.5							0.5				0.5				2.5
Samoa	1.0	1.0	1.0																							3.0
Seychelles																1.0	1.0	1.0	1.0							4.0
Slovak Republic				0.5	0.5											1.0	1.0	1.0	1.0				1.0			6.0
St. Kitt and Nevis																			0.5			0.5	0.5	0.5		2.0
St. Lucia	0.5	0.5	0.5																							1.5
St. Vincent & Gren.*				0.5									0.5	0.5				1.0				1.0				3.5
Turks and Caicos				1.0									1.0	1.0												3.0
Ukraine*	0.5	0.5	0.5	0.5	0.5	0.5	0.5	1.0		1.0	1.0		1.0	1.0	1.0								1.0	1.0	1.0	12.5
Uruguay		1.0	1.0																				1.0			3.0
Vanuatu													1.0	1.0	1.0											3.0

Data: FATF, www.oecd.org/fatf

References

Acemoglu, D., Johnson S. and Robinson, J.A. (2001), The colonial origins of comparative development: an empirical investigation, *American Economic Review*, 91, 1369-1401.

Alchian, A. A. (1950), Uncertainty, Evolution, and Economic Theory, *Journal of Political Economy*, 58, 211.

Ayres, I. and Gertner, R. (1989), Filling Gaps in Incomplete Contracts: An Economic Theory of Default Rules, *Yale Law Journal*, 99, 87.

Banoun R., Cephas, D. and Fruchtman, L.D. (2002), US Patriot Act and Other Recent Money Laundering Developments Have Broad Impact on Financial Institutions, *Journal of Taxation of Financial Institutions*, 15, 4.

Basel Committee on Banking Supervision (1988), *Prevention of Criminal Use of the Banking System for the Purpose of Money-Laundering*, Basel.

Beck, T., Demirguc-Kunt A. and Levine R. (2002), *Law, Endowments and Finance*, NBER Working Paper, n. 9089.

Becker, G. (1962), Irrational Behaviour and Economic Theory, *Journal of Political Economy*, 70, 1.

Boeschoten, W. and Fase M. (1992), The Demand for Large Bank Notes, *Journal of Money, Credit and Banking*, 24, 3.

Blomberg, B.S., Hess D.G. and Weerapana A. (2002), *Terrorism from Within: Model of Terrorism*, Paper presented to the DIW Workshop 'The Economic Consequences of Global Terrorism', Berlin, 14-15 June.

Drazen, A. (2000), *Political Economy in Macroeconomics*, Princeton University, Princeton.

Errico, L. and Musalem, A. (1999), *Offshore Banking: An Analysis of Micro and Macro Prudential Issues*, Working Paper, International Monetary Fund, n. 5.

Ferri, G. and Masciandaro, D. (2003), *Migration and Finance: Remittances, Banking and Informal Networks in the Italian Case*, mimeo.

Financial Action Task Force (2000), *Review of Non-Co-operative Countries or Territories: Increasing the Worldwide Effectiveness of Anti-Money Laundering Measures*.

Financial Action Task Force (1990), *The Forty Recommendations*, Paris.

Financial Stability Forum (2000), *Report of the Working Group on Offshore Financial Centres*, Basle.

Gilson, R. J. (2000), Globalizing Corporate Governance: Convergence of Form or Function, *Columbia Law School Working Paper*, n. 174.

Grandy, C. (1989), Can Government Be Trusted to Keep Its Part of a Social Contract? New Jersey and the Railroads, 1825 – 1888, in *Journal of Law, Economics, and Organisation*, 5, 249.

Grilli, V., Masciandaro, D. and Tabellini, G. (1991), Institutions and Policies. Political and Monetary Institutions and Public Financial Policies in the Industrial Countries, *Economic Policy*, 13, 341-376.

International Monetary Fund (1998), *Money Laundering. The Importance of International Countermeasures*, address by Michel Camdessus, Plenary Meeting of the FATF, pp. 1-4, Paris, mimeo.

Johnson, J. and Desmond Lim, Y.C. (2002), Money Laundering: Has the Financial Action Task Force Made a Difference?, *Journal of Financial Crime*, 10, 1.

La Porta, R. Lopez-de-Silanes, F. Shleifer, A. and Vishny, R.W. (1998), Law and Finance, *Journal of Political Economy*, 106, 1113.

Macneil, I. (1978), Contracts: Adjustments of Long -Term Economic Relations under Classical, Neoclassical, and Relational Contract Law, *Northwestern University Law Review*, 72, 854.

Madison, J. (1787), The Federalist n. 10, in J.E. Cooke (ed.), *The Federalist Papers*, Wesleyan University Press, Middletown, Connecticut, 1961.

Masciandaro, D. (2000), The Illegal Sector, Money Laundering and Legal Economy: A Macroeconomic Analysis, *Journal of Financial Crime*, 2, pp. 103-112.

Masciandaro, D. (1999), Money Laundering: the Economics of Regulation, *European Journal of Law and Economics*, 3, pp. 245-240.

Masciandaro, D. (1998), Money Laundering Regulation: the Micro Economics, *Journal of Money Laundering Control*, 2, pp. 49-58.

Masciandaro, D. (1996), Pecunia Olet? Microeconomics of Banking and Financial Laundering, *International Review of Economics and Business,* 10, pp. 817-844.

Masciandaro, D. and Portolano, A. (2003), It Takes Two to Tango: International Financial Regulation and Offshore Centres, *Journal of Money Laundering Control*, 6, 4.

North, D. (1990), *Institutions, Institutional Change, and Economic Performance*, Cambridge University Press, Cambridge.

Olson, M. (1965), *The Logic of Collective Action*, Harvard University Press, Cambridge MA.

Persson, T. and Tabellini, G. (2000), *Political Economics: Explaining Economic Policy*, MIT University Press, Cambridge MA.

Rider, B.A.K. (2002), Weapons of War: the Use of Anti-Money Laundering Laws against Terrorist and Criminal Enterprises, *International Journal of Banking Regulation*, 4, 1.

Rogoff, K. (1997), *Foreign and Underground Demand for Euro Notes: Blessing or a Curse?*, mimeo.

Romano, R. (1999), Corporate Law and Corporate Governance, in G .R. Carroll and D.J. Teece (eds), *Firms, Markets, and Hierarchies*, Oxford University, Oxford.

Romano, R. (1993), *The Genius of American Corporate Law*, American Enterprise Institute for Public Policy Research, Washington, D.C.

Romano, R. (1985), Law as a Product: Some Pieces of the Incorporation Puzzle, *Journal of Law, Economics, and Organisation*, 1, 225.

Sinn, H.W. and Westermann, F. (2001), *Why has the Euro been Falling?*, CESIfo Working Paper, 493, May.

Wasserman, M. (2002), Dirty money, *Regional Review*, Federal Reserve Bank of Boston, 12, 1.

Williamson, O. (1996), *The Mechanisms of Governance*, Oxford University Press, Oxford.

Williamson, O. (1985), *The Economic Institution of Capitalism*, Free Press, New York.

Williamson, O. (1983), Credible Commitments: Using Hostages to Support Exchange, *The American Economic Review*, 73, 519.

Williamson, O. (1979), Transaction Cost Economics: The Governance of Contractual Relations, *The Journal of Law and Economics*, 22, 233.

Chapter 5

Public Policy: Offshore Centres and Tax Competition: The Harmful Problem

Julian Alworth and Donato Masciandaro

Introduction

Chapter 4 analysed the relationship between money laundering and offshore financial centres. Tax evasion is also often associated with offshore centres and is related to money laundering in many ways.

To begin with, they both entail some form of concealment. In the former case, tax evaders conceal assets or do not fully declare the income that they have lawfully or unlawfully earned. Similarly, the ultimate objective of money laundering is to disguise the source and, sometimes, the nature of wealth. It inevitably involves resorting to real or imagined transactions designed to confuse onlookers and to confound inquiry.

Money laundering and tax evasion also accompany or are an accessory to one another: the proceeds from unlawful activities are generally not reported to the tax authorities and tax evasion often necessitates financial transactions to conceal undeclared income or proceeds from sales. Similarly, both tax evasion and money laundering often rely on cash for concealing transactions.

Finally, tax enforcement and measures to deter money laundering are part of the more general policy area of law enforcement. Both tax enforcement and efforts to curtail money laundering differ, however, from other forms of law enforcement. In the case of tax compliance, government agents do not start from a crime and endeavour to detect suspects; rather they scan tax records looking for evidence of evasion. Identifying money laundering is a means to an end: the ultimate objective is to unearth other underlying criminal activities. Tax evasion may be one such criminal endeavour, although the underlying economic activity may be legitimate.

The possibility of sheltering income through the use of a multiplicity of different jurisdictions expands the scope for both money laundering and tax evasion. Typically the incentives to carry out these activities in other jurisdictions will be higher where the possibility of detection is low and the returns to sheltering income from taxation are significant. It is obvious that one should focus on offshore financial centres (OFCs) with their low tax rates and legislation protective of banking secrecy as a set of preferred locations for these activities.

This chapter examines the interrelationships between money laundering, tax evasion and OFCs. It discusses various conceptual frameworks for examining the degree of overlap between money laundering and tax evasion, and the role of offshore financial centres in these activities.

The different facets of money laundering and tax evasion can only be understood by relying on an assortment of assumptions regarding information, enforcement costs and asymmetries in behaviour by policy makers across jurisdictions. In addition, we provide empirical evidence regarding factors that may give rise to an overlap between lax financial centres offering de facto money-laundering services and tax havens. The evidence which is provided should be treated with extreme caution since it does not point to tax evasion per se but rather to the importance that tax considerations and lax financial regulation may have in determining the location of financial investments.

This chapter also seeks to identify those aspects of anti-money laundering and anti-tax evasion policies that could be usefully co-ordinated across various international regulatory bodies. In particular, we examine what forms of enforcement can be contemplated in a framework of imperfect information characterised by a multiplicity of jurisdictions.

The first section provides an overview of money laundering and tax evasion activities. It delineates the area of interest of the paper and identifies the principal policy concerns in an international dimension. It also highlights the difficulties encountered in identifying illicit activity, particularly with a multiplicity of jurisdictions.

Money laundering and tax evasion involve different types of strategic interactions. In the following section, we describe typical models of tax evasion and money laundering where individual agents operate within a given tax and regulatory environment. In this context, governments are taken as imposing a particular framework on individuals, and in turn individuals are assumed to take actions based on varying degrees of understanding of how the institutional framework operates.

This approach provides guidance on how different law and tax enforcement policies affect individual incentives to engage in money laundering or evade taxes. It may also incorporate different levels of private agent information.

This private agent approach provides little guidance, however, to government behaviour. Government is only viewed as a benevolent law enforcer, and private agents in turn respond to the incentive structure established by governments. Many of the international policy concerns have been with the behaviour of governments themselves. Lax regimes are viewed as having been established purposefully by certain jurisdictions to attract capital income (i.e. to abet income shifting) or investments. Organised crime, terrorism and corruption appear to go hand in hand; lax tax administration malfunctioning governments.[1] Then we look at diff governments with different objectives act vis-à-vis ta laundering. We examine potential interactions between the and the nature of regulatory and tax regimes as well as governments.

The penultimate section examines empirical evidence regarding the interrelationships between lax financial regulation and tax havens. Finally, the concluding remarks draw attention to some of the policy implications of the analysis.

Basic Facts on Tax Evasion and Money Laundering

As Chapters 3 and 4 have pointed out, there is a widespread perception that money laundering and tax evasion have increased in recent years despite more stringent law enforcement in many countries.

Money laundering has attracted a great deal of attention because it has been closely associated with the vast profits generated in recent decades from the illicit trade in narcotics and more recently with the financing of terrorism.

It is arguable that without the possibility of laundering vast sums of money through the financial systems, these criminal activities would not have been viable. As discussed in Chapter 2, over the years it appears that money laundering has grown into an autonomous activity that is no longer merely ancillary to other criminal endeavours. Consequently, as we shall argue at some length below, it should be analysed independently of the criminal endeavours that it supports.

In the pioneering phase of the 1960s and 1970s, currency was the favourite means of laundering. In a context of closed banking systems and low capital mobility, currency –thanks to its anonymity – was the best tool to conceal the source of illegal revenues. The increasing efficiency of banking and financial markets somehow contributed to improving the effectiveness of money-laundering techniques. Over time, it appears to have been a shift from cash to bank-related laundering and, more recently, to laundering through the financial markets. These developments have been supported by a growing demand for money-laundering coming from all types of potential users (organised crime, tax-evaders), as well as other subjects guilty of extortion or corruption). In turn, money laundering has represented an essential tool for criminal activities, corruption and the informal economy.[2]

---

[1] Tanzi (1998, 2000).
[2] See Naylor (2000).

velopments in technology, communications and travel have also given
minal enterprises the ability to straddle jurisdictions and conduct business
beyond the reach of traditional systems of law enforcement. In particular, attention
has been focused on those financial centres that appear to operate a lax regulatory
environment.

The concerns with the growth of tax evasion have been of two types. On the
one hand, there is considerable evidence – in Chapter 3, too – suggesting that tax
evasion arising from the 'shadow' or 'underground' economy has increased in
recent years.

Within the OECD area, by the end of the 1990s the shadow economy was
estimated to account for nearly 17 per cent of GDP, up from less than 14 per cent
at the beginning of the decade.[3] The underground economy is much larger in non-
OECD countries and has also by most measures grown considerably. By its very
nature this activity is difficult to define and it adjusts to the economic environment,
which consists of both legal and illicit activities.

On the other hand, the liberalisation of financial transactions, including the
lifting of withholding taxes on interest income paid to non-residents, has
encouraged individuals to shift their savings offshore ('tax havens') and companies
to relocate parts of their business.[4]

Both the growth of the underground economy and the expansion of tax havens
can be loosely associated with money laundering. Concealing taxable economic
activity often entails cash transactions, the purchase of bearer securities or the
acquisition of financial assets in other tax jurisdictions.

However, for both money laundering and tax evasion there is at times a thin
borderline between licit and illicit activity.

For example, as see in Chapters 1 and 2, covert transfers of funds may at times
arguably have a legitimate origin when money is escaping a country that is
imposing a repressive regime on its population.

Moreover, the definition of criminal activities varies across countries and
within countries over time. Some regimes have imposed very stringent restrictions
on the export of currency and shortly thereafter abolished exchange controls
completely.

Finally, money laundering may not only be the result of criminal activities; as
has been discussed in Chapters 1 to 4, it may be used as way of funding terrorism.

Tax evasion is also time- and place-specific. Tax administrations vary in the
degree to which they sanction various types of behaviour. Misreporting in some
instances is considered a misdemeanour, whereas in others it is treated with greater
severity. In addition, the authorities are constantly redefining the boundary
between legitimate tax avoidance and illegal tax evasion.

---

[3] Schneider and Enste (2000).
[4] Alworth and Andersen (1991).

Similar ambiguities arise in respect of the definition of tax haven. As it has been noted:[5]

> The term 'tax haven' has been loosely defined to include any country having a low or zero rate of tax on all or certain categories of income, and offering a certain level of banking or commercial secrecy. Applied literally, however, this definition would sweep in many industrialised countries not generally considered tax havens, including the United States (the U.S. does not tax interest on bank deposits of foreigners).

Finally, it should not be forgotten that the imposition of restrictions has indirectly promoted the growth of illicit activities (as in the case of prohibition in the United States) and fostered the existence and long-term viability of criminal endeavours.

Private Agent Approaches

The motivations of individuals for engaging in criminal activity and tax evasion have been analysed at great depth independently of one another. In this section we will assume a *closed* economy. In an international environment, one would need to account for the presence of a wider range of players and of separate heterogeneous national regulations.

Broadly speaking, formal models have been based on the approach à la Becker[6] to analysing criminal behaviour. These models have the following basic characteristics: (a) illegal returns from criminal activity exceed the proceeds from legal business; (b) individuals are aware that they shall be sanctioned if and when they are apprehended.

These assumptions entail that at the margin there is a trade-off between the gain from the illegal activity and the cost of being apprehended (perfect information models). The basic message of these models is that taking 'profits out of crime' or, alternatively, that sanctions should be commensurate to the harm produced, is the most efficient strategy for dealing with crime.

We discuss below various extensions of these models in some detail, because much can be learned about the basic features of tax evasion and money laundering and about the nature of enforcement policies. However, most of these models are mute regarding an important feature of both money laundering and tax evasion: these activities are consciously or unconsciously supported by financial intermediaries. In order to examine the issues affecting financial intermediaries, it is best to extend the analysis to imperfect information models.

---

[5] Gordon (1981).
[6] Becker (1968).

Perfect Information: Tax Evasion and Money Laundering

Tax evasion Tax evasion and money laundering have been examined at great lengths independently of one another. Since the first works,[7] a large body of literature has addressed the determinants of income tax evasion.

The basic model is an application of the expected utility framework used for analysing decision-making under uncertainty. Individuals can choose to declare all their income (Y) and be taxed at a rate t, or, alternatively, declare only a part of their income (D) and face a fixed probability of being audited (p). If they are audited, a fine (F) is levied on each dollar of undeclared income *(Y-D)*. Under the assumption that individuals are risk averse, maximising expected utility (EU) from the evading strategy is given by:

$$EU = (1-p)U(Y- tD)+pU(Y- tD-F[Y-D])$$

Or:

$$EU = (1-p)U(N)+pU(C)$$

where N and C refer to the levels of net income if the individuals are not caught or caught respectively. Maximising this expression with respect to D yields the first order condition:

$$(1-F/t) = -\frac{(1-p)}{p}\frac{U'(N)}{U'(C)}$$

As can be seen from this expression, the marginal rate of substitution between not being caught and being caught will depend on the level of fines relative to the tax payable and the probability of being detected. Indeed, in this simple model the two policy instruments – fines and the probability of detection – are perfect substitutes. Given that increasing the probability of detection requires expenditures on monitoring behaviour, whereas fines are socially costless, fines should be set as high as possible to deter evasion. Conversely, fewer resources should be spent in identifying tax evasion.[8]

Comparative static analysis shows that reported income (D) varies positively with income and deterrence (i.e. the probability of detection and the level of the fine). However, the tax rate effect is ambiguous; it depends on attitudes toward risk and the penalty structure. If the penalty is based on the amount of taxes being

---

[7] Allingham and Sandmo (1972) and Yitzhaki (1974).
[8] See Myers (1990) and Polinsky and Shavell (2000) for a discussion of this apparent policy prescription in a number of contexts.

understated, then lower taxes may lead to more evasion[9] under the plausible assumption of decreasing absolute risk aversion.

The ambiguity of the tax rate effect is robust to the introduction of more complications, such as labour supply choice.[10] Indeed under these more general assumptions, the effects of deterrence become equally ambiguous.

A model[11] of taxpayer compliance has been proposed with the provision of a public good financed with taxes subject to non-compliance. The authors show that policies designed to increase tax and audit rate uncertainty have a generally ambiguous effect on compliance. Using an experimental design with student subjects to simulate taxpayer responses, they find that the tax and audit rate response depends upon the presence or absence of a public good. When individuals perceive that they receive a public good in exchange for their taxes, uncertainty always lowers compliance.

Finally, a model[12] examines the effect of information that helps the tax enforcement authority predict tax evasion on the strategic choices made by the taxpayer and the enforcement authority. The author finds that such strategic behaviour can increase tax evasion.

In general, the theoretical literature shows that tax rates have an ambiguous effect on compliance, depending upon taxpayer attitudes toward risk and audit selection criteria, among others.[13]

These models provide useful insights into the incentive structure behind tax evasion. However, they suffer from several drawbacks: (a) they assume that the probability of audit is constant; (b) they do not take into account non-economic factors such as taxpayer morality; (c) they do not focus on the role of other players (such as financial intermediaries) in fostering evasion.

They are less useful in addressing the issue of the relationships between economic infrastructure and evasion. In the specific case of capital income where financial intermediaries and, in some instances governments, wittingly or unwittingly play a significant role in fostering evasion, these models do not appear to be particularly appropriate because the supply side is totally absent.[14]

---

[9] Yitzhaki (1974) and Graetz et al. (1985).

[10] Pencavel (1979).

[11] Alm et al. (1992a).

[12] Sansing (1993).

[13] Surveys of the tax evasion literature and of tax compliance more generally can be found in Cowell (1990) and Alm et al. (1992b).

[14] The models also fail to distinguish between different types of tax evasion and their wider implications. For example, if tax compliance for companies operating in various countries differs, the effective rate of taxation, and hence – ceteris paribus – the competitiveness of companies, may differ. The implications of this case differ markedly from that of exportation of capital to escape inheritance taxes.

Money laundering   The interactions between criminality and financial markets have only recently been studied systematically.[15] These studies assume that the basic function of money laundering is to turn *potential* liquidity into *usable* or *effective* purchasing power.

Money laundering services are used to eliminate any relationship between 'whitewashed liquidity' and the illegal or criminal activity from which it was generated. Independence reduces the risk of identification of the source of the laundered liquidity. It is for this reason that money laundering is best thought of as an independent economic endeavour unconnected to the underlying crime that it supports.

The microeconomic model that applies in this instance is similar in spirit to that discussed in the previous pages. The individual must decide whether or not to launder money. An individual is assumed to receive proceeds from illegal pursuits; these proceeds cannot be consumed directly because they would increase the probability of detecting the criminal activity. A laundered dollar of income consequently has greater value (at a cost) than a dollar of income that has not been laundered.

The greater the probability of detection, the larger the size of the fine, and the higher the cost of using the laundering technology, the lower will be the expected utility from money laundering. Conversely, the decision to launder will be positively related to the return on the undetected proceeds.[16]

This framework yields interesting insights into some of the features of anti-money laundering regulation. At the optimum, governments balance the social costs resulting from money laundering with the costs regulations impose on the economic system, particularly in terms of compliance. Different relative preferences of legislators towards the damages of crime and the costs of regulation will result in different levels of tolerance for money laundering across countries. Regulation also has an impact on the efficiency of banks and of the financial system. It can be shown that the less the legislation impairs the bank's efficiency, the more the legislation is effective.

Money laundering can also be viewed as having multiplier effects on criminal activity – the lower the opportunity cost for money laundering; the larger the share of reinvestment in illegal activities and the need to finance this reinvestment with clean liquidity; the higher the differential between the real return on illegal and legal activities, and the lower the expected relative risk of the illegal activities; the higher the initial volume of revenues from illegal economic activity.

In a former model,[17] the multiplier effects of money laundering are induced by the re-investment rate in illegal activities. The portion that is destined to the illegal

---

[15] Masciandaro (1996, 1998, 1999, 2000a and 2000b).
[16] See Masciandaro (1999) for a more detailed description of this model.
[17] Masciandaro (1999).

sector will further produce some other revenues from illegal activity that in turn will undergo a laundering process.

The money-laundering cycle takes off, and each step – provided that no obstacle hinders the process – contributes to strengthen the economic and financial power of criminals.

The more widespread those crimes that need money laundering services, the greater the growth of the supply of these services. As a result, the real and financial sectors of the illegal economy tend to strengthen each other.

Finally, money laundering can also be viewed as producing three types of externality:[18]

- It can raise the incidence of *financial pollution*, due to the fact that the laundering process requires a more or less conscious involvement of financial intermediaries;
- Money laundering can also increase the rate of *economic pollution* by boosting illegal revenues and the financial assets that criminals can re-invest in their activities;
- Greater economic power in the hands of criminal organisations inevitably leads to their stronger influence on a country's social and political life, with a subsequent exacerbation of *social pollution* standards.

Public damage is even more serious when the money-laundering operation aims at controlling a company by the acquisition of a majority share. Besides social and economic pollution, we must now face the creeping presence of sectoral and/or territorial pollution: dangers lie in the outcome of a biased company management, which responds to the criminal subject's extra-economic goals rather than to fair economic principles.[19]

Money Laundering and Tax Evasion Two studies[20] are the only contributions that attempt to capture the overlap between tax evasion and money laundering.

In the first work,[21] individuals are assumed to allocate their work effort between legal and illegal activities. In order to enjoy the returns from illegal activities, the proceeds must be laundered either by being declared as part of income from legal activities or by being channelled overseas through the financial system at a cost. In contrast to most treatments of tax evasion, this model distinguishes between the act of concealment and the act of evasion. The proceeds from crime are concealed but in order to enjoy the proceeds of the illegal activity they must somehow be revealed.

---

[18] Masciandaro (2000b).
[19] Masciandaro (2000a).
[20] Yaniv (1994 and 1999).
[21] Yaniv (1994).

A number of penalties (on tax evasion and on illegal activities) serve to link together further tax evasion and money laundering. In equilibrium, the differential gain between illegal and legal business must equal their differential cost. Not surprisingly, this will depend on the severity of penalties, the relative tax rate and laundering costs associated with channelling funds abroad. From a policy standpoint, limiting money laundering may increase tax revenues indirectly.[22]

The basic premise of the second study[23] is that money laundering is ancillary to tax evasion. In attempting to avoid being caught by the tax authorities, individuals engage in (costly) money laundering to conceal their income. Individuals consequently face a two-tiered decision: how much to evade and, subsequently, how much of the evaded income to conceal by engaging in money laundering.

Similarly, the authorities engage in a two-stage enforcement policy: they audit taxpayers selectively and investigate further a proportion of those they initially audit.

This second model shows that combating money laundering (i.e. increasing the probability of in-depth audits) has the effect of reducing the optimal levels of both tax evasion by individuals and money laundering. In other words, there is an indirect benefit for the tax authorities from devoting resources to combating money laundering.[24] Furthermore, the amount of effort devoted to detecting money laundering may have an important impact on the resources spent on auditing taxpayers.

This analysis highlights the important synergies that can potentially exist between law enforcement in respect of money laundering and taxation.

However, it is limited in several respects. First, as already noted, it presumes that money laundering is ancillary to tax evasion. This may not necessarily be the case. The reasons for engaging in criminal activity, or more generally concealing the source of income, may be unrelated to taxation. It is also difficult to argue that tax evasion is ancillary to crime although, in some instances (Al Capone), criminals have been put on trial for tax evasion because they did not declare the proceeds from their illegal activities.

Secondly,[25] the framework focuses on the demand side of money laundering. The supply side, i.e. the role of financial intermediaries, deserves attention as well, particularly because this is the area on which law enforcement has dedicated most of its efforts.

---

[22] The paper also considers the case of tax amnesties. Their success is shown to depend crucially on the nature of money laundering (domestic or international).

[23] Yaniv (1999).

[24] The existence of an internal solution is predicated on the costs of money laundering being an increasing function of the amount laundered. If this were not the case it would always be optimal for taxpayers to evade their entire liability as long as the cost of money laundering was lower than the gross-up tax rate.

[25] As noted even by Yaniv (1999).

Imperfect Information

As we have already noted the literature on tax evasion and money laundering does not generally discuss the supply side.

In theory, one could consider the incentives of suppliers of tax evasion and money laundering services along the lines of those employed for the demand side. As with the analyses that focus on the demand side, the degree to which intermediaries would support money laundering would clearly depend on the level of explicit punishment, implicit penalties (e.g. reputation) and the probability of detection.

But this would capture only imperfectly the role of intermediaries, because by assumption they would be *wilfully* engaging in money laundering with criminals and tax evaders. The perfect information models also assume that it is always possible to draw a clear distinction between legal and illegal activities, although the probability of detection may in some ways capture the difficulty of identifying illegitimate activity.

In order to address the real issues of concern to financial intermediaries, one must turn to the role played by financial intermediaries in the economy and bear in mind that the distinction between criminal and legitimate activity is not always apparent.[26]

Within the financial sector, banks provide deposit contracts that fulfil monetary and payment needs, as well as credit contracts that are usually not negotiable on financial markets. Banks therefore have a special intermediating function resulting from credit and deposit contracts that allow them to reach economies of scale and diversification in the management of informational assets. In markets where information is incomplete and hard to gather, it is then clear how crucial it can be for a bank to conceal the purchasing power produced by illegal transactions.

As a consequence, banking intermediaries represent an ideal target for criminal organisations; the presence of either collusive or simply inefficient bank operators dramatically raises the chances of using credit or payment financial services in order to achieve criminal goals of money laundering and control upon the economic system.

We shall name the two cases of collusive bankers and inefficient bankers as 'criminal bank' and 'honest bank', respectively.[27]

Criminal Intermediaries

A criminal bank can be seen as a particular form of legal enterprise whose property and control actually belong to criminals. The reason why criminals might show a

---

[26] As pointed out by Rider (2002), responsible banking is a nebulous concept particularly in an international context.

[27] Masciandaro (1996, 1998 and 1999).

great interest in casting their influence upon such an enterprise – beyond the specific need of implementing the money-laundering process – is linked to the additional need to carry out some types of legal activity.

A bank's peculiar function in money laundering can be identified as its ability to use the supply of both asset and liability services for the purpose of concealing the illegal source of a given amount of money. On the liability side, bank deposits optimally allow users to exploit all forms of payment services: therefore criminal banks may offer to criminal subjects the best available guarantees – net of identification and punishment costs – in terms of legalising illegal money. As a consequence, any intermediary that supplies payment services represents a desirable target in the perspective of implementing money-laundering strategies.

On the credit side, besides engaging in money-laundering operations, dishonest bankers can arbitrarily grant credit to unworthy recipients – members of the criminal organisations or their men of straw – thus meeting the criminal goals rather than pursuing shareholders' and savers' interests. Such behaviour not only fuels the development of a criminal economy but also induces mismanagement in one of the most relevant and delicate banking functions, which is to monitor creditworthy projects thanks to banks' exclusive set of information.

The above mismanagement of the credit function brings about a biased concept of the implicit insurance that banks provide about the worthiness of companies in terms of investment projects. By granting credit to a company on the basis of its information set, a bank implicitly expresses a positive evaluation of the company. Such a favourable statement can then be used by the company itself in dealing with other counter -parties, including other financial intermediaries. As a consequence, if a bank's credit allocation policy is driven by distorted economic principles, the rating service offered by bank credit ultimately becomes polluted and therefore unreliable.

Honest Intermediaries

In most instances, money laundering is ultimately channelled through financial intermediaries that are unwitting parties to the final objective of the chain of transactions.

Authorities seek to limit the possibility of these transactions by imposing regulations and due diligence rules on financial intermediaries, who ultimately act as agents for governments. The willingness of financial intermediaries to assume a monitoring role will depend on two types of cost: the costs relating to investments needed to establish a system for monitoring clients and the indirect costs associated with the lifting of bank secrecy on the activities of clients (reputational costs).

There is a clear asymmetry of information between the regulator (the principal) and the financial intermediary (the agent). The difficulty in monitoring the degree of effort spent by intermediaries to report suspicious transactions is compounded by the lack of clearly identifiable indicators of laundering in most circumstances.[28]

The initial hypothesis is that any form of regulation tends to alter the structure of the incentives, and thus the conduct, of intermediaries. The effectiveness of regulation depends on the ability to influence the choices of banks and, at least, in part on the extent of regulation-related '*compliance costs*', i.e. the charges imposed by the very existence of rules and regulations, which produce risks of avoidance.

As the cost of regulation rises, the level of its acceptability to intermediaries declines, altering the structure of incentives, and thus conducting and distorting the objectives of regulation. The upshot is that each regulatory system must possess a sufficient level of acceptability for the regulated intermediaries to be effective. The costs of anti-laundering regulation must be weighed against the gains expected from regulation, so that the final net result is a lowering of the money-laundering risk.

A distinction must be made, however, between expected gains at the system level and expected gains for the individual intermediaries, for both the regulation aimed at defining the honest intermediaries as *agents* and for that aimed at deterring *criminal* intermediaries.

At the aggregate level, it is possible to show[29] that there is an evident incentive for the economic system in general, and for the industry of regulated intermediaries in particular, to accept rules that present a deterrent for potentially *corrupt* intermediaries.

Financial institutions must come to understand that they are just as much a stakeholder in upholding the integrity of a financial system.[30] Reputation and integrity are a public good and regulation must be designed to avoid the risks of free-riding.

In other words, intermediaries may choose to benefit from the reputation for integrity of a financial system in order to carry out a low level of diligence in vetting their customers.

As has been noted[31] in the specific case of the OFCs, confidentiality is still an economic asset in the national and international banking and financial industries. The less effect the definition of the role and obligations of intermediaries in the anti-laundering function has on their incentives, the greater will be the risks that each intermediary will seek to expend the minimum effort.

The design of effective regulation must therefore consider the role of incentives on behaviour. The intermediaries must find it optimal to perform their agent function effectively.

---

[28] See Filotto and Masciandaro (2001).
[29] Masciandaro (2000a and 2000b).
[30] Baity (2000).
[31] Antoine (1999).

If the regulation design is incentive-compatible, the bank disclosure strategy is easier to implement. It is important to remember[32] that, in general, any decision to disclosure can only be made after a fair, analytical and practical assessment of the facts and consequences in line with the corporation's policies, remedies and culture, and, in turn, all these variables are more or less dependent on the features of the rules of games.[33]

Among these it is important to mention the possible role of reputation. If an intermediary operates in markets that assign value to its endowments, be they linked to profits, assets or reputation, the regulation must take them into consideration. It will then be the intermediaries themselves who are endogenously driven to ensure that the structure of their internal incentives in the individual job positions (from manager to window clerk) moves toward the active effective collaboration that they produce with an effective anti-laundering commitment.

Government Interactions

In the preceding pages we discussed the relationship between money laundering and taxation under the assumption that government behaviour was exogenous and benevolent.

To be sure, in these models governments could alter their policies in response to private agents' behaviour, but these reactions assumed that governments aimed at both enforcing tax compliance and minimising the risks of money laundering.

In recent years, policy concerns at an international level have arisen because some jurisdictions have been perceived as actively encouraging money laundering through lax regulatory regimes or fostering undesirable tax competition or tax evasion, and in several instances both types of behaviour.

An analysis of this type of issue must go beyond the models described in the previous section and focus on two aspects. The first is the nature and size of the externalities produced by various governments. The second is the interaction between jurisdictions. In these instances, governments must be viewed as acting strategically along various dimensions.

Taxing Foreign Source Income

Taxing foreign source income under existing institutional arrangements faces a number of insurmountable problems and gives rise to strategic interactions between different jurisdictions.

---

[32] Moscarino et al. (2000).

[33] We shall return to discuss these factors at greater length in the following section. A good example of the importance of the cost-benefit approach for the analysis of intermediaries and regulators in the money laundering issues is KPMG (2003).

In the case of personal income, most countries apply taxes under national law regardless of whether the source is domestic or foreign (residence principle).[34] In certain instances, foreign source income is exempted even under national law, if the income was earned overseas under temporary work arrangements.

The core problem on foreign source income is enforcement. There is considerable evidence to suggest that a large proportion of assets held abroad by individuals go undeclared.[35] There is also a strong presumption that certain jurisdictions may seek to establish a reputation for providing services that facilitate concealing income (e.g. banking secrecy) from the tax authorities of the jurisdictions in which the individuals ultimately reside.

With the corporation tax, under current international law, foreign subsidiaries operate as independent legal entities. As a general principle, this means that they are subject to taxation in the country in which they are incorporated (source principle).

The residence principle generally applies only to dividends distributed to the parent company. Tax treaties between countries are often signed with the purpose of mitigating the double taxation of dividends and other remittances in the source and residence countries. Differential tax treatment of similar streams of income across centres results in strong incentives to relocate taxable income and/or to shift real business activity (and capital) to low-tax jurisdictions. It creates an ex ante incentive for countries wishing to attract tax base or capital to their jurisdictions to establish a favourable tax environment.

Interactions between various elements of the tax code affecting individuals and corporations are often exploited jointly. In many instances financial institutions locate in low-tax jurisdictions to reduce their own tax liability and to create a favourable tax environment for their clients. Hence, there is a complex interaction between corporation tax and the taxation of income accruing to non-residents.[36]

Tax Competition

There is a longstanding interest in the international arena regarding the consequences of jurisdictions trying to set up favourable regimes with the explicit

---

[34] Any withholding tax that may have been levied abroad can be credited against personal income tax in the country of residence of the taxpayer.

[35] In 2002, over €60 billion were repatriated to Italy following a tax amnesty for undeclared assets held abroad.

[36] See Alworth and Andresen (1990).

objective of attracting capital,[37] and they have generally been discussed under the heading of tax competition.

Tax competition seems to be defined broadly as any form of non-cooperative setting of taxes by independent governments that influences the location of a mobile tax base (typically capital).

More specifically, the OECD has harmful tax practice as one that 'meets one of the three operative criteria of no effective exchange of information, lack of transparency, and "no substantial activities"/ring fencing, and at the same time offers a low/no/nominal rate of tax'.

The literature on tax competition tends to focus on fiscal externalities that occur when capital or firms are not taxed efficiently. Tax base externalities arise when raising levies unilaterally in one country drives some part of the internationally mobile tax base to another jurisdiction. This results in a positive externality for the recipient country. It also leads to tax rates and public goods supply being too low relative to a situation where tax policies had been coordinated across jurisdictions.[38]

The literature also pays a great deal of attention to the various incentives to attract mobile tax bases faced by countries of different sizes. One general conclusion is that small countries have an incentive to undercut large countries if they can compete internationally for capital. If a country is sufficiently small, it will do so and gain from it, since the elasticity in these countries tends to be higher.

Differences in size are modelled by assuming that regions diverge in population size (only) but that per capita capital endowments are identical. This implies that capital will not move between regions unless taxes differ across jurisdictions.

Since large regions play a major role in international capital markets, any changes in their tax treatment of capital income will have a significant impact on the return on capital to savers in that jurisdiction but leave international pre-tax returns largely unchanged.

Conversely, small countries will have limited fiscal autonomy, since small changes in tax rates will entail large inward or outward movements of capital relative to the size of the population. This creates an asymmetry across countries. An important result in this context is that if small countries are sufficiently small, they set lower tax rates than the large countries and attract an over-proportional

---

[37] This definition of tax competition is somewhat narrow. A broader definition of tax competition to include 'uses of the tax system to foster the competitiveness of a country' would allow a number of other important enforcement problems to be addressed. For example, if expenditures on corruption are considered a 'deductible expense' item in country A this may facilitate tax evasion in country B by over-invoicing of exports by country A and 'side payments' made to a third country.

[38] Tax exporting externalities may occur when domestic tax authorities aim to tax rents accruing to foreigners. Terms of trade externalities may arise when taxes can be used to shift international commodity prices. See Haufler (2001).

share of the total capital stock. By doing so they 'win' the competition for capital in that they achieve a higher per capita utility in the tax equilibrium.[39]

The predictions of one important strand of the theoretical literature are very strong. First, capital mobility results in capital taxes that are too low from a social perspective; raising the tax rate lowers the tax base. Moreover, the supply of public goods is less than it would be in the presence of tax coordination.

Second, it is not in the national interest of small countries to participate in an international agreement that will curb their ability to attract capital.

Third, the smaller the country, the more likely it is that it will become a tax haven and large countries should export capital to small countries. Indeed, both these predictions have been verified by empirical studies, which find that there is a positive relationship between the size of taxes on capital and country size.[40]

These conclusions appear at first sight to match with a number of stylised facts. In order to 'win' the competition over mobile capital, tax havens seek to prevent the functioning of the residence principle. Investors wishing to evade resident taxation can do so with relative ease if they can rely on tax havens not to transmit information to their resident countries. The privacy of investors is secured mainly through two types of laws: secrecy laws and blocking laws. Blocking laws prevent the disclosure of any economic activity by a foreign investor to a third party. Secrecy laws prohibit the general disclosure of information concerning investors for the purpose of complying with foreign tax authorities. The effectiveness of these laws hinges on various measures such as penal sanctions against infractions (e.g. Switzerland) or criminal penalties (e.g. Luxembourg).

Secrecy laws can be used not only by individual households wishing to evade resident taxation, but also by financial intermediaries such as commercial banks to bypass domestic rules. As was discussed above, this appears to have been the case in Germany, where German banks were instrumental in the transfer of funds to Luxembourg in order to help their depositors evade the German tax on interest income. German banks were sheltered from revealing any information about its depositors as long as their branches were located in Luxembourg.

This reading of the limited empirical evidence must be taken with some degree of caution, particularly if the aim is to single out individual favourable tax regimes.

As has been noted,[41] certain tax provisions of major developed countries can be used by non-residents as a way to evade tax in their country of residence. To a great extent these favourable provisions result from the absence of source-based taxes on income accruing to non-residents and the lack of exchange of information agreements between countries. Consequently, one should be careful to extrapolate certain findings of the tax competition literature to particular types of countries.

---

[39] Bucovetsky (1991) and Wilson (1991).

[40] Hines (1999).

[41] Langer (2000) and McLure (1986).

The small versus large country paradigm clearly does not capture the phenomenon of Latin American flight capital seeking refuge in Miami banks.

Another note of caution regards the more general issues of whether tax competition is undesirable and always leads necessarily to lower tax rates.[42] More generally, the issue of tax competition is related to attitudes towards the desirable size of governments. As Chapter 1 pointed out, a sharply contrasting view to that described in the previous paragraphs considers that the downward pressure on tax rates resulting from tax competition 'would in general be desirable, providing an essential antidote to the built-in pressures for increased public expenditure and taxation'.[43]

Finally, the existence of tax avoidance opportunities and harmful tax competition in tax havens should be distinguished from tax evasion. As we have already noted, tax competition may exist without entailing tax evasion in other countries.

Lax Financial Regulation and the Supply of Money Laundering Services

Summarising what we analysed in Chapter 4, countries aiming to promote an influx of hidden funds operate, in many respects, in the same manner described by the tax competition literature.

However, the specific characteristics of a lax financial environment differ from those involving the non-cooperative setting of taxes. We focus on the actions of a national policymaker in what can be defined in Chapter 4 as a Lax Financial Regulation (LFR) country, in which the features of financial regulation increase the probability that money laundering services will be offered to criminal organisations and terrorist groups:

- An LFR country will be one that, in terms of economic characteristics, has relatively scant physical resources that can be devoted to international trade, and this is an initial channel of *national benefit* expected from lax regulation;
- At the same time, an LFR country has the potential for developing financial services, also useful for money-laundering purposes, and this is a second channel of *national benefit* expected from lax regulation;
- An LFR country also has geographical and social characteristics that shield it to some extent from the risks of terrorism and/or organised crime, thus reducing the *expected cost* of lax regulation;
- An LFR country is relatively indifferent to the *expected costs* due to international reputation risks.

---

[42] Wildasin and Wilson (2002).
[43] UK Treasury (1988).

Measuring the Overlap Between Money Laundering and Tax Evasion

Now we can examine the degree of potential overlap between money laundering activities and tax evasion, which can be detected from data collected from various sources.

Our purpose is to see whether the data that are available can be used to draw any inferences regarding the manner in which tax evasion and money laundering overlap. We focus on cross-border capital flows, but undoubtedly it is important to realise that both money laundering and tax evasion often start at home.

We also assess the criteria used by the authorities in defining tax havens and lax financial centres. It is important to bear in mind that any conclusion that can be derived from such empirical studies should be taken with extreme caution, since by definition the estimations are subject to very large measurement errors and biases. Moreover, as has been noted in several instances, there is a subtle line between tax avoidance and tax evasion. For many of the empirical findings that are discussed below, it is not possible to distinguish between tax reducing behaviour resulting from outright tax evasion and tax avoidance.

This section is structured as follows. We first examine the relationship between the lists of countries that have been identified as encouraging tax evasion and money laundering. Another series of tests are performed to examine the relationship between the size of the shadow economy, tax factors and lax financial regulation.

Using both public and confidential data supplied by the Bank for International Settlements, we examine the extent to which international banking activity is determined by lax financial regulation and tax factors. We look at both demand factors (in the country of origin of depositors) and supply factors (in the country in which banks are located).

While, as we have stressed in previous pages, there is a theoretical presumption that international tax evasion and money laundering through offshore centres should overlap, this is not necessarily the case.

In Chapter 4, Figure 4.1 shows the list of countries that, from time to time, were not complying with the Guidelines of the Financial Action Task Force (FATF). Here, Table 5.1 shows the countries that have been identified by the OECD as engaging in Harmful Tax Competition.

As can be seen by comparing the figure and the table, countries that were not compliant with FATF criteria do not necessarily qualify as tax havens. For example, Hungary, Israel and Russia are not widely considered to be locations that enjoy an advantageous tax status. However, owing to a lax regulatory and supervisory environment, banks in those countries were considered potential targets for money laundering. Similarly, a number of blacklisted locations from a tax standpoint are not NCCTs (Non-Cooperative Countries and Territories) under FATF.

While this finding may appear to contradict the hypothesis that money laundering and tax evasion are intimately related, this is not altogether surprising in light of the criteria utilised for constructing the blacklists for NCCTs and centres engaging in harmful tax competition.

The members of FATF did not seek to list a series of transactions that could be identified as money laundering and then seek to identify centres in which such transactions were more likely to occur. Rather, they used 40 criteria basically relating to the degree of transparency of the financial system and to the degree of law enforcement for defining NCCTs.

In drawing up the blacklist, FATF was also careful not to avoid a number of complex issues, such as the definition of criminal activity, which can vary from centre to centre. This is especially important for tax evasion, which is treated very differently under the law in various jurisdictions. As a consequence, the emphasis on non-transparency, degree of supervision and law enforcement has led to a very disparate series of jurisdictions appearing as NCCTs.

In the case of the OECD harmful tax competition studies (1998) and EU Report of the Primarollo Group, the focus was on identifying tax provisions or preferential regimes in some instances of a very specific nature or relating to a specific type of industry (for example, shipping).

The focus was on transactions that could lead to the shifting of the tax base and not necessarily to tax evasion, which entails the concealment of income. The coverage included regimes in OECD countries, and chapters were dedicated to a number of specific topics: artificial definition of the tax base; failure to adhere to international transfer pricing principles; foreign source income exempt from residence country tax; negotiable tax rates or tax base; existence of secrecy provisions; access to a wide network of tax treaties; regimes which are promoted as tax minimisation vehicles; and regimes encouraging purely tax-driven operations or arrangements.

There is also another important distinction that can be made between countries engaged in harmful tax competition and NCCTs. Given the complexity of many money laundering schemes, highly sophisticated intelligence and policing operations may be needed to control and eradicate money laundering.

This may be difficult for many small centres, particularly because money laundering by its very nature involves circumventing the rule of law, and small financial centres may not have the resources to police these activities. Consequently, the efforts of FATF aimed at improving the workings of the financial systems of small financial centres may at times actually assist the development of more efficient tax havens.

Therefore, with the same worldwide data set used in Chapter 4, we carried out another Probit analysis where the dependent variable is now an Offshore Binary Probit Variable, that is equal to 1 for the OECD offshore countries and 0 otherwise. The structure of the estimated equation is equal to that of the FATF countries, used in Chapter 4, with the same independent variables.

The estimated equation is as follows:

$$(BinaryLI)_t = \beta_1 + \beta_2(A1)_t + \beta_3(B1) + \beta_4(C1)_t + \beta_5(E1)\varepsilon_t$$

with $t = 1...N$
where:

$A1$ = Land use;
$B1$ = GDP per Capita;
$C1$ = Foreign Deposits per Capita;
$E1$ = Terrorism and Organised Crime Index.

Table 5.1   Comparing Binary Offshore Index and Binary Laxity determinants (130 countries and territories)

Dependent Variable	Binary Laxity Index	Binary Offshore Index
Landuse	0.007***	-0.002
	(0.003)	(0.005)
Gdpcapita	-7.07E-05****	-2.04E-07
	(1.92E-05)	(2.60E-07)
Fordepostcapita	3.18E-06****	1.71E-06
	(1.36E-06)	(1.33E-08)
Terrorismorgcrime	-0.508***	-1.888****
	(0.224)	(0.448)

Standard Errors in parenthesis. Asterisks indicate statistical significance at 0.01 (****), 0.02 (***), 0.05 (**), 0.10 (*).

As can be seen, with the exception of the crime and terrorism index, none of variables have any explanatory power. This seems to suggest that the underlying economic characteristics of offshore centres and blacklisted countries tend to differ. In general, therefore, we can reject the hypothesis that the causes of LFR decisions and of offshore activities are exactly the same.

Now, one useful starting point for examining the potential interrelationship between lax financial regulation and tax evasion is the above-quoted model[44] on the demand for money laundering services.

The principal conclusion of that model is that there is a positive relationship between financial laxity and tax evasion. Devoting resources to combating money

---

[44] Yaniv (1999).

laundering has the effect of reducing tax evasion. Furthermore, the amount of effort devoted to detecting money laundering may have an important impact on the resources spent on auditing taxpayers.

The shadow economy

Quantification of the size of the shadow economy and the examination of explanatory factors has been the object of considerable research in recent years.[45] Tax evasion and criminal activities give rise to informal economic activity. Money laundering is an important factor – even in the most basic form of cash transactions – in permitting the functioning of the informal sector.

Understanding the determinants of the shadow economy at the domestic level is also an important element in trying to construct a model of the international spillovers of lax financial regulation and tax evasion. One would presume that the larger the size of the shadow economy, the greater will be the demand for using offshore banking activities.

In estimating the relationship between the size of the informal economy, money laundering and tax evasion, we expand on existing literature by examining a broader range of countries.[46] The inferences that can be drawn from estimations of the determinants of the size of the shadow economy must be taken with great caution. Many potential independent variables tend to be highly collinear and causality may not be necessarily one-directional (for example, a low tax pressure may induce a smaller shadow economy or be the result of the existence of a sizeable shadow economy). Such problems are best dealt with in a simultaneous equation system. In what follows we limit ourselves to inferring broad relationships between various potential factors that may affect the size of the shadow economy.

Independent variables affecting the size of the shadow economy can be clustered into five groups:

- tax factors (both rates and burdens),
- macroeconomic determinants (such as domestic inflation or other measures of contingent financial uncertainty),
- proxies for the degree of financial laxity (crime and corruption, severity of supervision etc),

---

[45] Schneider and Ernst (2002).

[46] In particular, we rely on figures compiled by Schneider (2002) and on data compiled by various researchers at the World Bank on the regulatory framework of financial systems and on the structure of governance in various countries. We also take as our starting point the estimations carried out by Friedman et al. (2000).

- political and structural socio-economic variables (stability, effectiveness of government, level and distribution of income etc),
- structural variables (size, legal system, geography etc).

The first four sets of variables are closely interrelated. Political and economic instability affect the level of inflation and the structure of the tax system. Political stability in turn may be affected by deeper socio-economic factors such as ethnic fragmentation and the nature of constitutional arrangements. These deep-seated factors in turn affect the degree and character of corruption. The level of government involvement in the economy and high tax burdens may also be associated with corruption (Tanzi, 1998).[47] Owing to the endogeneity of many of the variables and possibility of reverse causality, it is difficult to draw strong inferences of causal relationships. Consequently the estimates reported in Tables 5.2-5.4 must be treated with caution.[48]

Table 5.2 confirms to a large extent the principal finding of Friedman et al. (2000), i.e. that the size of the shadow economy is related to socio-economic variables. In particular, greater political stability and lower levels of corruption – the higher the index the less the corruption – tend to be associated with lower levels of informal activity in all country groupings. We also find that higher inflation rates tend to accompany larger shadow economies (which may also be associated with lower levels of political stability). By contrast, the degree of openness of the economy and the tax pressure variable do not appear to influence the size of the shadow economy. Indeed, for the latter variable, the coefficient often has a negative sign, indicating that greater tax pressure will lead to a smaller shadow economy.

---

[47] It is also the case that some of the countries with the highest tax burdens (Denmark, Sweden, Finland) are those with the lowest level of corruption.

[48] The estimates for the size of the unofficial sector in GDP were taken from Schneider (2002) and based on private consumption of electricity. For details on the methodology used for calculating these numbers see Schneider and Enste (2000).

**Table 5.2   Regression of Shadow Economy to GDP on Number of
Independent Variables taken one by one (Coefficients)**

Independent Variable	Total	Latin America	Africa and Middle East	Asia Pacific	Transition	OECD
Tax Revenues/ GDP	-0.46*	0.04	-0.32	0.44	-0.71*	0.20
Freedom	9.60*	-0.09	7.11**	1.94	2.68	9.90*
Political Stability	-11.04*	-7.50	-7.69*	-10.47*	-13.66*	-13.13*
Index of Corruption	-4.13*	-5.28**	-3.30*	-3.63*	-6.50*	-2-21*
Inflation	2.39*	0.79	31.17*	2.28*	2.30*	184.50 *
Interest Rate Spread	0.98*	0.43	1.12*	0.57**	0.81*	1.32**
Trade	-1.14	8.29	1.54	-8.22	-13.09	1.95
(Tax/GDP)/goverm. effectiveness	0.352*	0.393	0.18	0.49*	0.092	0.90*
Num. of observations	107	16	24	22	22	21

* Significant at the 5% level, ** Significant at the 10% level

These results however are very sensitive to the choice of conditioning variables. In fact, as shown in Table 5.3, these conclusions must be somewhat revised once allowance is made for differences in the level of income per capita.

While corruption and political stability continue to appear as important determinants of informal activity at the overall level and for OECD countries, for other country groupings these factors do not appear to be statistically significant. The shadow economy appears to be more closely related to macroeconomic factors as proxied by the level of inflation.

The results reported in Tables 5.2 and 5.3, which are broadly in line with those reported by Friedman et al. (2000), suggest that the tax burden does not affect the size of the shadow economy.

This literature tends to suggest that higher tax rates (and revenue to GDP ratios) are associated with higher levels of unofficial activity but that these relationships tend to break down once account is taken of the burden of bureaucracy and corruption. This result would also appear to suggest that the tax revenue to GDP ratio might be eroded by the size of the shadow economy.

Table 5.3 **Regression of Shadow Economy to GDP on GDP per Capita and Number of Independent Variables taken one by one (Coefficients)**

Independent Variable	Total	Latin America	Africa and Middle East	Asia Pacific	Transition	OECD
Tax Revenues/ GDP	0.06	0.03	0.06	0.55	-0.34	0.17
Freedom	0.34	-5.58	0.80	-4.05	-0.23	7.14*
Political Stability	-6.48*	-3.64	-3.60	-10.33*	-9.43	-9.17**
Index of Corruption	-2.51*	-2.86	-0.84	-4.74	-1.86	-1.49**
Inflation	1.76*	0.09	19.27**	2.11*	1.78*	132.55**
Interest Rate Spread	0.60*	0.32	0.77**	0.48	0.48	0.53
Trade	0.99	0.45	2.55	-4.60	-6.34	1.79
(Tax/GDP)/go vern. effectiveness	.169*	0.042	0.099	0.423**	-0.047	0.703*
Num. of observations	107	16	24	22	22	21

* Significant at the 5% level, ** Significant at the 10% level

One reason for this result is that tax revenue per se is not a sufficient indicator of the tax burden. The burden of government is very different if taxes are used to transfer income to inefficient government officials or to finance a high level and quality of services. In order to test whether this might be the case, we created a new variable that deflates the level of government expenditures by an index of government effectiveness, as measured by the governance centre of the World Bank. In other words, we considered the perceived tax burden for a specific level of tax revenues to GDP to be higher if government effectiveness were lower.[49] As can be seen from the last row of Tables 5.2 and 5.3, this measure of tax burden is positively correlated to the size of the shadow economy and is robust to the inclusion of GDP per capita as an explanatory variable.

Bearing these caveats in mind, we carried out a further set of estimates to examine the extent to which the size of the shadow economy was related to a broad number of variables taken together. These results are presented in Table 5.4.

As can be seen from Table 5.4, the size of the shadow economy is positively related to both tax variables and to variables related closely to criminal activities

---

[49] Schneider and Enste (2002, Chapter 9), provide a discussion of other studies that attempt to measure the quality of public goods as a determinant of the size of the underground economy.

(and potentially money laundering), such as the index of corruption. It is interesting to note that institutional variables are major determinants of the size of the underground economy as well as variables that proxy for the degree of social cohesiveness such as the Gini coefficient. We also ran a series of regression that allow for the interaction between tax variables and crime-related variables. However, the inclusion of these interacted variables under varying specifications proved inconclusive. These preliminary results suggest that climatic and fiscal variables are important factors in determining the size of the shadow economy. It does not appear, however, that where crime is accompanied by high taxes there is a greater probability of observing a large shadow economy.

Table 5.4 Regression of Shadow Economy to GNP (Coefficients)

Independent variable	Eq(4.1)	Eq(4.2)	Eq(4.3)	Eq(4.4)	Eq(4.5)
Log GDP per capita	-2.975*	-1.689	-2.554*		-0.809
GDP per capita				-0.001**	
Political Stability	-5.802*	-3.529**	-4.840*	-4.988*	-2.786
Revenue to GDP ratio	0.061	0.043			
Inflation	1.643*	1.435*	1.401*		1.279*
(Tax/GDP)/Government. Effectiveness			0.143**	0.086	0.163*
Govern. Effectiveness		-4.740*			
Index of Corruption				-1.068	-1.475**
Trade				1.758	
Civil Dummy					1.143
Gini					0.355*
R^2 Adjusted	0.545	0.558	0.568	0.491	0.626
Number of Observations	107	107	94	107	94

* Significant at the 5% level, ** Significant at the 10% level

The Determinants of External Deposits

Any study of international movements of capital associated with money laundering and tax evasion must necessarily examine banking data. While cursory evidence suggests that transactions through financial markets relating to money laundering and tax evasion have increased in recent years, bank intermediation (and the payment system) remains crucial.

Data collected by the Bank for International Settlements since the mid-1960s is the best source of information on international financial flows. Currently, these data are collected from banks located in over 30 major financial centres including a number of offshore centres. The individual data items that are reported include breakdowns of assets and liabilities vis-à-vis bank and non-entities in over 200 jurisdictions.

As shown in Figure 5.2, cross-border deposits by non-banks have expanded very rapidly across all jurisdictions, although growth has been particularly notable in Luxembourg, Switzerland and Ireland. At end-2002, non-bank deposits placed in these centres plus those in reporting offshore centres accounted for over 40 per cent of all non-bank deposits worldwide.

In this section, and that which follows, we examine some of the determinants of this deposit activity by non-banks. Our initial focus is on the determinants of deposits held abroad by residents of different countries. Table 5.5 reports a first series of results regarding the determinants of external deposits (as measured by the ratio of total deposits to GNP) by non-banking entities at end-2000.

As we noted in the previous section, the shadow economy is connected to a number of domestic climatic factors that are related directly or indirectly to money laundering and tax evasion. We test whether the size of the shadow economy affects depositing abroad, after allowing for a number of control variables – the most important of which is the depth of international trade relations as measured by the ratio of exports plus imports to GNP.

A first series of cross-section estimates (columns 1 and 2) revealed that the size of the shadow economy appears to contribute to the extent residents of a particular country place deposits abroad. This finding is in line with the theoretical conjectures proposed by Yaniv (1999).

Other elements that appear important are the degree of financial repression, as measured by capital controls, and the presence of foreign banks as a means for channelling funds abroad.

These findings, however, do not stand up to further scrutiny. Adding in dummy variables for the OECD list of jurisdictions engaged in tax competition outside the OECD (Blacklist) or having harmful tax practices within the OECD, has a dramatic impact on the results, as shown by the rise in the overall explanatory power of the regression.

One possible interpretation of these results is that the dummy variables for countries engaged in tax competition captures the activities of non-banks operating in these centres. Tax factors are involved in the location of non-bank entities in these jurisdictions, and it is the effect of these entities (affiliates or, in some instances, pooled investment vehicles) that in turn invest elsewhere. Cross-border deposits cannot be explained by the shadow economy or indeed by many of those same variables that explained the shadow economy.

Indeed, 'Blacklist' and 'harmful' change the sign of the coefficient on the shadow economy. The significance of coefficients on a number of other independent variables (such as foreign banks) also changes very markedly in response to the inclusion of new variables.

Global Financial Crime

Table 5.5 Determinants of Cross-Border Non-Bank Deposits

Independent variable	Dependent variables					
	Non bank deposits			Interbank deposits		
(Exports+Imports)/GDP	77.715	87.290	28.331*	1.616	263.02*	252.91*
Shadow Economy to GDP	9.674*	10.405*	-0.956		-1.107	
Revenue to GDP ratio						-35.562
Capital Controls	-87.444**	-57.198	-20.529**	59.096	-103.2*	694.24
Interest rate spread	-11.313*	-13.08*	-0.459		-3.303	
Number of Foreign Banks		3.725**	0.739**	8.409*	8.290*	32.345
Latin America Dummy		203.99*	30.954		4.462	
'Blacklist'			3190.49*	2951.1*		13273.2*
Harmful			19.203*	45.155		153.61
(Tax/GDP)/ Government Effectiveness				-1.009		
Gini				-3.696		-7.634
Num. Tax Treaties				-4.901*		
Rule of law			-27.676*			622.659
Inflation				-3.305		
Index of Corruption				-1.038		
Individual Income Tax				0.438		-37.634
R^2 Adjusted	0.102	0.166	0.959	0.582	0.348	0.428
Number of Observations	91	91	91	121	91	121

* Significant at the 5% level, ** Significant at the 10% level

While the results of these regressions suggest that tax factors are correlated with the size of external deposits, it should not be inferred that deposits are necessarily associated with tax evasion. International investors often have at their disposal numerous legitimate alternative methods of structuring and financing their investments, arranging transactions between related parties located in different countries, and returning profits to investors. These alternatives are often tax-driven, evidence that tax considerations strongly influence the choices that firms make.

No direct evidence could be found linking external deposits to crime or other forms of illegal activity. A number of crime-related variables were included in various specifications, but none resulted in significant coefficients.

However, in part these factors may be proxied by the size of the shadow economy or through the existence of non-bank entities in blacklist countries. Finally, the last three columns show the results of regressions carried out for cross-border deposits by banks in order to test the robustness of our results. As can be seen, these regressions appear to indicate a significantly different behaviour from depositing by non-banks, particularly in respect of 'blacklist' and 'harmful'.

The Determinants of the Deposit Location Decision

The BIS data also provide a means of examining the factors that affect the location ecision of depositing. We focus on deposits by non-banks, since this variable may likely capture tax evasion or money laundering. For the group of BIS reporting banks, non-bank deposits account for roughly a quarter of total liabilities. Interestingly, non-bank liabilities are highest in Switzerland, the Cayman Island and Luxembourg, where they account for over 40 per cent of total liabilities.

Table 5.6 Determinants of the Location of Deposits

Independent variable	Dependent variable					
	Non bank deposits				Interbank deposits	
(Exports+Imports)/ GDP	-0.790				-1.506	
Share of Trade		0.112	0.277*	0.289*		0.570*
Regulatory Quality	9.685*	9.732*	8.216*	7.112*	7.152*	2.743*
Corporate Tax Rate	-0.077	-0.113	-0.10**	-0.075	-0.039	-0.047
Bank Secrecy	1.640*		1.359*	1.772*	0.522	0.841*
Number of Tax Treaties	0.118*	0.137*	0.110*	0.594**	0.134*	0.038**
Index of Corruption	-2.280*	-2.025*	-1.823*	-1.245**	-2.408*	-.653*
Common Law	2.205			-0.522	4.76*	0.175
Severity of Supervision		0.544*				
Ratio of Interbank to Total Deposits		-16.12*	-12.54*			
Dummy UK				10.234*		15.424*
Constant	5.447	11.790*	13.478*	2.181	7.632**	1.825
R^2	0.528	0.731	0.642	0.688	0.502	0.925
Number of Observations	28	24	28	28	28	28

* Significant at the 5% level, ** Significant at the 10% level

Table 5.6 reports some cross-sectional evidence regarding factors affecting the location of deposits at end-2000. In the spirit of competition across centres, the dependent variable was calculated as the share of cross-border non-bank deposits reported by individual countries in the total cross-border non-bank deposits reported by the BIS. In order to test the robustness of our results, we estimated a further set of regressions for interbank deposits on the same set of independent variables.

The relatively small sample places a constraint on the number of independent variables that could be tested and it also limits the degree of significance of the results. The most important conditioning variable shown in Table 5.6 is the ratio of the sum of exports and imports to GDP or the share of world trade as measured by the ratio 'export plus imports of individual reporting countries to total exports and imports'.

Trade-related transactions find their way into the international banking statistics although it is difficult to be specific as to their precise nature, because the financing can be reflected in different fashions (i.e. claim on non-banks, interbank liabilities etc). As can be seen from the table, from the standpoint of the reporting centres trade appears more closely related to interbank than non-bank depositing. This rather surprising result may be partly related to the manner in which trade financing is actually recorded in the BIS statistics.[50]

Regulatory quality and the severity of supervision appear to be important determinants of the location of deposits, particularly in the case of non-bank deposits.

Given that all the countries shown in the table no longer apply withholding taxes on cross-border deposits, such a variable could not capture any of the tax advantages to locating deposit-taking in specific centres.

Indeed, from the standpoint of financial intermediaries deciding on a location in which to set up their activities, it would appear that the rate of corporate tax would be far more important. This rate would naturally bear little relationship to tax evasion by non-residents and should be interpreted as a factor determining the supply of financial services in a specific centre.[51] A far more important variable, which captures some of the features of tax evasion, is the extent of bank secrecy in specific centres. Indeed, such a dummy variable appears to be marginally significant in the case of non-bank deposits whereas, as one would expect, it is not statistically significant in the case of interbank deposits.

Corruption in individual financial centres can have two types of effect on depositing for the purposes of money laundering. On the one hand, the less corrupt the financial centre, the more likely it is that the ultimate proceeds of the laundering activity will be usable in legitimate activities without attracting the

---

[50] The recording of a trade related transaction will depend on the type of involvement by banks in the financing.

[51] The number of tax treaties variable may capture two effects: (a) for corporate deposits the assurance of transparency in dealing with the local tax authorities, (b) the degree of linkage with the rest of the world (a measure of openness).

attention of the authorities. In this sense, as pointed out in Chapter 4, if it is possible to place deposits in a jurisdiction that is perceived as being uncorrupted, launderers will choose such centres.

On the other hand, the process of transformation and storage of illegal proceeds will be easier in those jurisdictions where money can more easily be invested without too many questions being asked or where corruption is rife. As can be seen from the results of our estimates, for bank deposits, the index of corruption (the higher the index the less the corruption) is negatively related to the volume of deposits, whereas for interbank deposits this variable appears to be only less significant.

Finally, the United Kingdom appears to be a financial centre with characteristics that are not fully captured by the set of independent variables shown in the table. One can only infer that the pivotal role of this centre in all forms of financial intermediation has given rise over time to economies of scale and scope that cannot be otherwise quantified.

Conclusion

This paper has examined the relationship between money laundering and tax evasion. Both activities originate in attempts to conceal transactions. Money laundering conceals the proceeds of illegal activities or finances criminal endeavours. Tax evasion involves concealing income or wealth from the tax authorities. There appears to have been a sharp expansion in both forms of activity as a result of globalisation and financial innovation, which have reduced the cost of concealing these activities. Moreover, tax evasion may be facilitated if proceeds from the shadow economy can be concealed more easily by money laundering. Criminal activity by its very nature in most instances entails tax evasion.

These analogies extend to the modes of analysis that can be applied to the two subjects. The Becker model of crime can illuminate many aspects of both tax evasion and money laundering behaviour by private agents. Tax competition and regulatory competition models also share many similarities. These similarities in approach also lead to some similarly strong conclusions: small jurisdictions are likely to attempt to adopt predatory policies by applying low tax rates and lax financial regimes.

While there are many reasons to believe that there is considerable overlap between these activities, great caution must be taken in valuing the actual extent to which criminal activity and tax evasion do indeed interact with one another and to draw strong policy conclusions. Tax evasion is not synonymous with tax avoidance. As our rough empirical estimates suggest, it is difficult to disentangle these two types of activity, particularly in an international context. High levels of corruption and political instability in a particular jurisdiction do not tend to attract foreign capital; on the contrary, financial centres with low levels of corruption and high credit standing appear to attract foreign deposits. These different facets suggest that, while there is scope for policy measures that take account of the

interactions between money laundering and tax evasion, a good deal of caution
needs to be applied in drawing analogies across countries identified as encouraging
these activities.

Table 5.7 Offshore Countries (Dummy=1 for OFCs, 0 otherwise)

Countries	Dummy	Countries	Dummy
Algeria	0	Liechtestein	1
Andorra	1	Lithuania	0
Angola	0	Luxembourg	1
Antigua	1	Macau	0
Argentina	0	Malaysia	0
Aruba	1	Malta	0
Australia	0	Morocco	0
Austria	0	Marshall Islands	1
Bahamas	1	Mauritius	1
Bangladesh	0	Mexico	0
Banhrain	0	Monaco	1
Barbados	1	Mozambique	0
Barbuda	0	Myanamar	0
Belgium	0	Nauru	1
Belize	1	Netherlands	1
Bermuda	1	Netherlands Antilles	1
Brazil	0	New Zealand	0
British Virgin Islands	1	Nicaragua	0
Brunei	0	Nigeria	0
Bulgaria	0	Niue	1
Cameron	0	North Korea	0
Canada	0	Norway	0
Cayman Islands	1	Oman	0
Chile	0	Pakistan	0
China	0	Panama	1
Colombia	0	Papua New Guinea	0
Cook Islands	1	Paraguay	0
Cote d'Ivoire	0	Peru	0
Croatia	0	Philippines	0
Cyprus	1	Poland	0
Czech Republic	0	Portugal	0
Denmark	0	Qatar	0
Dominica	0	Romania	0
Ecuador	0	Russia	0
Egypt	0	Samoa	1
Finland	0	Saudi Arabia	0
France	0	Senegal	0
Germany	0	Seychelles	0
Ghana	0	Slovak Republic	0
Gibraltar	1	Slovenia	0
Greece	0	South Africa	0
Grenada	0	South Korea	0
Guatemala	0	Spain	0
Guernsey	1	St. Kitt and Nevis	1
Honduras	0	St. Lucia	0
Hong Kong	1	St. Vincent & Gren.	0
Hungary	0	Sweden	0
Iceland	0	Switzerland	1
India	0	Syria	0
Indonesia	0	Taiwan	0
Iran	0	Tanzania	0
Iraq	0	Thailand	0
Ireland	1	Trinidad and Tobago	0
Isle of Man	1	Tunisia	0
Israel	0	Turkey	0
Italy	0	Turks and Caicos	1
Japan	0	Ukraine	0
Jersey	0	United Arab Emirates	0
Jordan	0	United Kingdom	0
Kenya	0	Uruguay	0
Kuwait	0	USA	0
Latvia	0	Uzbekistan	0
Lebanon	0	Vanuatu	1
Liberia	0	Venezuela	0
Libya	0	Vietnam	0

Figure 5.1 External Deposits by Non-Banks: Country of Residence of Reporting Banks ($ 3,164 billion at end-2002)

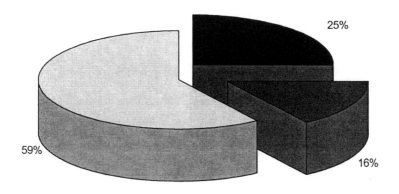

■Offshore ■CH, IE, LU □Other Countries

Figure 5.2 Growth of Non-Bank Deposits from 1984

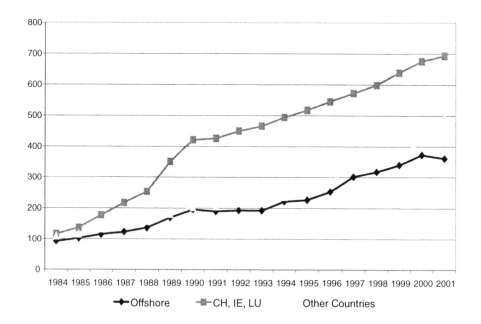

References

Alligham, M.G., and Sandmo, A. (1972), Income tax Evasion: A Theoretical Analysis, *Journal of Public Economy*, 1, pp. 323-35.

Alm, J., Jackson, B.R. and McKee, M. (1992a), Deterrence and Beyond: Toward a Kinder, Gentler IRS, in J. Slemrod (ed.), *Why People Pay Taxes: Tax Compliance and Enforcement*, University of Michigan Press, Ann Arbor, pp. 311-29.

Alm, J., Jackson B.R. and McKee M. (1992b), Estimating the Determinants of Taxpayer Compliance with Experimental Data, *National Tax Journal*, 45, pp. 107-14.

Alworth, J.S. and Andersen S. (1991), The Determinants of Cross Border Non-Bank Deposits and the Competitiveness of Financial Market Centres, *Money Affairs*, 5, pp. 105-133.

Antoine, R.M. (1999), Analysis: The Protection of Offshore Confidentiality. Policy, Implications and Legal Trends, *Journal of Financial Crime*, 7, 1.

Baity, W. (2000), Banking and Secrecy – The Price for Unfettered Secrecy and Confidentiality in the Face of International Organised Crime and Economic Crime, *Journal of Financial Crime*, 8, 1.

Becker, G., (1968), Crime and Punishment – An Economic Approach, *Journal of Political Economy*, 76, pp. 169-217.

Bucovetsky, S. (1991), Asymmetric Tax Competition, *Journal of Urban Economics*, 30, pp. 167-181.

Cowell, F. (1990), *Cheating the Government*. MIT Press, Cambridge M.A.

Filotto, U. and Masciandaro, D. (2001), Money Laundering Regulation and Bank Compliance Costs. What Do Your Customers Know? Economics and Italian Experience, *Journal of Money Laundering Control*, 5, pp. 133-145.

Friedman, E., Johnson, S., Kaufmann, D. and Zoido-Lobaton P. (2000), Dodging the Grabbing Hand: The Determinants of Unofficial Activity in 69 Countries, *Journal of Public Economics*, 76, pp. 459-493.

Gordon, R.A. (1981), *Tax Havens and their Use by United States Taxpayers: An Overview*, US Treasury, Washington D.C.

Graetz, M.J., Reinganum, J.F. and Wilde, L.L. (1985), The Tax Compliance Game: Toward an Interactive Theory of Tax Enforcement, *Journal of Law, Economics, and Organization*, 2, pp.1-32.

Haufler, A. (2001), *Taxation in a Global Economy*, Cambridge University Press, Cambridge.

Hines, J.R. (1999), Lessons from Behavioural Responses to International Taxation, *National Tax Journal*, 52, pp. 305-323.

KPMG (2003), *Anti Money Laundering*, mimeo.

Langer, M.J. (2000), Harmful tax competition: who are the real tax havens?, *Tax Notes International*, 18, pp. 1-9.

Masciandaro, D. (2000a), White Caterpillar, Grey Chrysalis, Black Butterfly: Organized Crime, Financial Crimes and Entrepreneur Distress, *Journal of Financial Crime*, n.1, pp. 274 - 287.

Masciandaro, D. (2000b), The Illegal Sector, Money Laundering and Legal Economy: A Macroeconomic Analysis, *Journal of Financial Crime*, 2, pp.103-112.

Masciandaro, D. (1998), Money Laundering Regulation: the Micro Economics, *Journal of Money Laundering Control*, 2, pp. 49-58

Masciandaro, D. (1996), Pecunia Olet? Microeconomics of Banking and Financial Laundering, *nternational Review of Economics and Business*, 10, pp. 817-844.

Masciandaro, D. and Portolano, A. (2003), It Takes Two to Tango: International Financial Regulation and Off-shore Centres. A Law and Economics Approach, *Journal of Money Laundering Control*, 6, 4.

McLure, C.E. (1986), Tax Competition: Is What's Good for the Private Goose also Good for the Public Gander?, *National Tax Journal*, 39, pp. 341-348.

Moscarino, G., Parcher, L. and Shumaker, M. (2000), To Disclose or not to Disclose: if that is the question what is the answer?, *Journal of Financial Crime*, 7, pp. 308-323.

Myers, G. (1990), Optimality, free mobility and the regional authority in a federation, *Journal of Public Economics*, 43, pp. 107-121.

Naylor, R.T. (2002), *Wages of Crime: Black Markets, Illegal Finance and the Underworld Economy*, Cornell University Press, Ithaca.

Pencavel, J.H. (1979), A Note on Income Tax Evasion, Labor Supply, and Nonlinear Tax Schedules, *Journal of Public Economy*, 12, pp. 115-24.

Polinsky, A.M. and Shavell S. (2000), The Economic Theory of Public Enforcement of Law *Journal of Economic Literature*, 38, pp. 45-76.

Rider, B.A.K. (2002), Weapons of War: the Use of Anti-Money Laundering Laws against Terrorist and Criminal Enterprises - Part 1, *International Journal of Banking Regulation*, 4, pp. 13-31.

Sansing, R.C. (1993), Information Acquisition in a Tax Compliance Game, *Accounting Review*, 68, pp. 874-884.

Schneider, F. (2002), *The Value Added of Underground Activities: Size and Measurement of the Shadow Economies of 110 Countries all over the World*, mimeo.

Schneider, F. and Enste, D. (2002), *The Shadow Economy: Theoretical Approaches, Empirical Studies, and Political Implications*, Cambridge University Press, Cambridge.

Schneider, F., and D. Enste (2000), Shadow economies: size, causes and consequences, *Journal of Economic Literature*, 38, pp. 77-114.

Tanzi, V. (2000), *Policies, Institutions and the Dark Side of Economics*, Edward Elgar, Cheltenham.

Tanzi, V. (1998), Corruption Around the World: Causes Consequences Scope and Cure. *IMF Staff Papers*, 45.

UK Treasury (1988), *Taxation in the Single Market. A Market-Based Approach*, UK Treasury Press Office, London.

Wildasin, D.E. and Wilson, J.D. (2002), *Tax Competition: Bane or Boon?*, Working paper prepared for the Office of Tax Policy Research Institute for Fiscal Studies, Michigan State University, London.

Wilson, J.D. (1991), Tax Competition with Interregional Differences in Factor Endowments, *Regional Science and Urban Economics*, 21, pp. 423-452.

Yaniv, G. (1999), Tax Evasion, Risky Laundering, and Optimal Deterrence Policy, *International Tax and Public Finance*, 6, pp. 27-38.

Yaniv, G. (1994), Taxation and Dirty Money Laundering, *Public Finances/Public Finance*, 49 (Supplement), pp. 40-51.

Yaniv, G. (1994), Taxation and Dirty Money Laundering, *Public Finances/Public Finance*, 49 (Supplement), pp. 40-51.
Yitzhaki, S. (1974), A note on income tax evasion: a theoretical analysis, *Journal of Public Economy*, 3(2), pp. 201-202.

Chapter 6

Politics: Offshore Centres, Transparency and Integrity: The Case of the UK Territories

Chizu Nakajima

Introduction

The globalisation of financial markets and those who use them have produced for regulatory authorities one of the most difficult problems that any legal system has had to address.[1] In the previous chapters, the analysis was focused mainly on the reactions and policies of 'onshore' authorities. In this final chapter, attention is concentrated on the offshore policymakers' actions to contribute to the international efforts in pursuit of financial stability and integrity, on the one hand, and tax policy coordination, on the other.

The dematerialisation of financial assets and the rapid development of information technology, together with deregulation to allow competition increasingly on a global basis,[2] have created tremendous opportunities for efficiency and innovation in the financial world.

Vast sums of money can be transmitted around the world with the click of a mouse, wealth can be held in multiple currencies in any number of financial centres and be controlled by a single person. In the context of these momentous developments, the simple balance between the promotion of efficiency, essentially

---

[1] Commentators have drawn a distinction between 'globalisation' which denotes 'a process of denationalisation' and 'internationalisation' which refers to 'the co-operative activities of national actors', see G. Walker, S. Mellor, M. Fox and S. Francis, 'The concept of globalisation', *Company and Securities Law Journal*, 14, 59, 1994.

[2] For example, on the developments leading to 'Big Bang' in the UK, see B.A.K. Rider, C. Abram and E. Ferran, *Guide to the Financial Services Act*, CCH, Bicester, 1986 (2nd ed, 1989), pp. 11-25. For an analysis of the deregulation of leading financial centres, including New York, see S.J. Khoury, *The Deregulation of the World Financial Markets: Myths, Realities and Impact*, Quorum, New York, 1990. For an analysis of the abolition of separation of banking and securities business in Japan, see C. Nakajima, 'Conflicts of interest in Japan', in B.A.K. Rider and T.M. Ashe (eds), *The Fiduciary, the Insider and the Conflict*, Sweet & Maxwell, London, 1995.

by promoting free competition and removing fiscal and bureaucratic constraints, on the one hand, and ensuring an appropriate level of fairness to protect and advance confidence, on the other, is a very much more complex exercise.

A clear example is the worldwide concern to fight serious criminal enterprises by depriving criminal organisations of the profits they make through their subversive and illicit activity.[3] Added to the fight against organised crime is the 'war on terror' initiated after the attacks on the US in September 2001, to starve Al Qaeda and other terrorist organisations of funds.

The integration of the financial world has made the fight against organised crime and terrorism in many ways more difficult, as any framework is only as secure as its weakest link.

As highlighted on different occasions in the above chapters, many developed economies have identified offshore financial centres (OFCs) as the weakest link, and a number of international organisations have initiated measures to eliminate those problems associated with OFCs, such as engaging in harmful tax practices, undermining financial stability and facilitating money laundering and terrorist financing.

Indeed, the recent spate of large-scale corporate scandals in the US has highlighted, amongst other things, those weaknesses in relation to some of the OFCs. For example, it has been alleged that bankrupt energy giant Enron Corp. avoided paying any income taxes in four of the last five years by using some 900 subsidiaries in tax haven countries in the Caribbean[4] and other techniques.[5]

The present chapter addresses these issues in relation to what is described as 'UK Offshore' – Guernsey, Isle of Man and Jersey – and Gibraltar.

Offshore Financial Centres

As was noted in Chapter 1, and then discussed in Chapter 5, the OECD uses the term 'tax haven' rather than OFC in discussing issues relating to tax avoidance and

---

[3] See further, C. Nakajima, *Conflicts of Interest and Duty: A Comparative Analysis in Anglo-Japanese Law*, Kluwer Law International, London, 1999, in particular Chapters 1 and 8.

[4] Reuters, 17 January 2002, Miami, quoting the *New York Times*, 16 January 2002.

[5] See, for example, a study conducted by S.J. Pak and J.S. Zdanowicz and released by Senator Byron Dorgan, which showed that multinational corporations avoided $45 billion dollars in US taxes the previous year by artificially fixing prices for transactions with foreign affiliates, a practice known as transfer pricing, referred to in M. Godfrey, 'US study reveals multinationals avoided paying billions in taxes', *Tax-News.com*, New York, 26 November 2001. Such practice shifts company profits out of the US by either overpricing products sold to US operations by foreign affiliates or by under-pricing goods that are bought by the same foreign affiliates, thus moving company profits away from the reach of the Internal Revenue Department.

tax evasion, but makes reference to 'offshore regimes' being used for the purpose of tax avoidance.[6]

In its report, published in 1987,[7] the OECD recognises the difficulty in providing an objective definition of a tax haven. However, it concludes that a good way to determine whether a jurisdiction is a tax haven or not is to apply the 'reputation test'[8] – whether a country or territory offers itself or is generally recognised as a tax haven.

The report – as has been noted in Chapter 5 – also identifies several salient features indicative of a tax haven. Firstly, whether the jurisdiction imposes no or nominal taxation and offers itself, or at least is perceived to offer itself, as a place to be used by non-residents to escape taxation in their countries of residence.

Other key factors which are indicative of the existence of a tax haven are a lack of effective information exchange due to banking secrecy laws or administrative practices, a lack of transparency allowing investors to hide their true identities, thereby facilitating tax evasion or money laundering, and the absence of 'substantial activity' requirement – consequently it may be 'purely tax-driven'.[9] It also refers to a number of non-tax factors, including a form of 'free-riding', whereby the tax haven's attractiveness is accentuated by its close ties with non-haven countries. It gives an example of a tax haven that, as a dependency, benefits, at no cost to itself, from the home country's diplomatic, financial and other infrastructure provisions.[10]

It is arguable that the four jurisdictions that are the subject of the present chapter are such dependencies of the UK as their home country, thus putting them squarely within the remit of the OECD initiatives to combat harmful tax practices.

As discussed in Chapter 1, another international organisation that has taken an interest in issues relating to OFCs is the IMF. The IMF identifies the traditional characteristics of OFCs as being jurisdictions that have financial institutions engaged primarily in business with non-residents and financial systems with external assets and liabilities out of proportion to domestic financial intermediation designed to finance domestic economies.

The centres provide some or all of the following opportunities: low or zero taxation, moderate or light financial regulation, banking secrecy and anonymity.[11]

---

[6] OECD, *Harmful Tax Competition: An Emerging Global Issue*, Paris, 1998, p. 39. See also *ibid*, p. 78, Annex II, Statement by Switzerland. In opposing the OECD's proposals, Switzerland refers to 'offshore centres' where it argues that 'the selective and repressive approach that has been adopted does not give territories that make tax attraction a pillar of their economies an incentive to associate themselves with the regulation of the conditions of competition and will therefore fail to combat effectively the harmful excesses of tax competition that develops outside of all rules. On the contrary, it could reinforce the attraction of offshore centres, with all the consequences that this implies.'

[7] OECD, *International Tax Avoidance and Evasion Four Related Studies*, 1, Paris, 1987.

[8] OECD, *International Tax Avoidance and Evasion Four Related Studies*, 1, Paris, 1987, p. 22.

[9] OECD, *Harmful Tax Competition: An Emerging Global Issue*, 1998, p. 24.

[10] OECD, *Harmful Tax Competition: An Emerging Global Issue*, 1998, p. 25.

[11] IMF, *Offshore Financial Centres – The Role of the IMF*, 23 June 2000, Chapter 1.

The IMF has taken an interest in the OFCs, as their existence affects the work of the Fund in several ways.

> First, a better understanding of the activities taking place in OFCs can contribute to strengthening financial system surveillance by improving abilities to identify and deal with surrounding risks at an early stage.
>
> Second, OFCs are generally used not only by major industrial countries, but also by emerging market economies whose financial systems are perhaps more vulnerable than others to reversals in capital flows, rapid accumulation of short-term debt, unhedged exposure to currency fluctuations, and selective capital account liberalization.
>
> Finally, the operation of OFCs has implications for the Fund's work on the promotion of good governance because it can reduce transparency, including the exploitation of complex ownership structures and relationships among different jurisdictions involved.[12]

International efforts, including those initiated by the IMF, are aimed at encouraging 'offshore financial centres to improve their regulatory environment and to improve the transparency and operation of financial markets, including the functioning of offshore financial centres'.[13] Although these initiatives differ in scope and emphasis from the OECD project on harmful tax competition, as it points out, there is 'a common ground in seeking greater transparency and information disclosure'.[14]

Guernsey

The Bailiwick of Guernsey (Guernsey) is a Dependency of the British Crown comprising the islands of Guernsey, Alderney and Sark with a population of around 60,000. The United Kingdom Government is responsible for the Islands' international relations and defence but matters of taxation and other domestic issues are the responsibility of the Islands' authorities. The Islands are part of the customs territory[15] of the European Union, but other EU rules do not apply. The Islands have a legislature and judiciary that is separate from the UK Parliament and courts, although the Judicial Committee of the Privy Council is the supreme court of appeal for Guernsey.

Guernsey has a higher per capita GDP than the UK and a level of unemployment below the UK average. Finance and related services contribute about 60 per cent of GDP. Banking businesses hold assets and liabilities of about £53 billion[16] and around £20 billion in collective investment schemes.

The financial services conducted in Guernsey include banking, investment and securities business, insurance, pensions and trust services. The principal types of banking business conducted by banks in Guernsey are community banking, deposit

---

[12] IMF, *Offshore Financial Centres – IMF Background Paper*, 23 June 2000, Chapter 1.
[13] IMF, *Offshore Financial Centres – IMF Background Paper*, 23 June 2000, Chapter 1.
[14] Statement by Gabriel Makhlouf, Chairman of the Committee on Fiscal Affairs, 26 June 2000.
[15] Protocol 3 to the United Kingdom's Treaty of Accession to the European Community.
[16] Figures as at 31 March 1998.

gathering and international private banking, while the investment business conducted in Guernsey includes management, administration and custody of collective investment schemes, discretionary and non-discretionary asset management, stockbrokerage; and provision of investment advice. Guernsey has a large number of trust schemes with total assets estimated at £30 billion. It has established a niche in providing complex and innovative insurance products.

The reason for banks choosing to establish operations in Guernsey is almost always client-led.[17] The attractions of Guernsey as an offshore financial centre are self-evident. It offers financial services subject to international supervisory and regulatory standards in a politically stable, low taxation economy with a sound commercial infrastructure and no exchange controls or capital gains tax.

Isle of Man

The Isle of Man is a Dependency of the British Crown with a population of around 73,000. The UK Government is responsible for international relations and defence, but matters of taxation and other domestic issues are the responsibility of the Isle of Man authorities. The Island is part of the customs territory[18] of the European Union, but other EU rules do not apply. The Island has a legislature and judiciary that are separate from the UK Parliament and courts, although the Judicial Committee of the Privy Council is the supreme court of appeal for the Isle of Man.

Isle of Man GDP and unemployment are lower than the UK. Financial services contribute 37 per cent of GDP and employ 18 per cent of the workforce.

The financial sector includes banks and building societies, CISs, fund management, investment businesses and life assurance. Bank deposits are £20 billion, managed funds £16 billion and insurance £12.3 billion.[19]

Jersey

Jersey is a British Crown Dependency with a population of around 85,000. The United Kingdom Government is responsible for international relations and defence, but there is autonomy in relation to taxation and other domestic matters. Jersey is part of the customs territory[20] of the European Union, but other EU rules do not apply. The legislature and judiciary are separate from the UK Parliament and courts, although the Judicial Committee of the Privy Council is the supreme court of appeal for Jersey.

---

[17] As was identified in the 'Edwards Report', see A. Edwards, 'The Guernsey finance centre', *Review of Financial Regulation in the Crown Dependencies,* Part III, HMSO, London, November 1998.

[18] Protocol 3 to the United Kingdom's Treaty of Accession to the European Community.

[19] See further A. Edwards, 'The Isle of Man finance centre', *Review of Financial Regulation in the Crown Dependencies*, Part IV, HMSO, London, November 1998.

[20] Protocol 3 to the United Kingdom's Treaty of Accession to the European Community.

Per capita GDP is higher than in the UK, while the unemployment level is below the UK average. Financial and related services contribute 55 per cent of GDP and employ 20 per cent of the workforce.

The main areas of business are personal and corporate banking, global custody and securities, treasury operations, mutual fund management and administration, trust and company administration, investment management and advice and bond issues and securitisation. Bank Deposits total £135 billion,[21] managed funds in excess of £200 billion, and collective investment schemes of £38 billion.[22] Jersey has an extremely large trust sector estimated to hold assets in excess of £100 billion.[23]

Gibraltar

Gibraltar is a UK Overseas Territory with a population of 27,000. Spain maintains a claim of sovereignty over the territory. Gibraltar entered the European Union at the time of the accession of the United Kingdom. The UK government is responsible for international relations and defence, while matters of taxation and other domestic issues are the responsibility of the Gibraltar government. The common law and the rules of equity in force in England apply to Gibraltar. The Judicial Committee of the Privy Council is the supreme court of appeal for Gibraltar.

Gibraltar's financial services sector dates back to the enactment of the Companies (Taxation and Concessions) Ordinance in 1967, which made provision for a special tax regime for international business. Recently, Gibraltar won a case in the European Court of Justice against the European Commission for categorising the tax exemption provided to foreign companies as unfair state aid. The financial services sector provides a broad spectrum of professional services, including private banking, portfolio management, trading on Eurex, insurance management and securitisation. Together with the shipping trade it forms a substantial component of the economy. The financial sector accounts for 20 per cent of GDP.

Harmful Tax Practices

The OECD project on Harmful Tax Competition commenced pursuant to a request from Ministers to 'develop measures to counter the distorting effects of harmful tax

---

[21] See further *Jersey Financial Services Commission Quarterly Report*, 29 May 2002, for the period 1 January 2002 to 31 March 2002, at http://www.jerseyfsc.org/pressreleases/releas93.htm

[22] See A. Edwards, 'The Jersey finance centre', *Review of Financial Regulation in the Crown Dependencies*, Part II, HMSO, London, November 1998, par. 3.10.

[23] *Ibid*, par. 3.14.

competition on investment and financing decisions and the consequences for national tax bases'.[24]

The project subsequently obtained support from G7 Heads of State, who were concerned about the impact of globalisation on tax policy.[25] The *Report on Harmful Tax Competition, An Emerging Global Issue* (OECD, 1998) deals with the 'dark side of globalisation'[26] – the manner in which the tax policies of one economy can affect the domestic tax base of another economy and generate negative externalities.

A distinction is drawn between tax evasion, tax avoidance – action by the taxpayer to circumvent or subvert the law to avoid taxes – and acceptable tax planning.[27] The project restricts its focus to geographically mobile activities, including financial and other services.

The OECD considers tax practices and competition to be harmful in several ways. Tax policies aimed at diverting capital flows for pure 'financial', as opposed to investment, reasons distort patterns of trade and investment. Some jurisdictions use low or no taxation as a unique selling point and spearhead a 'race to the bottom'.[28]

Such jurisdictions benefit from the ability to finance government spending without recourse to the taxation of income and actively promote themselves as locations for non-residents to avoid domestic tax liability. The tax base of countries is eroded by the migration of capital to low tax locations as a result of tax arbitrage or active 'poaching'.[29]

The erosion of a tax base leads to a fall in revenue, affects public spending decisions and causes an alteration of tax structures with less mobile services such as income and consumption bearing the greater burden. Further, taxpayers with savings in low tax locations act as 'free riders – benefiting from public services without contributing towards them.[30] Discouraging compliance by taxpayers and imposing increased enforcement costs on revenue authorities causes additional harm.

Identifying harmful tax practices involves a balancing of the factors considered above. A taxation practice is considered harmful if 'the spillover effects [of the practice] are so substantial that they are concluded to be poaching other countries'

---

[24] Ministerial Communiqué of May 1996.

[25] 'Globalisation is creating new challenges in the field of tax policy. Tax schemes aimed at attracting financial and other geographically mobile activities can create harmful tax competition between States, carrying risks of distorting trade and investment and could lead to the erosion of the national tax bases.' Communiqué issued by Heads of State at 1996 Lyon Summit.

[26] Statement by G. Makhlouf, Chairman of the Committee on Fiscal Affairs, OECD, Paris, 26 June 2000.

[27] D.J. Johnston, Introductory remarks of Secretary General of the OECD, High-Level Symposium on Harmful Tax Competition, Paris, 29-30 June 2000.

[28] OECD, *Harmful Tax Competition – An Emerging Global Issue*, Paris, 1998, p. 20, par. 43.

[29] OECD, *Harmful Tax Competition – An Emerging Global Issue*, Paris, 1998, p. 16, par. 29.

[30] OECD, *Harmful Tax Competition – An Emerging Global Issue*, Paris, 1998, p. 14, par. 24.

tax bases.'[31] Effectively the practices impose negative externalities on other countries. When considering harmful tax practices the OECD distinguishes between tax havens and harmful preferential tax regimes in member and non-member countries.[32]

A preferential tax regime is designed to attract economic activity that is most susceptible to tax arbitrage. The key features of a preferential tax regime are:[33]

- Low or zero effective tax rate on relevant income;
- 'Ring fencing' of regimes either by a prohibition on resident participation or a prohibition on domestic operation;
- Lack of transparency – details of the regime or its application are not apparent; and
- Lack of effective information exchange.

Additional features include artificial tax base, failure to adhere to international transfer pricing principles, exemption of foreign source income from taxation, negotiable tax rate or base, existence of secrecy provisions, access to a wider network of tax treaties, regimes that are promoted as tax minimisation vehicles and regimes that encourage purely tax-driven operations and arrangements.[34]

The 1998 Report makes 19 Recommendations for counteracting harmful tax competition.[35] The recommendations fall into three broad categories: recommendations concerning domestic legislation, tax treaties and for intensification of international co-operation.[36] The Recommendations address all aspects of harmful tax competition – refraining from adopting harmful practices, counteracting the benefits to taxpayers, and addressing demand for such services by taxpayers.

Member countries are urged to consider terminating current tax conventions and to avoid future tax conventions with tax havens. The abolition of double taxation treaties removes the economic benefit of using tax havens.[37]

It is proposed that a Forum on Harmful Tax Practices (Forum), created under the auspices of the OECD's Committee on Fiscal Affairs, is to co-ordinate international co-operation in response to harmful tax competition, evaluate existing and new regimes, and to analyse the effectiveness of counteractive measures.[38] The Forum is required to prepare a list of tax havens in accordance with the criteria identified in the Report.[39] Such a list is to be designed to have a readily identifiable

---

[31] OECD, *Harmful Tax Competition – An Emerging Global Issue*, Paris, 1998, p. 16, par. 31.

[32] OECD, *Harmful Tax Competition – An Emerging Global Issue*, Paris, 1998, p. 20, par. 44.

[33] OECD, *Harmful Tax Competition – An Emerging Global Issue*, Paris, 1998, p. 27, box II.

[34] OECD, *Harmful Tax Competition – An Emerging Global Issue*, Paris, 1998, pp. 30-34.

[35] See OECD, *Harmful Tax Competition – An Emerging Global Issue*, Paris, 1998, Appendix I for a full list of 19 Recommendations.

[36] OECD, *Harmful Tax Competition – An Emerging Global Issue*, Paris, 1998, p. 39, par. 92.

[37] Recommendation 12.

[38] Recommendation 15.

[39] Recommendation 16.

group with whom the Forum could liaise and co-ordinate the international response.

Countries with links to tax havens are to ensure that such links do not cause harmful tax competition and countries with dependencies are to ensure that these do not increase or promote harmful competition.[40] This Recommendation applies to the United Kingdom in relation to the Crown Dependencies and UK Overseas Territories in Gibraltar and the Caribbean.

As described in Chapter 1, the OECD's progress report, published in 2000,[41] listed 47 jurisdictions meeting the criteria of a tax haven as identified by the Forum by factual review and technical evaluation in accordance with Recommendation 16. The British Crown Dependencies of Guernsey, Isle of Man and Jersey and the UK Overseas Territory of Gibraltar were included in the list.[42]

The 2000 progress report adopted a carrot-and-stick approach towards tax havens. All tax havens were invited to make a written commitment to eliminate harmful tax practices. The commitment required is 'a public political commitment by a jurisdiction to adopt a schedule of progressive changes to eliminate its harmful tax practices by 31 December 2005'.[43]

Any jurisdiction failing to make the commitment would be included in a List of Uncooperative Tax Havens that would be subject to co-ordinated defensive measures.[44] The OECD formulated defensive measures designed to impede severely the functioning of such havens and to make transactions with havens unattractive. This would be achieved by increasing the cost and complexity of transactions. The defensive measures include:[45]

- Removal of deductions, exemptions, credits, or other allowances related to transactions with havens or to transactions taking advantage of their harmful tax practices;
- Comprehensive information reporting requirement for transactions involving havens or using harmful tax practices;
- Enhanced audit and enforcement with respect to havens and transactions;
- Imposition of withholding taxes on certain payments to residents of havens;
- 'Transactional' charges on certain transactions;

---

[40] Recommendation 17.

[41] OECD, *Towards Global Tax Co-operation – Progress in Identifying and Eliminating Harmful Tax Practice*, Report to the Ministerial Council Meeting and Recommendations by the Committee on Fiscal Affairs, Paris, 2000.

[42] Other UK Overseas Territories, identified as tax havens, are Anguilla, British Virgin Islands, Montserrat, Turks & Caicos.

[43] OECD, *Towards Global Tax Co-operation – Progress in Identifying and Eliminating Harmful Tax Practices*, Paris, 2000, p. 19, par. 21.

[44] OECD, *Towards Global Tax Co-operation – Progress in Identifying and Eliminating Harmful Tax Practices*, Paris, 2000, p. 18, par. 19-20.

[45] For a list of possible defensive measures identified, see OECD, *Towards Global Tax Co-operation – Progress in Identifying and Eliminating Harmful Tax Practices*, Paris, 2000, p. 23, par. 25.

- Any fees incurred in establishing or acquiring entities in the haven would not be recoverable.

The robust resistance of many OFCs and the Bush administration's opposition caused the project to lose momentum. The Bush administration claimed the OECD's initiative had become 'too broad' and therefore needed to be 'refocused' on the 'common goal', which was to enable 'countries to obtain specific information from other countries upon request in order to prevent the illegal evasion of their tax laws by the dishonest few'.[46]

The US Treasury Secretary, Paul O'Neil, expressed his concern about the OECD's underlying premise that low tax rates were 'somehow suspect and by the notion that any country, or group of countries, should interfere in any other country's decision about how to structure its own tax system.' He clearly stated that the US 'will not participate in any initiative to harmonize world tax systems'.[47]

Subsequently, the OECD shifted the project's emphasis toward achieving effective information exchange and eliminating tax non-compliance without limiting the ability of taxpayers to engage in legitimate tax planning.[48] The removal of 'no substantial domestic activity' from the criteria applied to decide whether or not a tax haven is uncooperative reflects an acknowledgement from the OECD that it is difficult to determine.[49] It was, thus, decided that commitments from a tax haven would be sought 'only with respect to the transparency and effective exchange of information'.[50]

As of 28 February 2002, over 30 of the initially listed tax havens had made a commitment to improve information exchange and transparency policies, while seven jurisdictions are on the OECD List of Uncooperative Tax Havens.[51] US Treasury Secretary Paul O'Neil attributed the commitments as resulting from US action to refocus the project on information exchange and transparency.[52]

Some speculate that the US's staunch opposition to imposing punitive sanctions on uncooperative havens may well relax as a result of the tragic events of 11th September 2001, which necessitated the tracking of terrorist funds. It has been reported that the US authorities have encountered difficulties whenever the money trail led offshore, and an official was quoted as saying 'If necessary, we will use the considerable persuasive powers of the US to close certain [offshore] centres

---

[46] Office of Public Affairs, *Treasury Secretary Paul O'Neil Statement on OECD Tax Havens*, PO-366, London, 10 May 2001.

[47] *Ibid.*

[48] R.M. Hammer and J. Owens, *Promoting Tax Competition*, mimeo, 3 June 2001, p. 2.

[49] OECD, *The OECD's Project on Harmful Tax Practices: The 2001 Progress Report*, Paris, November 2001, p.10, par. 27.

[50] *Ibid.*, par. 28.

[51] Seiichi Kondo, Deputy Secretary General, OECD, 'Ending Tax Abuse' 18 April 2002. The seven jurisdictions on the List are: Andorra, Liechtenstein, Liberia, Monaco, The Marshall Islands, Nauru and Vanuatu.

[52] Office of Public Affairs, *Treasury Statement on the Success of the OECD Harmful Tax Practices Project*, PO-3008, London, 18 April 2002.

down'.[53] However, it may be that it would only reinforce the US's approach, which is to enhance information exchange and transparency in regard to tax havens but 'without stifling tax competition'.[54]

Indeed, to reflect US concern to retain tax competition, as soon as Israel was removed from the list of non-cooperative countries and territories (NCCTs) in relation to combating money laundering, it announced its intention to introduce low tax measures designed to attract foreign companies to relocate their operations to Israel. It also has plans to introduce a low tax rate for company dividends withdrawn from Israel by foreign shareholders, thereby creating a sort of tax haven.[55]

More recently, the G7 Finance Ministers, at their meeting held in June 2002 in Halifax, Nova Scotia, issued the following statement emphasising their commitment to transparency and exchange of information:

> We agree that the administration and enforcement of tax laws depend increasingly on transparency and effective international exchange of information. We call on all countries to permit access to, and exchange, bank and other information for all tax purposes; OECD countries should lead by example. Progress in this area is urgently needed and we intend to review developments at our next meeting.[56]

Notwithstanding US eagerness to enhance information exchange and transparency with regard to tax havens, it is interesting to note that the order, issued by the US SEC on 27 June 2002, requiring all CEOs and finance chiefs of US companies with turnovers of more than $1.2 billion to swear under oath that their books have not been 'cooked', does not apply to offshore-based US companies.

The exclusion of offshore US companies from such a requirement is thought to be for greater efficiency and speed of implementation but has added 'fuel to the already furious debate over offshore reincorporation'.[57] This is not surprising as some of those offshore-based US companies, such as Tyco International and Global Crossing, are currently under investigation by the US government for accounting and bookkeeping irregularities.[58]

---

[53] J. Gorringe, 'US Reconsidering OECD Proposals on Tax Havens', *Tax-News.com*, London, 25 September 2001.

[54] Office of Public Affairs, *Statement of Paul H. O'Neil before the Senate Committee on Governmental Affairs Permanent Subcommittee on Investigations OECD Harmful Tax Practices Initiative*, PO-486, London, 18 July 2001.

[55] A. Banks, 'Israel to Unveil Tax Haven Plans Following FATF Delisting', *Tax-News.com*, London, 27 June 2002.

[56] Statement of G7 Finance Ministers, 15 June 2002, Halifax, Nova Scotia, see the website of Department of Finance, Canada, at www.G7.ca/final_halifax_e.html (print out with author).

[57] L. Baker, 'Offshore Based US Companies Won't Have to Swear to Accuracy', *Tax-News.com*, New York, 9 July.

[58] L. Baker, 'Offshore Based US Companies Won't Have to Swear to Accuracy', *Tax-News.com*, New York, 9 July.

It is to be noted that exchange of information with other tax authorities, in the case of the OECD proposals, would be on request, while under the EU Savings Tax Directive, discussed below, it would be automatic.[59] It should also be noted that the UK, in practice, accepts that the Isle of Man should deal direct with the OECD.[60]

Guernsey

Guernsey made a political commitment to the principles of transparency and effective information exchange. The commitment is subject to a level playing field existing for all parties and OECD members conforming to their commitment. Guernsey agreed to:

- Exchange tax information;
- Make available information on beneficial ownership of companies, partnerships and other entities, including managers of collective investment schemes and trustees and beneficiaries of trusts;
- Require account keeping, the auditing of accounts to international standards and the filing of accounts in support of tax returns.

Guernsey reiterated the need for a level playing field and a commitment to fair tax competition.

Isle of Man

The Isle of Man became the first Crown Dependency to acquiesce to the demands of the OECD, issuing a Commitment letter to the OECD on 13 December 2000. Initially, the authorities committed to effective exchange of information, transparency and no substantial activities, but the commitment in regard of 'no substantial activities' was dropped when the OECD changed the emphasis of the project. Following the change announced in the 2001 Report, jurisdictions that had committed are allowed to review the commitment with regard to no substantial activities. Further to the commitment on effective exchange of information, the Isle of Man has agreed to provide information on criminal and defined civil tax matters, to alter its laws to facilitate such exchange, to maintain sufficient regulatory and tax resources and to avoid banking secrecy laws. To facilitate transparency, information on beneficial ownership of companies, partnerships and other legal entities, including managers of collective investment schemes and trustees and beneficiaries of trusts, will be available to tax and regulatory authorities. Internationally accepted accounting and audit practices will be required from all legal entities with a presence in the Isle of Man.

---

[59] Standing Committee on Economic Initiatives, *Annual Report 2002*, Isle of Man, par. 4.
[60] Standing Committee on Economic Initiatives, *Annual Report 2002*, Isle of Man, par. 12.

Jersey

Jersey made a political commitment to the principles of transparency and effective information exchange. The commitment is subject to a level playing field existing for all parties, OECD members conforming to their commitment. Jersey agreed to:

- Exchange tax information;
- Make available information on beneficial ownership of companies, partnerships and other entities including managers of collective investment schemes, and trustees and beneficiaries of trusts; and
- Require account keeping, the audit of accounts to international standards and the filing of accounts in support of tax returns.

Jersey reiterated the need for a level playing field and a commitment to fair tax competition.

Gibraltar

Gibraltar made a political commitment to the principles of transparency and effective information exchange. The commitment is subject to a level playing field existing for all parties and OECD members conforming to their commitment. Gibraltar agreed to:

- Exchange tax information;
- Introduce no new banking secrecy laws;
- Enable beneficial ownership information of companies, partnerships and other entities and information on settlers and beneficiaries of trusts to be available;
- Abolish the ability of investors to negotiate tax rates; and
- Ensure that future laws comply with the principles and effective information exchange and to modify any current laws not in conformity.

Victor Chandler, a high street bookmaker in the UK, pioneered a move to Gibraltar to take advantage of the zero tax levied on bets. Other big bookmakers such as William Hill, Ladbrokes and Corals followed suite. Due to the threat posed by the offshore activities of the bookmakers, the UK government abolished the 9 per cent betting tax. This is a good example of a geographically-mobile service taking advantage of tax arbitrage. This occurred without Gibraltar actively 'poaching' the bookmakers.

EU Savings Tax Directive

Under the proposed information-sharing regime, participating governments (27 prospective EU members plus the UK's dependent territories plus Switzerland) would report savings income to the tax authorities in the home states of depositors or investors. Jersey, Guernsey and the Isle of Man have given in to pressure from the UK to join the regime.[61]

The Isle of Man's Standing Committee on Economic Initiatives, in its 2002 annual report, states that 'the impact on business which exchange of information with other tax authorities would have is difficult to assess'.

However, the Committee believes that 'the problems posed by demands for exchange of information are essentially transitional and that, given sufficient time for business to adapt to them, the proposals emanating from the EU should not be too seriously disadvantageous to the Island. There could be an initial negative impact on the banking sector for automatic exchange, but the inevitability of some exchange along these lines is to some degree becoming accepted'.[62] However, the Committee emphasises the importance of taking full opportunity to achieve as much in the way of reciprocal benefit for the Isle of Man as possible, in terms of 'the recognition of the "level playing field" principle, unimpeded access to financial markets and equal treatment with EU states, and the establishment of double taxation agreements'.[63]

The Committee raises the question of the Isle of Man's possible membership in the EU, as at present it is represented by the UK. It is not oblivious to the potential conflict of interest with the UK, whereby in seeking to protect the City of London, the Isle of Man's interests might 'have a lesser priority in the UK Government's eyes'[64] and would prefer to negotiate directly with the EU alongside the UK, as it has been doing vis-à-vis the OECD.

This would not only ensure proper representation in EU decision-making, of the kind that is satisfactorily emerging in the context of the OECD, but would also obtain access for Isle of Man financial products to EU financial markets.[65]

Financial Stability

OFCs are a key component of the global financial architecture, providing vital services such as bank intermediation, fund management, insurance, trust business, asset protection, corporate planning and tax planning.[66]

In contrast to the OECD's approach to OFCs, which focused on their negative aspect of potentially engaging in harmful tax practices, the IMF recognises that:

> OFCs can be used for *legitimate reasons*, taking advantage of: (1) lower explicit taxation and consequentially increased after-tax profit; (2) simpler prudential regulatory

[61] U. Lomas, 'EU Turns Heavy Artillery on the Swiss', *Tax-News.com*, Brussels, 4 July 2002.
[62] Standing Committee on Economic Initiatives, *Annual Report 2002*, Isle of Man, par. 20.
[63] Standing Committee on Economic Initiatives, *Annual Report 2002*, Isle of Man, par. 21.
[64] Standing Committee on Economic Initiatives, *Annual Report 2002*, Isle of Man, par. 15.
[65] Standing Committee on Economic Initiatives, *Annual Report 2002*, Isle of Man, par. 16.
[66] IMF, *Offshore Financial Centres Background Paper*, Washington, 23 June 2000, Chapter II.

frameworks that reduce implicit taxation; (3) minimum formalities for incorporation; (4) the existence of adequate legal frameworks that safeguard the integrity of principal-agent relations; (5) the proximity to major economies, or to countries attracting capital inflows; (6) the reputation of specific OFCs, and the specialist services provided; (7) freedom from exchange controls; and (8) a means for safeguarding assets from the impact of litigation etc.

However, the IMF does also point out their use for '*dubious purposes*, such as tax evasion and money-laundering, by taking advantage of a higher potential for less transparent operating environments, including a higher level of anonymity, to escape the notice of the law enforcement agencies in the 'home' country of the beneficial owner of the funds'.[67]

The key role played by OFCs means they can have an adverse effect on the global financial system, threatening its stability, and can be a cause of systemic risk. OFCs can pose a threat by engaging in regulatory competition or using lax regulation as an incentive to do business in the territory, thus facilitating the growth of rogue financial institutions.

Furthermore, branches of major institutions in OFCs may take advantage of regulatory arbitrage and lax supervision or regulatory gaps to conduct activities that place the parent institution at risk.

The Financial Stability Forum's (FSF) Working Group on Offshore Financial Centres was set up to review the uses and activities of OFCs and their significance for global financial stability. It published its findings in 2000.

The report noted that offshore financial activities are not inimical to global financial stability, provided they are well supervised and supervisory authorities co-operate. It recognised that some OFCs are well supervised and co-operate with other jurisdictions. At the same time, it concluded that OFCs that are unable or unwilling to adhere to internationally accepted standards for supervision, co-operation, and information sharing create a potential systemic threat to global financial stability.

Such OFCs constitute weak links in an increasingly integrated international financial system and hinder broader efforts to raise standards of soundness and transparency in the global financial system. Those OFCs with weaknesses in financial supervision, cross-border co-operation, and transparency were thought to allow financial market participants to engage in regulatory arbitrage, undermining efforts to strengthen the global financial system. The FSF considers that the key to addressing most of the problems with these OFCs is through the adoption and implementation of international standards, particularly in cross-border co-operation.

The FSF has identified the relevant international standards whose implementation would address these issues, is considering mechanisms for

---

[67] IMF, *Offshore Financial Centres Background Paper*, Washington, 23 June 2000, chapter II. See also UN Office for Drug Control and Crime Prevention, *Financial Havens, Banking Secrecy and Money Laundering, Global Programme Against Money Laundering*, Vienna, 1998.

assessing compliance in the implementation of the standards, and is looking at appropriate incentives to enhance such compliance.[68] The FSF has asked the IMF to take on the main responsibility for conducting these assessments, drawing on expertise from supervisory agencies and elsewhere.[69]

To alleviate OFCs' potential danger to the stability of the global financial system, the Basle Committee on Banking Supervision issued Minimum Standards for the supervision of international banking groups and their cross-border establishments, which established the following four main principles:[70]

- A home country authority that capably performs consolidated supervision should supervise all international banks;
- The creation of a cross-border banking establishment should receive the prior approval of both host and home country authority;
- Home country authority should possess the right to gather information from cross-border banking establishments; and
- If the host authority determines that any of the three standards is not being met, it could impose restrictive measures to prohibit the establishment of banking offices.

A working group, consisting of members of the Basle Committee on Banking Supervision and the Offshore Group of Banking Supervision (OGBS), was set up in 1994 to come up with practical solutions to problems encountered in implementing the above four principles.[71]

These four principles are derived from the Basle Core Principles[72] that require banking supervisors to practise global consolidated supervision,[73] contact and information exchange with host country,[74] and the host country to require equal standards in local operations from cross-border banks and share information with the home supervisor.[75]

Effective consolidated supervision requires a group-wide approach to supervision whereby all the risks run by a banking group are accounted, with operation escaping supervision and all risks being evaluated globally. Nevertheless, consolidated supervision is not a panacea.

---

[68] See further Financial Stability Forum, *Report of the Working Group on Offshore Financial Centres*, Basle, 5 April 2000.

[69] IMF, *Offshore Financial Centres Background Paper*, Washington, 23 June 2000, chapter. 3.

[70] Basle Committee on Banking Supervision, *Minimum Standards for the Supervision of International Banking Groups and their Cross-border Establishments*, Basle, July 1992.

[71] Basle Committee on Banking Supervision, *The Supervision of Cross-Border Banking*, Report by a working group comprising the Basle Committee on Banking Supervision and the Offshore Group of Banking Supervisors, Basle, October 1996.

[72] Basle Core Principles for Effective Banking Supervision.

[73] Principle 23.

[74] Principle 24.

[75] Principle 25.

The IMF identifies effective consolidated supervision as one of the more difficult aspects of supervision to implement in practice. There is likely to be problems with information access, information flows between supervisors, the verification of data, and potential supervisory gaps. The IMF suggests practical safeguards such as punitive capital charges, consolidation of parallel bank and memoranda of understanding with host regulators when there is a danger of failure in consolidated supervision.[76]

While Michel Camdessus, then Director General of the IMF, identified OFCs as the weak link in the system of banking supervision,[77] Howard Davies, Chairman of Financial Services Authority (FSA), found 'no evidence to suggest OFCs are a major cause of systemic risk'.[78] Given the venue at which his address was delivered and the sensitivity required in regard to the UK's own OFCs, this remark was perhaps not surprising. The FSA has a statutory obligation, however, to maintain confidence in the financial sector and to protect consumers in the UK, and is therefore required to deal with any threat that OFCs may create to the achievement of its obligations.

Guernsey

The Guernsey Financial Services Commission (GFSC), established in 1988, is responsible for the regulation of all aspects of the financial services industry, including banking, investment business, pensions, insurance and trusts. The style of financial services supervision and regulation is strongly influenced by that in the United Kingdom, and many laws concerning financial services business are based on UK law. The duty of the GFSC is to protect and enhance the reputation of Guernsey as a finance centre. The creation of new business is dependent on approval by the GFSC.

Guernsey is a founding member of the Offshore Group of Banking Supervisors and is in accordance with the Core Principles of Effective Banking Supervision. There is no financial secrecy legislation, although the common law principles of confidentiality are applied. The Financial Stability Forum's Working Group on Offshore Financial Centres Report (FSF Report) placed Guernsey in Group I – jurisdictions generally viewed as co-operative, with high quality of supervision, which largely adhere to international standards.

The authorities ensure only bona-fide companies are incorporated, there are no shelf company facilities and no avoidance of the obligation to disclose initial beneficial ownership. The authorities are committed to ensuring that proceeds of

---

[76] IMF, *Offshore Financial Centres: The Role of IMF*, Washington, 23 June 2000.

[77] 'Money Laundering: the Importance of International Countermeasures'. Address by Michel Camdessus, Managing Director of the International Monetary Fund at the Plenary Meeting of the Financial Action Task Force on Money Laundering, 10 February 1998, Paris, in FATF, *Annual Report 1997-98*, Annex A, 1998, p. 40.

[78] Howard Davies, 'Offshore Financial Centres in the Spotlight', speech delivered at the Financial Supervision Commission, Douglas, Isle of Man, 26 September 2001.

drug trafficking, tax evasion and other criminal activity are not laundered through the financial system. The FATF Forty Recommendations are fully endorsed.

Isle of Man

The Financial Supervision Commission established in 1983 regulates most financial services. Insurance and pensions are regulated by the Insurance and Pensions Authority established in 1986. The style of financial services supervision and regulation is strongly influenced by that in the UK, and many laws concerning financial services business are based on UK law. The Financial Stability Forum's Working Group on Offshore Financial Centres Report (FSF Report) placed the Isle of Man in Group I – jurisdictions generally viewed as co-operative, with high quality of supervision, which largely adhere to international standards.

Jersey

The Jersey Financial Services Commission (JFSC), established in 1998, is responsible for the regulation of all aspects of the financial services industry, including banks, insurance business and collective investment fund business. The JFSC administers the registers of companies and limited partnerships. Jersey is a designated territory for the marketing of collective investment schemes into the UK. Jersey is a member of OGBS and IOSCO. The Financial Stability Forum's Working Group on Offshore Financial Centres Report (FSF Report) placed Jersey in Group I – jurisdictions generally viewed as co-operative, with high quality of supervision, which largely adhere to international standards.

Recently, the Director-General of the JFSC, Richard Pratt, expressed his wish to extend the Commission's powers to impose fines on those companies that conduct unauthorised business in the jurisdiction. At present, the Commission is only permitted to issue a public statement about the offending service provider in the *Jersey Gazette*.[79]

Gibraltar

The Financial Services Commission, established in 1989, is responsible for regulating all aspects of the financial services industry. The style and standard of regulation is modelled on UK financial services regulation. Gibraltar is a member of the OGBS. The Financial Stability Forum's Working Group on Offshore Financial Centres Report (FSF Report) placed Gibraltar in Group II – jurisdictions generally seen as having procedures for supervision and co-operation in place, but where actual performance falls below international standards, and there is

---

[79] *Jersey Evening Post*, 2 July 2002, quoting Richard Pratt, the Director General of the JFSC. Even though public shaming may be sufficient punishment for large and well-known companies conducting the majority of their business on the island, it is unlikely to act as a deterrent for small companies based in Jersey but operating elsewhere, as their customers are not likely to see the public statement.

substantial room for improvement. Gibraltar has been the subject of scrutiny by the OECD, the EU and a report from the French Parliament into money laundering.

Money Laundering[80]

The globalisation of finance, with highly mobile capital and new payment technologies, has significantly increased the tools for money laundering. The proliferation of offshore financial centres with minimal or no regulation, strict banking secrecy and an unwillingness to engage in international efforts against money laundering threatens the integrity of the international financial system and attempts to combat money laundering.

The Financial Action Task Force on Money Laundering (FATF) was established in 1989 at the G7 Summit as an inter-governmental body whose purpose is the creation of an international consensus and the development and promotion of policies to combat money laundering.

As mentioned several times in the previous pages, in 1990 the FATF issued the Forty Recommendations for action against money laundering. These were subsequently revised in 1996 and 2003 to reflect changes in money laundering trends. Membership of the FATF comprises 29 governments, including the United Kingdom.

The FATF focuses on three main tasks, namely: spreading the anti-money laundering message to all continents and regions of the globe; improving members' implementation of the 40 Recommendations; and strengthening the review of money laundering methods and countermeasures.[81]

The 40 Recommendations have been recognised, endorsed, or adopted by many international bodies. They set out the basic framework for anti-money laundering efforts and are designed for universal application. They cover the criminal justice system and law enforcement, the financial system and its regulation, and international co-operation.

The Recommendations are principles for action, recognising the diversity of legal and financial systems by allowing flexibility in application. Gibraltar, Guernsey, Isle of Man and Jersey have subscribed to the Forty Recommendations through membership of the Offshore Group of Banking Supervisors (OGBS).

The FATF aims to combat money laundering by employing several methods. Strengthening the comments in Chapter 4, and starting from Recommendation 4, it states that each country should criminalise money laundering as specified by the 1988 United Nations Convention against Illicit Traffic in Narcotic Drugs and Psychotropic Substances (the Vienna Convention).

---

[80] For extensive work on money laundering and its control and prevention, see B.A.K. Rider and C. Nakajima (eds.), *Anti-Money Laundering Guide*, Sweet & Maxwell, London, 1999.
[81] FATF, 'More about the FATF and its work'; the updated file is available at http://www1.oecd.org/fatf/AboutFATF_en.htm (print out with author).

The main countermeasures against money laundering are through 'know your customer' and suspicious transaction reporting requirements on banks and non-bank financial institutions.

Recommendations 10, 11 and 12 state that financial institutions should identify, on the basis of reliable documentation, and record key customer data such as name, address and legal incorporation. In addition, they are expected to identify beneficial owners when intermediaries are used and to maintain records for five years, engage in due diligence and be informed of the business of customers.

The FATF has identified suspicious transaction reporting as crucial in generating new cases of money laundering, supplementing and linking to others and illustrating gaps in regulation. Recommendation 15 states that financial institutions should be required to report transactions where it is suspected the funds stem from criminal activity. A good knowledge of the client and his business will enable institutions to spot unusual patterns or large transactions.

Other Recommendations include confiscation of laundered proceeds, multilateral co-operation and requiring financial institutions to develop programmes against money laundering. The Wolfsberg AML principles are additional guidelines for financial institutions to combat money laundering effectively.[82]

Implementation of the 40 Recommendations is observed by a two-stage process. Firstly, each Member State conducts an annual self-evaluation exercise in which it examines the status of implementation of the Forty Recommendations. Secondly, each member is examined by a FATF team as a mutual evaluation.

The FATF examines the methods and trends of money laundering in an annual typologies exercise[83] to ensure the 40 Recommendations are up to date. The most recent exercises have discovered that methods and intermediaries, such as online banking and Internet gambling, alternative remittance systems, correspondent banking, trade, trusts, bearer securities and professional service providers, have been used to avert detection through the mechanisms set by the Forty Recommendations.

The FATF identified several methods by which OFCs facilitate money laundering.[84] It is possible to route multiple financial transactions through an OFC using nominees or other intermediaries to manage the transactions – this achieves a 'starburst'.[85]

FATF members reported problems in pursuing anti-money laundering investigations with links to offshore financial centres. Obtaining information from offshore jurisdictions on the true owners or beneficiaries of foreign registered

---

[82] Global Anti-Money Laundering Guidelines for Private Banking: Wolfsberg AML Principles (revised May 2002), available from www.wolfsberg-principles.com.

[83] FATF, *Report on Money Laundering Typologies 2001-2002*, Paris, 1 February 2002.

[84] FATF, *Report on Money Laundering Typologies 1998-1999*, Paris, 10 February 1999, para. 20 et seq.

[85] A technique used at the 'layering' stage of the laundering cycle to disguise the audit trail and provide anonymity by dividing the original sum into hundreds of smaller sums that are scattered via numerous financial centres prior to returning to a single location.

business entities – shell companies, international business companies, offshore trusts – appears to be the primary obstacle in investigating transnational laundering activity. The lack of an official registry or strict banking secrecy laws makes identification of the beneficial owners of legal entities very difficult.[86]

The FATF identified rules and practices that in its view impaired money laundering prevention and detection and international co-operation.[87] These rules and practices include inadequate financial regulation, inadequate customer identification requirements, excessive secrecy provisions, ineffective suspicious transaction reporting, legal and administrative obstacles to international co-operation and exchange of information.

Some centres were hindered in their activities by inadequate resources for preventing, detecting and repressing money laundering activities, while other centres lack the political will to do so. Pursuant to the criteria, the FATF has, from time to time, identified specific jurisdictions as non-cooperative countries or territories and in effect blacklisted them. Chapter 4 analysed the pros and cons of the blacklisting process.

Countermeasures were applied against the jurisdictions on the list by imposing rules and restrictions on the conduct of transactions between financial institutions in FATF countries and non-cooperative countries or territories.

The Basle Core Principles of Effective Banking Supervision state: 'Banking supervisors must determine that banks have adequate policies, practices and procedures in place, including strict "know-your-customer" rules, that promote high ethical and professional standards in the financial sector and prevent the bank being used, intentionally or unintentionally, by criminal elements.'

As was stressed above, Michel Camdessus, then Managing Director of the IMF, identified OFCs as playing a crucial role in money laundering: the proliferation of smaller offshore centres offering 'tax and regulatory services' including secrecy and confidentiality is a cause for concern. Some of the offshore centres feature prominently in international discussions of serious money laundering problems. Even with the government's best will, very small countries or territories tend to lack the expert resources needed to supervise a large number of offshore banks.[88]

---

[86] For example, see FATF, *Report on Money Laundering Typologies*, Paris, February 1997, at para. 24, stating that several countries indicated they had a problem in identifying the ordering customer in electronic funds transfer transactions where funds originated in offshore jurisdictions.

[87] FATF, *Report on Non-Cooperative Countries and Territories*, Paris, 14 February 2000, Annex.

[88] 'Money laundering: the importance of international countermeasures', Address by Michel Camdessus, Managing Director of the International Monetary Fund at the Plenary Meeting of the Financial Action Task Force on Money Laundering, 10 February 1998, Paris, in FATF, *Annual Report 1997-1998*, Annex A, 1998, p. 40.

Guernsey

The OGBS conducted a mutual evaluation of Guernsey to assess compliance with the FATF 40 Recommendations. The evaluation concluded that the standards set by Guernsey are close to complete adherence with the Forty Recommendations.[89] Guernsey has a robust arsenal of legislation, regulation and administrative practices to counter money laundering.

The authorities demonstrate the political will to ensure their offshore institutions and the associated professionals maximise their defences against money laundering, and co-operate effectively in international investigations into criminal funds.

The all-crimes anti-money laundering law is largely in line with the UK, covering a wide range of offences. There is a requirement on financial institutions to report suspicious transactions, and the authorities have confiscation powers. There is a comprehensive and effective system of financial services.

The mutual evaluations identified several areas of weakness – the indirect obligation to report certain suspicious transactions, the introduction of business rules whereby a regulated intermediary identifies the client, failure to ratify Council of Europe Convention on Laundering, Seizure and Confiscation of the Proceeds of Crime – and areas for improvement – enhanced confiscation powers and proactive investigation into money laundering. The absence of company law in Sark and insufficient oversight of the fiduciary sector were identified as particularly susceptible to money laundering.

Isle of Man

The OGBS conducted a mutual evaluation of the Isle of Man to assess compliance with the FATF 40 Recommendations. The evaluation concluded the standards set by Isle of Man are close to complete adherence with the Forty Recommendations and in some cases exceed relevant international standards.[90]

The Isle of Man has a robust arsenal of legislation, regulation and administrative practices to counter money laundering. The authorities demonstrate a political will to ensure their offshore institutions and the associated professionals maximise their defences against money laundering and co-operate effectively in international investigations into criminal funds.

Criminalisation of money laundering is largely in line with the UK, covering a wide range of offences. There is a universal requirement on financial institutions to report suspicious transactions, and the authorities have broad powers of confiscation. There is a good compliance culture within the financial services sector and a high number of suspicious transaction reports. There is a comprehensive and effective system of financial services.

---

[89] FATF, *Annual Report 2000-2001*, Paris, 22 June 2001, Annex C, 'Summaries of Mutual Evaluations undertaken by the Offshore Group of Banking Supervisors', pp. 2-4.

[90] FATF, *Annual Report 2000-2001*, Paris, 22 June 2001, Annex C, 'Summaries of Mutual Evaluations undertaken by the Offshore Group of Banking Supervisors', pp. 4-5.

Jersey

The OGBS conducted a mutual evaluation of Jersey to assess compliance with the FATF 40 Recommendations. The evaluation concluded the standards set by Jersey are close to complete adherence with the Forty Recommendations.[91]

Jersey has a robust arsenal of legislation, regulation and administrative practices to counter money laundering. The authorities demonstrate a political will to ensure their offshore institutions and the associated professionals maximise their defences against money laundering and co-operate effectively in international investigations into criminal funds.

Criminalisation of money laundering is largely in line with the UK, covering a wide range of offences. There is a requirement on financial institutions to report suspicious transactions, and the authorities have confiscation powers. There is a comprehensive and effective system of financial services regulation, and the authorities propose to tighten regulation in the company and trust sector.

The mutual evaluations identified several areas of weakness – the indirect obligation to report certain suspicious transactions, the introduction of business rules whereby a regulated intermediary identifies the client, a mixed compliance culture – and areas for improvement – enhanced confiscation powers and proactive investigation into money laundering.

Conclusion: The Challenge of the Terrorist Financing Risk

As has been remembered several times in the previous chapters, following the 11 September attacks on the US, the remit of the FATF was extended to combat terrorist financing.

The FATF issued eight Special Recommendations on Terrorist Financing that, in combination with the 40 Recommendations, set out the basic framework to detect, prevent, and suppress the financing of terrorism and of terrorist acts. Special Recommendations state that jurisdictions should implement the United Nations International Convention for the Suppression of the Financing of Terrorism,[92] to criminalise the financing of terrorism, of terrorist acts, of terrorist organisations, and establish terrorist financing offences as predicate offences for money laundering.[93]

Financial institutions should report transactions suspected of being linked to terrorist financing or where there are reasonable grounds to suspect the funds are linked to terrorist financing.[94] Action is recommended with regard to the freezing and confiscation of terrorist assets, international co-operation, alternative remittance systems, wire transfers and non-profit organisations.

---

[91] FATF, *Annual Report 2000-2001*, Paris, 22 June 2001, Annex C, 'Summaries of mutual evaluations undertaken by the Offshore Group of Banking Supervisors', pp. 1-2.

[92] FATF, *Special Recommendation on Terrorist Financing*, Recommendation I.

[93] FATF, *Special Recommendation on Terrorist Financing*, Recommendation II.

[94] FATF, *Special Recommendation on Terrorist Financing*, Recommendation IV.

Terrorist funds originate from direct support or revenue gathering by the organisations. Although direct state support of terrorism has fallen markedly, there has been a sharp increase in individual sponsorship of terrorism.[95]

Revenue gathering by terrorist organisations involves a mixture of legal and illegal methods: although the proceeds are applied to an illegal purpose some of the donors believe the proceeds are for charity. The FATF identifies little difference between laundering terrorist funds from illegal sources and traditional money laundering.[96] Chapter 2 discussed similarities and differences between money laundering and terrorism finance.

However, terrorists have access to funds from legal sources that can be transmitted above board.[97] As was testified before the US Senate

> Terrorist financing activities are unlike traditional money laundering in a very significant respect. Money used to finance terrorism does not always originate from criminal sources. Rather, it may be money derived from legitimate sources that is then used to support crimes. Developing programs that will help identify such funds before they can be used for their horrific purposes is a daunting task.[98]

Terrorist organisations often need to launder funds from legitimate sources[99] to disguise the link between the origin of the funds and the terrorist organisation and to avoid creating a financial trail via the fund transfers to the operatives, who in many instances will be sleepers.[100] When legal funds are used for terrorist financing, the existing scope of money laundering legislation may be inadequate unless terrorist financing is a predicate offence as recommended by the FATF.[101]

The detection of terrorist financing transactions is complicated by the relatively small amounts needed for such activity. In contrast to the estimated insured losses

---

[95] FATF, *Guidance for Financial Institutions in Detecting Terrorist Financing*, 24 April 2002, par. 11.

[96] FATF, *Guidance for Financial Institutions in Detecting Terrorist Financing*, 24 April 2002, par. 15.

[97] FATF, *Guidance for Financial Institutions in Detecting Terrorist Financing*, 24 April 2002, par. 13.

[98] 'Antiterrorism Initiatives', testimony of Richard Spillenkothen, Director, Division of Banking Supervision and Regulation, Federal Reserve Board, before the Committee on Banking, Housing, and Urban Affairs, US Senate, 29 January 2002 at www.federalreserve.gov/boarddocs/testimony/2002/20020129/default.htm (printout with author). He emphasises that they are trying to meet this responsibility in co-operation with the US Departments of Treasury and Justice, the Securities and Exchange Commission and other US and international regulatory and law enforcement agencies.

[99] FATF, *Guidance for Financial Institutions in Detecting Terrorist Financing*, 24 April 2002, par. 15.

[100] Chief of the Financial Crimes Section of the FBI distinguishes between 'Mission Specific Terrorist Cells' and 'Sleeper Cells', see Dennis M. Lormel, Congressional Statement before the House Committee on Financial Services, Subcommittee on Oversight and Investigations, 12 February 2002, Washington DC, http://www.fbi.gov/congress02/lormel021202.htm (printout with author).

[101] FATF, *Special Recommendation on Terrorist Financing*, Recommendation II.

resulting from the attacks of September 11, ranging from $30 billion to $90 billion,[102] the US Treasury estimated the total cost of launching the September 11 attacks to be US$ 500,000, with most of the funds having been transferred in individual transactions of less than US$ 10,000 that would not trigger suspicions. Chapter 3 estimated the total flows of terrorism finance.

The FATF[103] has identified the main methods used to transfer funds – cash smuggling, structured deposits and withdrawals, monetary instruments, wire transfers and alternative remittance systems. Certain methods, such as the unusual use of accounts and transactions to locations of concern, were highlighted as being indicative of use for terrorist purposes.

Notwithstanding its relatively small volume, terrorist financing is a major threat to the survival of OFCs. Following the tragic events of 11 September 2001, an executive order was signed authorising the Treasury Department 'to block funds and anyone associated with a terrorist or terrorism'.[104]

Treasury Secretary Paul O'Neil thus stated:

> We have the President's explicit directive to block the US assets of any domestic or foreign financial institutions that refuse to cooperate with us in blocking assets of terrorist organizations. This order is a wake-up call to financial institutions around the world. If you have any involvement in the financing of the Al Qaeda organization, you have two choices: cooperate in this fight or we will freeze your US assets. We will punish you for providing resources that make these evil acts possible.

Given such a strong stance by the US Government, the political mood has swayed against any jurisdictions that hinder the fight against terrorism, let alone abet terrorism.[105]

Indeed, Guernsey, Isle of Man, Jersey, and Gibraltar adhere to the FATF Special Recommendations on terrorist financing. Recently, Guernsey, Isle of Man, and Jersey introduced, as a joint action, new know-your-customer requirements to help in preventing their financial system being used for terrorist financing.[106]

---

[102] Office of Public Affairs, 'Economic Impact of the Lack of Terrorism Risk Insurance', Testimony of Mark J. Warshawsky, Deputy Assistant Secretary for Economic Policy, US Treasury Before the Financial Services Subcommittee on Oversight and Investigation, United States House of Representatives, PO-1050, Washington, 27 February 2002.

[103] FATF, *Guidance for Financial Institutions in Detecting Terrorist Financing*, 24 April 2002, par. 15.

[104] Office of Public Affairs, 'Statement of Secretary Paul O'Neil on Signing of Executive Order Authorizing the Treasury Department to Block Funds of Terrorists and their Associates', PO-630, London, 24 September 2001.

[105] See, for example, J. Gorringe, 'Offshore Jurisdictions will agree to US anti-terrorist demands', *Tax-News.com*, London, 26 September 2001 quoting Richard Pratt, Director General of the Jersey Financial Services Commission as saying, 'Jersey should be in a position to meet the demands of the US because one can find ways of doing so'.

[106] See Jersey Financial Services Commission, Overriding Principles for a Revised Know Your Customer Framework, Position Paper, 22 January 2002, available from http://www.jerseyfsc.org/knowyourcustomer.pdf (printout with author).

It appears, however, that, notwithstanding the tough US stance against terrorist financing, these measures to block Al Qaeda's access to funds have not been as successful as it was hoped.

Recently, the press reported[107] that the draft UN Report showed that while the US and other UN members where able to freeze more than US$ 112 million immediately after the attacks on the US in September 2001, only US$ 10 million has been blocked in the last eight months, showing that the efforts are somewhat running out of steam. Furthermore, it states that Al Qaeda has taken steps to shift its assets into precious metals and gems, and to transfer money through underground banking systems, such as Hawalah, described in the previous chapters.

The draft Report also points to a number of practical problems, including the existence of different lists of terrorists issued by various bodies and governments around the world, creating confusion, thereby undermining the efforts to freeze Al Qaeda. Indeed, this point and other practical problems faced by financial institutions were discussed in detail by the expert working group that was convened last year to look at various issues arising from the interdiction of terrorist property.[108]

The press report states, 'Al Qaeda is by all accounts "fit and well" and poised to strike again at its leisure',[109] and adds, 'The prime targets of the organization are likely to be persons and property of the United States of America and its allies in the fight against Al Qaeda, as well as Israel'.[110] While people feel nervous about further attacks, they must feel equally helpless in fighting the war against terror through conventional financial systems, notwithstanding the introduction of further measures taken against individuals and organisations linked to terrorism.

References

Baker, L., 'Offshore Based US Companies Won't Have to Swear to Accuracy', *Tax-News.com*, 9 July, New York.

Banks, A. (2002), 'Israel to Unveil Tax Haven Plans Following FATF Delisting', *Tax-News.com*, 27 June, London.

---

[107] Colum Lynch, 'War on Al Qaeda funds stalled', 29 August 2002, *Washington Post*.

[108] *Report by the Expert Working Group on the Interdiction of Terrorist Property*, convened under the auspices of the Society for Advanced Legal Studies, London, is to be published in September 2002. The author acted as convenor for the sub-group, comprising of lawyers, bankers and regulators, that was mandated to look at the impact of the initiatives against terrorist property on banks and financial institutions.

[109] The US Treasury wasted no time in criticising the UN report cited by the *Washington Post* by issuing a statement, which points out that it 'does not focus on other elements of the campaign against terrorist financing. As a result, it is an incomplete picture of the financial war against terrorism', see Office of Public Office, 'Treasury Statement on UN Terrorism Report', PO-3382, London, 29 August 2002.

[110] Colum Lynch, 'War on Al Qaeda funds stalled', 29 August 2002, *Washington Post*.

Basle Committee on Banking Supervision (1996), *The Supervision of Cross-Border Banking*, Report by a working group comprising the Basle Committee on Banking Supervision and the Offshore Group of Banking Supervisors, October, Basle.

Basle Committee on Banking Supervision (1992), *Minimum Standards for the Supervision of International Banking Groups and their Cross-border Establishments*, July, Basle.

Camdessus, M. (1998), Money Laundering: the Importance of International Countermeasures, in FATF, *Annual Report 1997-98*, Paris.

Davies, H. (2001), *Offshore Financial Centres in the Spotlight*, Financial Supervision Commission, 26 September, Douglas, Isle of Man.

Edwards, A. (1998), The Guernsey Finance Centre, in *Review of Financial Regulation in the Crown Dependencies*, November, London.

Edwards, A. (1998), The Isle of Man Finance Centre, in *Review of Financial Regulation in the Crown Dependencies*, November, London.

Edwards, A. (1998), The Jersey Finance Centre, in *Review of Financial Regulation in the Crown Dependencies*, November, London.

FATF (2002), *Guidance for Financial Institutions in Detecting Terrorist Financing*, 24 April, Paris.

FATF (2002), *Report on Money Laundering Typologies 2001-2002*, 1 February, Paris.

FATF (2001), *Annual Report 2000-2001*, 22 June, Paris.

FATF (2000), *Report on Non-Cooperative Countries and Territories*, 14 February, Paris

FATF (1999), *Report on Money Laundering Typologies 1998-1999*, 10 February, Paris.

FATF (1997), *Report on Money Laundering Typologies 1996-1997*, February, Paris.

Financial Stability Forum (2000), *Report of the Working Group on Offshore Financial Centres*, Basle, 5 April.

Godfrey M. (2001), 'US Study Reveals Multinationals Avoided Paying Billions in Taxes', *Tax-News.com*, 26 November, New York.

Gorringe, J. (2001), 'US Reconsidering OECD Proposals on Tax Havens', 25 September, *Tax-News.com*, London.

Hammer, R.M. and Owens, J. (2001), *Promoting Tax Competition*, 3 June, mimeo

IMF (2000), *Offshore Financial Centres – The Role of the IMF*, 23 June, Washington.

IMF (2000), *Offshore Financial Centres – IMF Background Paper*, 23 June, Washington.

Jersey Financial Services Commission (2002), *Overriding Principles for a Revised Know Your Customer Framework*, 22 January, http://www.jerseyfsc.org/knowyourcustomer.pdf (print out with author).

Khoury, S.J. (1990), *The Deregulation of the World Financial Markets: Myths, Realities and Impact*, Quorum, New York.

Kondo, S. (2002), *Ending Tax Abuse*, OECD, 18 April, Paris.

Lomas, U. (2002), *EU Turns Heavy Artillery on the Swiss*, 4 July, *Tax-News.com*, Bruxelles.

Lynch, C. (2002), *War on Al Qaeda Funds Stalled*, 29 August, Washington Post.

Nakajima, C. (1999), *Conflicts of Interest and Duty: A Comparative Analysis in Anglo-Japanese Law*, Kluwer Law International, London.

Nakajima, C. (1995), Conflicts of interest in Japan, in Rider, B.A.K. and T.M. Ashe (eds), *The Fiduciary, the Insider and the Conflict*, Sweet & Maxwell, London.

OECD (2001), *The OECD's Project on Harmful Tax Practices: The 2001 Progress Report*, November, Paris.

OECD (2000), *Towards Global Tax Co-operation – Progress in Identifying and Eliminating Harmful Tax Practices*, Report to the 2000 Ministerial Council Meeting and Recommendations by the Committee on Fiscal Affairs, Paris.

OECD (1998), *Harmful Tax Competition: An Emerging Global Issue*, Paris.

OECD (1987), *International Tax Avoidance and Evasion Four Related Studies No.1*, Paris

Rider, B.A.K and Nakajima, C. (1999), *Anti-Money Laundering Guide*, Sweet & Maxwell, London.

Rider, B.A.K., Abram, C. and Ferran, E. (1989), *Guide to the Financial Services Act 1986*, CCH, Bicester.

Spillenkothen, R. (2002), *Antiterrorism Initiatives*, U.S. Senate, 29 January. www.federalreserve.gov/boarddocs/testimony/2002/20020129/default.htm.

UN Office for Drug Control and Crime Prevention (1998), *Financial Havens, Banking Secrecy and Money Laundering*, Global Programme Against Money Laundering, Vienna.

Walker, G., Mellor, S., Fox, M. and Francis S. (1994), The concept of globalisation, *Company and Securities Law Journal*, 14, 59.

Warshawsky, M.J. (2002), *Economic Impact of the Lack of Terrorism Risk Insurance*, 27 February.

Conclusions

Donato Masciandaro

After 11 September 2001, it was clear to all that the principle of free circulation of capital is not absolute: if the financial flows are used to finance, or derive from, activities of terrorism or organised crime, they must be detected and intercepted.

The design of financial regulations, national and international, had to accommodate the need to develop policies to prevent and combat the phenomenon of terrorism. The financial war on terrorism, which, as illustrated in the first two chapters, was born of the experience of the international war against drugs and organised crime, in progress for at least the past two decades, was instituted on the basis of four fundamental assumptions. In this volume we have taken a multidisciplinary approach to analyse the robustness of these assumptions, inquiring into the causes and effects, to derive then the consequences for *policy*.

First Postulate (Vulnerability to Terrorism Financing Risk): the world network that today represents the banking and financial industry, beyond the specific awareness of the majority of individual intermediaries and professionals who work in it, is the linchpin of the mechanisms that permit the financing of international terrorism.

We have verified the robustness of the first postulate on the level of economic and institutional analysis, particularly in Chapters 2, 4 and 5. In fact, the banking and financial industry is physiologically vulnerable to the risk of becoming an instrument at the service of terrorist and criminal organisations, because of the accentuated phenomenon of information asymmetries. The banking and financial industry produces and distributes fiduciary services through exchanges in which at least one of the two parties, if for no other reason than uncertainty surrounding future events, lacks a complete and symmetrical quantity of important information regarding that exchange.

As claimed in Chapter 5, in most instances money laundering is ultimately channelled through financial intermediaries that are unwitting parties to the final objective of the chain of transactions.

Authorities seek to limit the possibility of these illegal transactions by setting due diligence rules on banks, who ultimately act as agents for governments. The willingness of financial intermediaries to assume a monitoring role will depend on two types of cost: the costs relating to establishing a monitoring system and the reputational costs associated with the lifting of bank secrecy.

There is information asymmetry between the regulators and the banks. The difficulty in monitoring the degree of effort spent by banks to report suspicious transactions is compounded by the lack of clearly identifiable indicators of laundering.

The design of effective regulation must therefore consider the role of incentives on behaviour. The intermediaries must find it optimal to perform their function of 'agent' effectively. Given the characteristics of intermediaries as complex organisations and their numerous relationships with various supervisory institutions, the system of rules must exert a positive impact on the resources deemed important by the intermediaries.

The widespread presence of information asymmetries thus makes that financial industry particularly well suited to the needs of those like terrorist organisations who need to conceal the destination, and often the origin, of certain financial flows, and financial flows of a particularly significant amount, as suggested by the analytical reconstruction and estimates proposed in Chapter 3.

Furthermore we have stressed, in Chapters 1, 2 and 4, that the vulnerability of the banking and financial sector concerns not only, or not so much, the forms of overt and legal intermediation but also the lesser known informal financial network, developed in recent years in part due to the growth of world migration flows.

Second Postulate (*Equivalence between Terrorism Financing Risk and Criminal Capital Laundering Risk*): the mechanisms that facilitate the financing of terrorism are the same as those permit the laundering of illicit capital by transnational criminal organisations.

The second postulate seems less robust than the first, in light of the analyses presented, especially in Chapters 1, 2 and 4. On the one hand, the laundering of capital (money laundering) is conceptually different from the financing of terrorism (money dirtying): in the first case, the objective is to transform financial flows of illegal origin into licit funds, while in the second case the purpose is to channel financial flows toward an illegal purpose, whether their origin was legal or not.

From another viewpoint, however, in both situations there is an interest in reducing the probability that the parties and organisations conducting criminal activity will be incriminated. In the case of money laundering, the desire is to reduce the probability that the financial flows originating from criminal activities might lead to the identification of the organisations that derive benefit from those activities. In the case of money dirtying, the intention is to decrease the probability that the identity and structures of the international terrorist associations will be discovered through tracking of the flows of financing.

And we must not forget that investigations have often determined that terrorist organisations finance themselves through the production and trafficking of illegal goods and services, such as drugs and arms, so money dirtying activity tends to overlap that of money laundering.

Thus, the mechanisms and channels that permit the financing of terrorism do not perfectly coincide with those for the laundering of capital from organised crime but may overlap and intermingle with them.

Third Postulate (*Offshore as a Catalyst of Terrorism Financing Risk*): the mechanisms of financing terrorism and laundering criminal capital can function in a world financial network, because in that network there are 'weak' nodes or 'black holes' represented by offshore financial centres (OFCs).

Throughout this volume, the theme of the potential vulnerability of the world financial network due to the presence of OFCs has been explored with various methodological approaches.

Firstly, beginning with the financial aspects, we began by observing that the onshore countries, represented by the major industrialized countries, view as vulnerable those countries and territories whose regulations are relatively accommodating compared with their own, in the sense that greater risks exist that money-laundering or terrorism financing transactions can be concealed.

But why do the offshore financial centres possess these lax regulations? This volume answers the question by applying the latest instruments of economic, institutional and political analysis. The two key terms are a surplus of economic benefits that the OFCs receive by having lax regulations, which forcefully clashes with a deficit of political legitimacy in the directives of the onshore countries and international institutions, as perceived by the OFCs. While Chapter 1 dealt specifically with the theme of legitimacy, Chapter 4 analysed the question of benefits, while Chapters 2 and 6 examined both themes transversely.

Thanks to an empirical analysis, it was demonstrated that the OFCs display relatively uniform structural characteristics, economic and institutional: they are countries and territories poor in natural resources, with a strong dependence on the income produced by their banking and financial services, devoid of particular problems associated with terrorism risk and organised crime risk. Therefore, the laxity of their financial regulation ultimately becomes a case of free lunch for the OFCs: the anticipated benefits of laxity, in terms of increasing the value produced by the financial industry, are evident, while the OFC's do not perceive the anticipated costs, represented by greater risks of increasing terrorism and organised crime. Furthermore, the action suggested by the international organisations suffers from a marked lack of legitimacy, in the eyes of jurisdictions that express more or less accentuated and consolidated forms of national sovereignty.

Thus, more than the robustness of the third postulate, which is tautological per se – OFCs are those jurisdictions defined as such by the onshore countries – this volume casts some light on the economic and political causes that may explain the birth and development – past, present and (alas!) future – of countries with relatively lax financial regulations.

Fourth Postulate (*Equivalence of Offshore Centers as a Catalyst of Terrorism Financing Risk and Fiscal Damage Risk*): the weak nodes in the network are particularly dangerous because they not only facilitate the financing of terrorism and the laundering of criminal capital but also facilitate unfair fiscal competition among sovereign nations.

This volume demonstrates that the fourth postulate is false, through the concepts developed in Chapters 1 and 2, and especially the empirical analysis offered in Chapter 5 and the country cases presented in Chapter 6. The decision of a few countries and territories to institute highly advantageous taxation policies, in some cases highly aggressive, and the relative determinants do not coincide with those who adopt lax financial policies, although areas of overlapping and partial coincidence do exist. Using a graphic image, the set of fiscal OFCs does not coincide with the set of financial OFCs, although there is an area of intersection. Fiscal competition, if regulated by the principles of transparency and correctness, tends to be different from financial laxity.

On the theoretical level, while a relative consensus exists regarding the potential damage of financial laxity, the same cannot be said for fiscal competition. Various theories exist regarding the possible effects of tax competition. To attempt a summary, we might identify two opposing positions: on the one hand, the advocates of perfect fiscal competition, on the other, the supporters of total tax harmonisation.

The supporters of perfect tax competition are those who feel that capital must be completely free to circle the globe, in search of the most advantageous tax regime. The possibility of capital to arbitrate freely among various national regulations becomes the key to an increasingly efficient allocation of resources. In other words, they are proposing the perfect demand of arbitrage: each citizen, in every nation of the world, must be free to choose the tax regime for his or her own capital. In parallel, each nation must have the possibility of providing a perfect supply of arbitrage, proposing its tax regime to capital throughout the world. The basic idea is that competition will punish the less efficient countries, characterised by harsher tax regimes, and thus reduce the risks of 'country failure', to the advantage of all.

The advocates of tax harmonisation, on the other hand, stress that the individual and collective advantages of perfect competition can be exalted only by those who conceal the 'market failures' that characterise the real functioning of the markets, national and international. First, the presence of various forms of transaction costs and information asymmetries make the actual mobility of the individual production factors, and the capacity of choice of the various categories of citizens, highly heterogeneous and variable from country to country, so the demand for arbitrage, if satisfied, might in reality produce allocation inefficiencies and inequalities.

At the same time, the supply of arbitrage and competition among tax regimes must take into account that, for each country, especially if it is characterised by a democratic regime, the design of public intervention, and therefore the relative fiscal burden, does not respond solely to the criterion of efficiency but must also consider other public priorities, which may be summarised as equity and sustainability.

Furthermore, the absolute neutrality of capital, in the sense that its origin and destination are irrelevant, can no longer be affirmed, especially since 11 September 2001, so the international objective of safeguarding integrity against the risks of capital contamination by terrorism and organised crime must be taken into account. This is another reason, therefore, for not allowing the debate on tax competition to coincide with that on the war on terrorism and organised crime.

Summing up, do the various analyses developed in the various chapters suggest common guidelines for the design of international rules for the financial war on terrorism? The possible indications, useful on both the microeconomic and macroeconomic levels, revolve around four fundamental words: specificity, information, incentives and legitimacy.

Firstly, the phenomenon of terrorism financing has a specificity of its own, linked to the coexistence of three characteristics: firstly, the transnational, damaging and illegal nature of the destination of the financial flows. Fiscal arbitrage and money-laundering operations are also transnational phenomena. There is a widespread consensus on the damaging nature of financial flows produced by crime. The origin of those flows is illegal, while in fiscal arbitrage, which arises from forms of evasion, neither the origin nor the destination of the funds is illegal, just the decision not to contribute part of the funds to tax revenues. The specificity of financing terrorism must always be borne in mind, since the definition of policies for preventing and combating it, national and international, must not passively follow the schemes of action devised in the past for combating organised crime or tax evasion.

Secondly, it is evident that the more widespread are the information asymmetries, to the detriment of various categories of authorities (sectoral, investigative, inquiring) in the banking and financial industry, the more developed and effective will be the financing of international terrorism. A necessary, but not sufficient, condition for designing effective rules and enforcement at both the national and international levels is the generation and collection of relevant information.

However, the production and collection of relevant information – and this is the third point – can never reach satisfactory levels unless it places us in the perspective of providing proper incentives to the various players involved, starting with the individual intermediaries and operators, passing through the authorities and arriving at the relevant countries, be they onshore or offshore. Combating the financing of terrorism must be beneficial at all the various levels that are potentially involved in the rather complex operations of terrorism financing.

The theme of incentives is thus strongly intertwined with that of information. There must be a clear separation between the objective of information accessibility in the financial and economic system and the potential collaboration of financial intermediaries, and operators and companies in general, in the generation of useful information.

This difference is fundamental. The first objective is to enable authorities investigating a suspect to collect relevant financial information effectively: this means being able to access information with minimal time and cost, thanks to the availability of the information assets of intermediaries, companies and professionals (passive collaboration).

A second, more ambitious objective is to activate inverse channels of information from economic agents to the authorities (active collaboration). In general, the action of active collaboration involves expected costs to economic agents – in terms of reputation, efficiency, reprisal – that are much higher than the expected benefits, and the path to follow is certainly not that of sanctions, including criminal sanctions, that seem perhaps unjust, and undoubtedly ineffective. Rather, to increase the active collaboration from the economic agents involved, the path to take is that of incentives and mutually agreed regulations, especially where sovereign offshore jurisdictions subject to blacklisting are concerned. On this point, the economic and institutional analyses in this volume stimulate some final considerations.

We have emphasized that countries deemed lax have some uniform structural elements in common, while there are significant differences between those countries and those judged accommodating on the fiscal level. Hence, three indications for designing international prevention and enforcement policies can been highlighted.

Firstly, the financial blacklist must be formulated and updated with particular care, so as to avoid errors in the formulation of relative incentives or sanctions. Secondly, the fact that a country simply brings its formal rules into compliance does not automatically mean that it is not a potentially lax country on the financial level, since the incentives to laxity in the war on terrorism may have deep-running structural, economic and institutional roots.

Thirdly, the international community must seek to act positively on these roots with specific country-by-country policies, precisely because the degree of laxity and its rationale may not be identical from case to case. On this respect, in June 2003 the FAFT explicitly recognised that countries have diverse legal and financial systems and so all cannot take identical measures to achieve the common objective to combat money laundering and terrorist financing.

However, most importantly, the theme of financial regulations mutually agreeable to both the onshore and offshore countries leads us to the decisive question of the political legitimacy of the action by international institutions. The more each country and territory, active or passive party to the action under an international code of conduct for the war against the financing of terrorism, recognises the political legitimacy of the international institutions guaranteeing that code, the more effective the code will be. The legitimacy problem is not restricted to the blacklisting phenomena; for example how can one clearly distinguish a political movement from the list of terrorist organisations that the United States and other industrial countries issue?

Economic incentives and political legitimacy are therefore the pillars on which to build rules governing international capital flows that observe the cardinal principles for the proper functioning of a market economy: efficiency and integrity.

Index